FIELDS OF FIRE

www.transworldbooks.co.uk
www.transworldireland.ie

Also by Damian Lawlor

I Crossed the Line
(with Liam Dunne)

Working on a Dream – a Year on the Road
with the Waterford Footballers

All In My Head
(with Lar Corbett)

FIELDS OF FIRE

The Inside Story of Hurling's
Great Renaissance

Damian Lawlor

TRANSWORLD IRELAND

TRANSWORLD IRELAND
an imprint of The Random House Group Limited
20 Vauxhall Bridge Road, London SW1V 2SA
www.transworldbooks.co.uk

First published in 2014 by Transworld Ireland,
a division of Transworld Publishers

A CIP catalogue record for this book
is available from the British Library.

ISBN 9781848272026

Addresses for Random House Group Ltd companies outside the UK
can be found at: www.randomhouse.co.uk
The Random House Group Ltd Reg. No. 954009

The Random House Group Limited supports the Forest Stewardship Council® (FSC®),
the leading international forest-certification organisation. Our books carrying the FSC label
are printed on FSC®-certified paper. FSC is the only forest-certification scheme supported
by the leading environmental organisations, including Greenpeace. Our paper procurement
policy can be found at www.randomhouse.co.uk/environment

Typeset in 12½/15¼pt Ehrhardt by
Kestrel Data, Exeter, Devon.
Printed and bound in Great Britain by
Clays Ltd, St Ives plc

2 4 6 8 10 9 7 5 3 1

To Ruth, Jamie and Chloe:

Having a place to go is home.
Having someone to love is a family.
Having both is a blessing.

Contents

Three – New Challenges for the Old Order

Prologue

Ger Loughnane's eyes twinkled when, in a conversation about Clare hurling and the magical year that was 2013, the name Podge Collins cropped up.

'There is a certain mystery as to where the 2013 Clare hurling team came from,' said the county's double All-Ireland winning manager of the nineties. 'But if anyone personifies that sense of mystery, and this new team, it's Podge Collins. He's one of the most intriguing characters I have ever met; everywhere he's gone his fame has preceded him. I think I knew about him when he was three.'

Loughnane was principal of St Aidan's NS, Shannon, where Catriona Collins, Podge's mother, also taught. Podge had yet to begin formal education, but over countless cups of coffee in the staff room, Loughnane and colleagues would listen enthralled as Catriona told of her little boy's exploits. And with each passing term the legend grew. Podge's brother Seán was already attending the school, a grand, quiet youngster who needed little or no looking after.

Podge, though, was different.

'He was dynamite,' Loughane laughed. 'He hardly slept at all and he was constantly breaking stuff. On the Friday before the 1995 All-Ireland final he outdid himself by jumping off a wall, catching his tongue between his teeth and severing part of his tongue. Colm Collins phoned the school and asked me to break the news to his wife. Sure that was only the start of it.'

Loughnane was the founding principal at St Aidan's, and in his thirty years there thousands of boys came and went, but he remembers well the day he finally got to meet Podge himself: 'And Jesus he did not disappoint.'

Each time Ger met Podge, the spring-heeled kid had a hurley close to hand. Already there was a passionate madness. Loughnane ran a schoolyard five-a-side league, which kicked in when classes finished for the day. In advance of those league games, impromptu sessions would break out in the morning schoolyard. And though the timber hurley in use had a rubber bas, those games were not for the faint-hearted, up to thirty kids skelping and digging for the sliotar.

The school principal imposed just two conditions for those skirmishes: helmets were barred – the master reasoning that kids wielding safety hurleys need not be mollycoddled – and only fourth-graders and above could participate.

'Podge, of course, was stone mad to be involved; he was itching for road,' his old teacher recalled. 'But I banned him. Sure he was only in first class. I told him that when he got to third class – or maybe grew a bit – I might let him in. He was fairly upset – it would break your heart to see his face.'

One morning, however, Loughnane arrived in the yard and there was the little fella – no higher than a chair – hacking like a lumberjack in a scrum of about twenty others. Loughnane thought about pulling him out of the commotion but, seeing the enjoyment on the wee face, held fire.

As luck would have it, the combatants included Conor Loughnane, the principal's son and a big chip off the old block, as the father admitted: 'Sure enough, Conor drew this big awkward belt and broke Podge's jaw. Off went Podge to hospital, leaving me to break the news to Catriona and Colm.'

Thankfully, both parents were already resigned to the reality – this was how it was going to be. The wounded warrior missed three weeks of school but on returning immediately sought out the battlefield again. Loughnane banned him a second time but that afternoon the bold Podge was back in action, keen to make his mark.

Loughnane, for once unsure how to proceed, spoke to the mother: 'Catriona, what will I do?'

The reply was instant: 'Let him off, Ger.'

And he did. At the age of seven Collins had defied everyone to play with kids three years older and two feet taller. Fourteen years later he was still beating the odds. When it came to hurling he refused to fail.

Like Podge Collins, many other hurlers have been blessed with ferocious will and determination. And several just happened to mature in tandem and play together on the Clare team that won the most exciting championship of all time, the 2013 All-Ireland. Five of that team's front eight stood less than six feet – anomalous in what is increasingly a game for giants. They all had to overcome obstacles to get where they wanted, but together they did it.

Along the way they also changed the face of modern-day hurling. Most of them had Munster minor medals; a fair number had two All-Ireland under-21 titles, and now they had the ultimate prize – an All-Ireland senior medal.

Despite his precocious passion for the game, Podge Collins got off to a slow start – his low stature one of the reasons he didn't get on a Clare team till he was sixteen – but the little lad from Cratloe soon made up ground. In 2013 he landed an All Star and was shortlisted for Player of the Year and Young Player of the Year. A rich harvest for one so young, the seeds of which had been sown many years before.

'He was completely one-sided at the start, his left was much stronger than his right,' Loughnane recalled. 'But he still couldn't hit the ball any distance. Not a huge amount was expected of him. By pure dint of determination he got there – just typical of this Clare bunch.'

Far away from boisterous crowds of 82,000, and long before they contested All-Ireland senior finals, these young Clare players were moulded by a group of willing, passionate volunteers: men of the quiet fields.

Collins would be the poster boy for all those who invested time and effort. In the best hurling season ever, he was arguably the classiest player on view. The paper-soft touch; that sublime reverse handpass against Galway; the point of the season in the drawn All-Ireland final – an audacious sprint, scoop and strike off his weaker right side, caressing the sliotar over the bar as four Corkmen bore down on him at a crucial stage in the game.

'Early in his school days he was only about four foot,' Loughnane explained. 'He was told his height would stop him from making it, but he got it into his head that if his hurling was good enough no one could stop him. He took to going down to the hurling field in Cratloe twice a week to hit a hundred balls – fifty off his left and fifty off his right. That was when he was a child.'

The small kid that pestered Loughnane to be allowed to play

with the big boys maintained and extended that obsessive ritual of peppering balls left and right. He practised until his hands were red raw and the grip unravelled from his hurley. He lived on brown rice, pasta, chicken and vegetables and pumped iron to compensate for lack of heft. He gave himself every possible chance to make it.

Off the field he led the way too. The week before Clare played in the 2010 All-Ireland minor final, their joint managers, Gerry O'Connor and Donal Moloney, found themselves on the horns of a dilemma. No fewer than twenty-five of the squad were graduating from St Flannan's just days before the big match. The clash of dates – sporting as well as romantic – had the coaches in a tizzy. It was Collins who came up with the compromise: let the lads collect their dates at eight, sup mineral water all evening and be tucked up in bed by half past midnight.

'That attitude from the entire group showed what a very special Clare hurling academy we have,' Loughnane remarked.

In 2013 Clare transported the game of hurling to grand new environs. For nine of the previous thirteen years Kilkenny had been almost untouchable. Tipperary and Cork did upset their momentum, but only sporadically. Between 2009 and 2011 the jousts between Kilkenny and Tipp, two traditional giants, were full-on collisions, emotion-fuelled clashes fought out under the dropping ball and in physical hits to determine who would be left standing. The day of the small, handy hurler seemed consigned to history.

Then Clare arrived. Under Davy Fitzgerald they were swift and fluent. They played hurling their own way. And in front of our eyes the game underwent a paradigm shift. Clare emerged on their own terms with an approach that, compared to Kilkenny's, was day versus night.

And how they gave hope to the other counties! As the 2014 championship loomed, Brian Cody's men were licking wounds and looking to reinvent themselves. Others, though, were ravenous for their own slice of the action. Like Clare, they hankered for days of revival. Hurling looked rejuvenated, with at least four counties harbouring realistic aspirations of soon winning a championship. This is the story behind that shift in power, a tale of how the others mobilized and finally caught up with a great Kilkenny team: men of the endless summer.

One

THE KILKENNY WAY

1

Men as Well as Giants

How Kilkenny became a team for the ages

They were the greatest hurling team we have ever seen. Kilkenny of the noughties; a side defined by unprecedented excellence, habitual success and rare consistency. They amassed unparalleled riches and drew us into their magnificent obsession throughout a decade and beyond. It's probable we will never see their likes again.

Eddie Brennan has told a story that encapsulates much of what they were about. Shortly before they played Galway in the 2007 All-Ireland quarter-final, Brennan decided to make a good impression on his manager, Brian Cody, by turning up early for training. In their opening two games, they had walloped Offaly and Wexford by a combined twenty-nine points, but Brennan had managed only three points of that total and was anxious about his position coming into the All-Ireland series.

He left work and headed for Nowlan Park, where training was to start at 7.30 p.m. He arrived shortly after six, let the car seat back and closed his eyes for twenty minutes before grabbing a bottle of Lucozade Sport and munching a few Jaffa Cakes. He walked in, togged out, got a rub and made his way on to the field at around 6.50 p.m., smiling contentedly as he passed Cody at the gate. The manager, after all, would often tell him to 'go in and hit a few balls'. When Brennan reached the field, however, the self-satisfied grin was wiped from his face.

'I looked down and saw four to five lads driving balls at each other and putting them over the bar on the turn. Worse still, they were all subs, and worst of all, they were all forwards looking for my place. It wasn't even seven o'clock. I bit my teeth and said, "Feck it, they're trying to steal a march on me here."'

As the sun set, those subs were still going at it hammer and tongs. Nowlan Park was a bear pit that bred and cultivated a ruthless, winning culture. You could never forget that. Brennan duly took note: 'Let's just say I was even earlier the next day.'

He had four All-Ireland medals in the cabinet by then but had never felt able to assume ownership of the jersey. His team-mates – especially those after his place in the team – were too unrelenting, their unwavering quest for perfection too great.

The heroes of that team embarked on an odyssey few others in the history of Gaelic games could dream of. The road they negotiated between 2000 and 2013 was dotted with glorious milestones, and though in 2013 they seemed submerged by a new wave, perhaps the odyssey did not end there. Even if it did, they can always claim they had achieved mighty deeds and crashed all manner of records.

'Before the 1999 All-Ireland final, I made the statement that I expected us to win seven out of the next ten All-Irelands,' D. J. Carey said. 'People must have thought I was off my rocker, but we had big guys coming in abundance and the teams that were coming at the same time didn't look in any way capable of matching us.'

Carey was right; over the next decade the Leinster champion-ship hit its lowest ebb in twenty-five years. Offaly were in decline, as were Wexford, and Dublin would struggle for several years. With little out there to trouble them, Kilkenny made hay.

'You basically looked at winning two matches to get out of Leinster and another two to win the All-Ireland,' Carey said. 'It sounded simple – it wasn't always, but several things were in our favour.'

By the start of the 2014 championship they were hunting for the thirteenth Leinster title of Brian Cody's reign, but the out-look was nowhere near as bright as it had been; nor were the production lines flowing with anything like the quality of the previous ten years. A succession of injuries and general wear and tear had clearly diminished a great team.

'The aura is gone, no doubt about that,' says James 'Cha' Fitzpatrick, who left the team aged twenty-six, by which time he had won five All-Irelands and three All Stars. 'Teams will fancy a crack at the boys now. But they won't go too far or too easy. Just look at what they achieved.'

There are signs of slippage. Given, however, that the great crusade had begun in earnest back at the dawn of the Millen-nium that process of attrition was entirely to be expected.

In 1999, the first graduates of a promising underage set-up came through: powerful men like Noel Hickey, solid stalwarts like Mick Kavanagh, swift and subtle virtuosi like Eddie Brennan.

Around the time this bunch of prodigies emerged, the Kilkenny chairman, Ned Quinn, took it upon himself to re-structure the county's underage set-up so as to ensure the production line kept rolling. They hadn't won an All-Ireland minor title between 1993 and 2002, and Quinn wasn't for leaving the future to chance – they would frame their own destiny. They convened a think-tank, sounded a call-to-arms to former players and created a development-squad system.

John Power, who won four All-Irelands with the county and enjoyed a senior career, albeit a fragmented one, that spanned the years between 1986 and 2002, said that Quinn deserves massive credit for complementing Cody's managerial style and paving the way for unprecedented success.

'I was left off the team in 1998 and when I got back in '99, Cody and Ned were leading the county like it was a different outfit. I returned from my first night's training with runners under my arm. The next evening I came home with wet gear. We were streets ahead of everyone else. Ned did things right. If you travelled from Mars to Nowlan Park for training you were paid accordingly in expenses. But if you took the piss that would be the end of you with him. Cody would get involved too. They'd see you hadn't the best interests of Kilkenny hurling at heart.'

Power feels, though, that the single biggest defining factor in paving the way for future glory was making changes to the club culture. 'Brian took power away from clubs. When I came on the scene in 1986 at the age of nineteen, Clara and Ballyhale were playing in a county final and there was wholesale war after it with the referee followed down a tunnel after Clara had scored a last-minute goal. I then went into a Kilkenny dressing room with their players on one side and Shamrocks players on another. We travelled away to one league match against Wexford and two of our players, Harry Ryan and Liam Fennelly, clashed because there was an open goal if one of them had passed to the other. That was the environment. It was not always good to be around. Cody changed so much. He gave county title-winning clubs the Kilkenny captaincy but cut all ties after that. When he took over there were no more rows. He let no club dictate. Can you imagine a scenario where a player like Colin Fennelly from the Shamrocks would be dropped for Walter Walsh [who comes from a small club in comparison] for the 2012 replayed All-Ireland final with Galway? It would never have happened before Cody took over.'

Apart from that change in mindset, the new structures worked.

'The board introduced a fantastic teacher system whereby former players came back and put something in,' Carey explained. 'The structures were always good in the schools, we had a great senior team in the making with an unbelievable manager, and soon we had underage squads and a platform for them to come right through to the senior team. Later, other counties copied us, but they had given us a head start of about eight years.

'Meantime, we had a group of freaks on our hands, and I mean freaks in the best possible sense of the word. Henry Shefflin hadn't featured to any great extent in the underage set-up; he struggled to make the Kilkenny under-16 team and battled initially to make college teams at Waterford IT. Derek Lyng also came from nowhere. He was at a small club [Urlingford] and not many people were aware of him. He couldn't make the college team in Waterford either.

'So, that's what I mean by saying what happened afterwards was freakish. To see these guys drive through, combine with the development-squad graduates and go on to win eight and nine All-Ireland medals was incredible.

'Cody was obviously the driving force but I would also pay tribute to Ned. He got things motoring underneath the surface.'

They soon got the rewards, winning four minor All-Irelands between 2002 and 2010 and four under-21 crowns between 2003 and 2008.

*

Still, they weren't satisfied. As the noughties ended, a delegation travelled to London in March 2010 for a close-up view of the Arsenal FC youth set-up.

Cody wasn't among the group; instead several of those who worked behind the scenes travelled, such as the former minor and under-21 manager Brendan O'Sullivan, a key figure behind the formation of the development squads, and Brian Ryan, a highly rated coach and games manager who would go on to become under-21 manager.

They went to Arsenal's training headquarters at Hale End, where they met Pat Rice, the club's assistant manager at the time. They also sat down with Steve Bould, manager of the youth team, and were given a rundown from top to bottom on how the Arsenal set-up worked and how talents like Cesc Fàbregas, Jack Wilshere, Ashley Cole and Aaron Ramsey were nurtured.

The first thing they noted was how everything revolved around the ball. Admittedly, language barriers were a factor – some of the players spoke little or no English, so communication had to be kept simple.

The visitors also observed that Arsenal had their footballers for several hours every day – whereas Cody and his assistants had their hurlers for only an hour or two each week. Thus the message was driven home: whatever time was available had to be used wisely.

The Kilkenny delegates were unlikely to admit it, but perhaps the salient message that emerged from the trip was that they were already doing most things right. The trick was to keep the good times coming. That foray to one of the lesser hurling counties – London – gave a snapshot of Kilkenny's approach during their period of supremacy.

*

They always went about their business with a minimum of fuss. Medals were amassed and handed for safe keeping to mothers or wives or girlfriends, while the players did their best to stay out of the spotlight. Scarcely a hubristic word escaped their lips.

The ethos prevailed as their winning run started to gain momentum. They had off-days in the 1999 All-Ireland final and 2001 All-Ireland semi-final but removed the bitter aftertaste of those setbacks when beating Offaly in the 2000 All-Ireland final and Clare two years later.

Some forty minutes before the 2002 final throw-in, John Hoyne, picked to play at half-forward, was split by an accidental skelp of a hurley while warming up. As blood streamed from his forehead minutes before the biggest game of his life, his nickname, Dougal, seemed more fitting than ever – it was like a scene from *Father Ted*.

He was leaden-footed and stunned – but clear-headed enough to know the flow needed to be stemmed quickly, so he asked for stitches. The wound, however, was too deep. Undeterred, he had four staples inserted, went out, hit a point and lasted until the fifty-sixth minute.

The shock and pain of the injury could have skewed his focus, but making the field was his only concern; a statement perhaps of his identity as a Kilkenny hurler – they carry on regardless.

Hoyne needn't have worried about loss of blood; Clare were the ones who proved anaemic on the day, the colour draining from their cheeks after just three minutes when D. J. Carey pounced for Kilkenny's first goal.

After winning the final by seven points and burying the torture of the previous year, the players might have lost the run of themselves in celebration. But in the Kilkenny dressing room, as the Liam MacCarthy Cup rested on top of a kitbag, the team captain, Andy Comerford, stood on a bench and spoke.

'You can all hold your heads high, lads. Thirty men got us here and every one of them was needed. I'll say one thing, lads – respect yourselves and respect your families. Celebrate for sure, but Kilkenny were always men that were humble.

'Always remember that you're Kilkenny hurlers. Whatever way you celebrate, do it with dignity and do it with pride. Be proud of what you achieved. Respect the jersey.'

He had spoken to a hushed room but stepped down to thunderous applause. It was as if those key words had found an echo in their hearts. The black-and-amber jersey. Dignity. Pride of place. Cornerstones of what they were all about. The foundations of a team's excellence.

When the cheering ended it was clear there would be no losing the run of themselves.

They were never seen making idiots of themselves around their home town. Their manager's words seemed to resound every-where they went: 'If you respect your opponents you'll respect yourself.' That is what Cody made sure they achieved and it goes a long way to explain why they won six All-Irelands in seven and nine in thirteen seasons.

They maintained their dignity off the field. After one big win, a player let his hair down with a few beers and a bit of River-dancing. Someone in the bar filmed his footwork and the footage found its way on to YouTube. Acutely embarrassed, the culprit immediately owned up to management.

Before they moved to have the clip taken down, one of the backroom team asked just how X-rated the footage might be. There was a pause before the guilty party fessed up: he had been dancing; without a shirt; maybe on top of a table.

In another county's social diary that bit of tomfoolery would be a mere warm-up for the night ahead. In Kilkenny, it was taken to mean success was going to your head.

Little wonder then that, while stories of the team's accomplishments stayed on the bestseller lists, their off-field activities were banned from publication.

There was a constant media glare, and countless times Corporate Ireland knocked on doors seeking endorsements, but more often than not the players declined the perks.

Inevitably, Henry Shefflin was in huge demand, but he too was very careful about who he chose to work with.

A team-mate of Shefflin's was invited in 2012 to turn up at Croke Park, pull on a sponsor's shirt and speak to the media. He scrutinized the list of participants, saw the name of a hurler with whom Kilkenny had had serious issues and declined the €1,000 on offer, preferring to do his talking on the field.

So self-effacing were Kilkenny that in the eyes of some they lacked interest. They seemed not to produce 'characters' of the type so beloved of commentators and casual observers. They had plenty of wonderful players but none whose private lives were punctuated with colour and drama.

As a result, hurling became for many a boring duopoly around the mid-noughties, with only Cork looking capable of challenging Cody's men, who were simply unstoppable in Leinster and only slightly susceptible elsewhere. Indeed, GAA officials became so concerned with the perennial one-horse race in Leinster that they held a crisis meeting.

'Perhaps the only one to cause controversy in the early days was myself,' Carey smiled, 'and that was with the formation of the Gaelic Players Association. As a big name in hurling I was asked to use my profile to look outside of Kilkenny and give other counties a hand in how their players were treated. I felt I did need to do it. I got no flak from Brian Cody but he asked me once or twice where the whole thing was going and wondered if I had an issue with the Kilkenny board.

'I had no issues at all. But I was presenting medals all over Ireland and travelling across the country and I saw others that did have problems. Not everyone was treated as we were.'

Much as Carey was in demand countrywide, there was a growing desire among coaches and players to visit Kilkenny in the pursuit of knowledge and excellence. Soon they flowed in from the four corners to Nowlan Park, eager to discern what was happening. They came from as far afield as Antrim looking for esoteric wisdom and arcane formulae – but left bemused at the simplicity, the sheer ordinariness, of the sessions. The secret, they learned, was merely the sum of a colossal effort day in, day out. The Kilkenny hurlers simply saw the training field as their gauge – the more they bled there in practice, the less they bled in battle.

Their run began in 2000. Cork softened their cough in the middle of the decade before they dusted themselves down and drove on, burying most teams that tried to block their path.

While they were still dominant in 2009, '11 and '12, hindsight would suggest they peaked in 2007 – when they destroyed all before them, beating Offaly by fourteen points, Wexford by fifteen and Galway by ten.

In the 2007 All-Ireland semi-final they thrashed Wexford, again by ten points, and hammered Limerick by the same margin in the final. Although that may not suggest an outright hammering, Kilkenny had effectively buried their rivals in the first sixteen minutes.

Limerick, desperate to end a famine stretching back to 1973, had arrived in Croke Park surfing on a gigantic green wave. They had left nothing to chance. Richie Bennis, their manager, was bred on traditional hurling but wasn't afraid to embrace new ways. For weeks they pored over tactical videos of Kilkenny. The Munster rugby great Paul O'Connell spoke to them about the tightrope they were walking, the delicate line separating success from failure on the big day. The night before the final, they stayed in Dunboyne, where the legendary motivator Seán Boylan was invoked to ensure they had ticked all the boxes.

During the pre-match formalities they behaved as if Croke Park were their second home. They almost embraced President Mary McAleese like you would an old friend. The video shows Stephen Lucey chortling heartily as they spoke, and the President obviously found Donie Ryan a hoot – whatever he said left her in stitches.

They strode around the field then, soaking up the atmosphere. People wondered if David had ever been so calm with Goliath bearing down on him. For good measure, Limerick's passionate supporters outnumbered Kilkenny's three to one. And then battle was joined.

Henry Shefflin went straight over on Stephen Lucey. Eddie Brennan went hunting for Séamus Hickey. After nine minutes, and before Limerick got their second breath, Kilkenny had 2-3 on the board. All over. At half-time Limerick could have done with forensics as they sifted through the wreckage.

As the half unfolded, Hickey, on course for Young Hurler of the Year, had taken more hits than Joe Dolan. A beacon of the new Limerick generation, Hickey had hurled a fair amount of ball – and did much to contain Brennan – but the psychological damage was done as early as the ninth minute when Brennan, who would end up with 1-5, discarded his man like a rag doll and buried one of the goals that would send his side to another title.

Kilkenny's tried and trusted strategy of zoning in on the opposition's best players had worked once more. Eoin Larkin filleted another defensive stalwart, Peter Lawlor, at the far side of the field, taking four points off him. Shefflin had 1-2 in the bag before a leg gave way. And though Limerick hung on heroically, the game was a dead duck by the break.

'After the game I went looking for Séamus,' said Limerick's Donal O'Grady. 'One by one the Kilkenny lads came over and shook hands, so it took me a while to reach him. When I did see him – and I still have this vision in my head – there was Eddie with his hands wrapped around Séamus. He was more or less saying, "Sorry lad, I had to do it."'

'That game summed up the [difference between] two teams,' O'Grady lamented. 'You have to be ruthless. They were.'

A year later they racked up seven goals and forty-five points in their first two championship games and went on to hammer Waterford 3-30 to 1-13 in the All-Ireland final. During that time they must frequently have known they had games won before they even took the field, but they were never outwardly cocky.

'We didn't actually like those scenarios,' Cha Fitzpatrick says. 'Sure, you could enjoy the second halves and start spraying a few passes around but at the final whistle you didn't celebrate those wins in the same way that you would have celebrated a one- or two-point win.'

Recalling that 2008 final, John Mullane spoke of a team possessed taking Waterford apart from the first whistle: 'They hit us like a train from the start, ran us over and cut the legs from under us with a hail of early scores. But they were even more relentless at the end.'

Mullane talked of picking himself off the ground after being flattened, wondering if the final whistle would ever sound. They were then twenty-seven points behind.

'I was on my knees and looking up at Henry Shefflin. There he was arguing with the referee for not getting a free and they had us absolutely pulverized by that stage. I just thought, "Ah here, give us a break!"'

Mullane stayed on the field that day to hear Kilkenny's trophy acceptance – not because he would enjoy it, but because he felt they were owed that respect: 'They had beaten us out of sight. But fair play to them for going for the jugular. There was nothing sly about it and they didn't rub it in either. In fact, I was marking Mick Kavanagh and he came over to me and kept apologizing. I swear he must have said sorry three times.'

Eddie Brennan, holder of eight senior All-Ireland medals, admitted they did sometimes feel invincible but insisted they treated every opponent with respect. The important thing was to harness that self-belief and not let it morph into arrogance: 'Confidence was surging through the team, but we never once took it for granted. Most of the lads – Tommy Walsh, J. J. Delaney, Jackie Tyrrell – had come up together from minor and under-21 and married in with my under-21 team of 1999. We knew we had the best hurlers in Ireland in our dressing room – that's about as far as the cockiness went.

'Cody would always say, "Look, the day ye stop challenging yourselves is the day ye become ordinary. But if your attitude is spot on there's no limit to what ye could achieve."'

Much has been made of their decade-plus of dominance. One could delve into the annals and return a blow-by-blow account of their deeds, but here it is sufficient merely to revisit some of the factors that made them unique.

Theirs was a pioneering run and yet their manager planned

for, say, their thirty-one-point demolition of Offaly in 2005 exactly as he would for Cork in the 2006 All-Ireland final. Before each game he spelled out his vision to players, prepared his match-ups for the battle ahead. Then they hit the training ground to maintain that absolute focus.

At the end of every session they were left fearful that their productive run was dangling by a thread. And everyone bar Shefflin was led to believe at some stage that his place was under threat from some hungry young cub who had thrown down a gauntlet in training. And rather than seeking to humiliate opponents on the field, they were simply focused on retaining the jersey. The best way to do that, and to respect the opposition, was to apply full force until the final whistle.

In 2005, when they beat Offaly out the gate, they could have pulled up when ten points ahead and started showboating. But they drove on with full intensity.

That single-mindedness has brought accusations of rubbing opponents' noses in the dirt, but the charge is simply incorrect. The surest way to insult beaten opponents is to saunter to breaking ball or start bouncing the sliotar off the turf or play keep-ball with a string of handpasses. But that was never the Kilkenny way. They always kept pedal to metal. Every opponent was there to be respected – and then chewed alive.

Yes, there was at times something almost machine-like or superhuman about it, but it was never calculated to make fools out of rivals. It was simply that neither sentiment nor sympathy was allowed to intrude. Nothing personal, just business.

Offaly's Brian Carroll studied at St Kieran's College, and thereby learned his trade in harness with most of Kilkenny's stars of that golden era. In 2005, Carroll was only twenty-two when Offaly had their rear ends handed to them on a platter by Kilkenny, and yet he has spoken of them only with admiration.

'They respected us enough to go on and drive the nail in and I wouldn't expect anything less. If the shoe was on the other foot I'd like to think Offaly would have done the same.

'They had us beaten off the pitch by half-time and yet there wasn't one loose comment passed. Eddie Brennan was obsessed with goals and Kilkenny had two or three in the bag early on. The most frustrating thing was that after twenty minutes we had seven scores and so had they – but they had three goals and we didn't.'

In the days after that drubbing, former Offaly hurlers like Aidan Fogarty and Damien Martin got together and phoned the players to offer support.

'I grew up looking at videos of those men, was starstruck by them and took their word to be gospel, so it meant a lot that they didn't turn their backs on Offaly hurling,' Carroll said. 'But they didn't. They knew we had just been taken apart by one serious team and they wanted us to know that not many teams could have survived the onslaught.

'We were mortified for months afterwards; I was too embarrassed to go out – but the words of those former players helped ease the burden a little.'

According to Brendan Cummins, every team suffered a hiding from Kilkenny but some lost on the field of play and some were beaten before a sliotar was pucked in anger.

'Consistency was their key,' he said. 'They had teams beaten before they went out on the field; there is no doubt about that.'

At ground level, Cummins got his fill of the black-and-amber shirt. From 2002 until he retired in 2013 the Tipp keeper came up against Kilkenny six times and ended up on the winning side only once. Despite the counties being long-time foes, he said, Tipp never had those defeats shoved down their throats.

'No, their players were never cocky. You could tell by their body language that they fully believed in themselves because they were always going around upright, the heads up and the shoulders up.

'The only time I got a glimpse that they were suffering was when we beat them in the 2010 All-Ireland final. I knew for all the world that we had them that day for one reason – they went quiet. They didn't give up but they stopped encouraging each other.

'Every other time I played them in the championship, though, they motored until the end. They had made so many sacrifices and they were so proud that they had got that jersey. They weren't going to give it up, because they knew how valuable it was and how hard they had worked to get it.

'That's been their secret, really. That – and they had aerial skills better than most other teams. Among the fifteen players they put out on any given day they had nine natural ball winners. That turned the tables massively in their favour, especially with four of those ball winners in the forwards. Not many teams had that.'

When encouraged to select the single biggest contributor to Kilkenny's sustained dominance, Cummins settled on one man – Henry Shefflin, who, up to and including 2013, played in every championship game bar three that Cody presided over.

In the process, Shefflin rattled off an astonishing sixty-two appearances on the trot, edged past immortals such as Christy Ring and became the greatest hurler in the history of the game, the all-time leading scorer and, along with Noel Hickey, the holder of nine All-Ireland medals.

*

During that era Kilkenny put together unbeaten runs that Katie Taylor might envy, falling just short of a five-in-a-row that would have been a first in senior intercounty hurling or football.

After their 2005 All-Ireland semi-final defeat in the goalfest against Galway, they didn't again lose a competitive match until well into the 2007 league. They won three games to capture the 2006 Walsh Cup; won seven more and drew once, with Limerick, en route to the Allianz League title; and then won a further five times to recapture the Liam MacCarthy Cup. That was sixteen victories, one solitary draw and no defeats. The unbeaten record stretched to eighteen months and nineteen games.

During that spell Shefflin was the embodiment of the team; when they needed to find out about themselves they looked at him. In subsequent years he minded himself, playing in only six league matches between 2006 and 2013.

It is widely assumed that 2014 may bring the curtain down on Shefflin's career. His departure would mark definitively the end of an era for Kilkenny.

'If Cody is the driving force, Henry is definitely the man on the field,' Cummins said. 'The one that always steadied the ship when they were in crisis. In the first half of the 2012 All-Ireland semi-final we had them on the ropes and he was at left corner-forward watching the Kilkenny puck-out land about fifty metres away from me.

'He could see that plenty of ball was breaking in front of him, but none of the scraps were coming his way. He tried to get the message to his team-mates to attack the breaks and hunt harder for possession. He was giving out and pointing but getting frustrated because no one heard him.

'Eventually he called for the ball. Put his hurl up to David Herity, signalled to a gap that only he could see and ran on to the puck-out, gathered the ball and burst through. We opened up and he swung the pass to T.J., who had switched corners into where Shefflin should have been. He buried it and that goal killed us.

'Hurling is a game of complete variables and chance – that was the only time Shefflin made that run. He went forward to react rather than waiting for it to go behind. He had read the previous few plays. More hurling intelligence than anyone else.'

In an interview with the *Kilkenny People* early in 2007, Cody was asked if their appetite had been sated. He replied that they were going out to win every game: 'It is hard to defend the alternative. I don't think there is an alternative. I don't think the alternative is of any use to anyone.'

With a manager that driven and his players so conscientious, it's little wonder they rewrote the record books. Before they arrived, the county knew what it was like to drink from the well of success, but once Cody came on the scene they took up permanent residency at the spring.

In the 1970s they had won four and lost three All-Ireland finals. The 1980s were decent too; they appeared in three finals and won two. And in the 1990s they made five finals and again won two. They were more than getting by. Tacking on a few titles here and there. Keeping there or thereabouts with Cork and keeping Tipp below them. How bad?

'That scenario was the norm for thirty years before Brian Cody came in,' said the former Kilkenny under-21 manager Richie Mulrooney. 'Throughout those three decades we were doing fine.'

But 'doing fine' wasn't a term Cody could ever identify with. After he took over in 1999 the landscape was for ever changed. Under his watch they went on to win nine All-Irelands between

1999 and 2013 and landed seven league titles from nine finals. To put that into perspective, Mick O'Dwyer's great Kerry football team won only three league crowns.

It is also pertinent that Cody's Kilkenny went to war following the 1990s, when all their main rivals had either stormed the summit or gained a close-up view of it.

They lost the 1999 decider to Cork, and even though it was only his first year, Cody found himself under pressure, not least because Cork had been no great shakes on the day. If Cody was to make his wine, he needed to discard the sour grapes of 1999. That was the beginning.

Before their era of dominance started, however, there were further painful lessons to be learned. If losing the 1999 final was a crushing blow, the harshest lesson was dished out by Galway, who beat them up physically in the 2001 All-Ireland semi-final. Indeed, Galway didn't just beat up Kilkenny – they went through them for a shortcut.

Early in the championship Offaly had tried to outmuscle Cody's youthful-looking side but lacked the heft for the job. Galway were up to it, though. From the throw-in, when the nineteen-year-old Richie Murray slammed into Brian McEvoy and sent him crashing to the turf, the tone for Galway's victory was set.

The Kilkenny lads spent much of that game tangling with opponents and complaining to match officials, looking for the protection that never came. They were boys in a man's world. After that mugging they swore they would never again be bullied.

It was a promise they held. Up to the end of 2013 they had played sixty-seven championship games under Cody, won fifty-six of them and lost only nine. An unprecedented spell of dominance, let alone consistency.

2

Nothing to See Here

How Cody's men kept outward calm
through every storm

When you have amassed a treasure trove as sizeable as Kilkenny's, you encounter challenges. As well as trying to guard your haul against covetous outsiders, you must maintain the high standards which helped you to win it.

With Cody's pragmatic style and a gallery of big names jostling for starting places, there were always bound to be squalls and dangerous reefs on Kilkenny's voyage, especially as that voyage was so long. And so it proved. What's fascinating, however, is that whenever the good ship black and amber entered stormy waters it emerged virtually undamaged and sailed blithely on.

In other hurling counties there were player strikes and stand-offs. Counties saw that just one high-profile defection, one big name shown the door, one drink-fuelled night out, one difference of opinion between players and officials, was sometimes enough to sink a season and leave wreckage washing the shore for years afterwards.

But Kilkenny let the seat back, munched popcorn and grew stronger while watching the soap operas unfold as county after county washed their grubby gear in public.

Kilkenny had plenty of issues of their own, and not all of them were kept under wraps, but most were. And the difference was they could cope even when an item of dirty linen ended up in the public thoroughfare. So many episodes that could have boiled over stayed simmering until the heat was turned off.

In September 2000, the rumour raced through the county that one of their starting forwards, Stephen Grehan, had been dropped for going on a solo run by playing in a soccer game just a week before the All-Ireland final.

Grehan had taken the field as a sub for Spa United in the second half of a game with River Rangers in the Maher Shield. He scored the winner, but it proved to be an own goal because it surely cost him an appearance in what would have been the biggest game of his life.

Hurling is really the only code that counts in Kilkenny, and Grehan had played in all three of their championship games that season before being surprisingly left off the All-Ireland final team.

The media dug deep and the line emerged that he had been punished for a breach of squad discipline. But Cody was adamant that John Hoyne had been selected ahead of Grehan purely on merit – even though Hoyne had scarcely featured that season.

Sensing a fuss, television, radio and newspaper reporters swooped on Kilkenny to cover what was now a running story – it had even made the front page of one tabloid.

As the tempest came to town, Cody kept repeating the party line: 'I have no control over what's being said about the team selection, either inside or outside Kilkenny, and, frankly, it doesn't bother me. The management's job is to select what we regard as the best team and that's what we've done. Our only concern is the wellbeing of Kilkenny hurling for this very important game.'

After a day or so trying to put flesh on the bones of the story, the press pack grew tired of hunting for scraps and, with no one in the county willing to feed their frenzy, threw away the carcass and left town. The storm had quickly passed.

Kilkenny hammered Offaly 5-15 to 1-14 in the final, and Grehan, who didn't even make it on as a sub, was barely mentioned in the aftermath.

One squall that raged slightly longer was Charlie Carter's withdrawal in 2003. Kilkenny's management had gradually lost faith in the sublimely talented Gowran man. His skill set was unquestionable but the feeling was that his work rate didn't fit the high-tempo, post-2001 template constructed on the back of a crushing defeat to Galway.

Carter lost his place for the 2002 championship, regained it and then lost it again. His club won the 2002 county senior title and proposed him as Kilkenny captain for the 2003 season. He trained exceptionally hard over the winter, but to little avail – Carter was no longer seen as a seventy-minute player, but didn't see himself as an impact sub. Something had to give.

A darling of the galleries, he was always driven to win, but his effortless, languid style didn't seem to fit the new way. His absence from the 2003 championship starting fifteen and subsequent departure from the panel baffled many supporters, who couldn't understand that their captain would leave the squad in mid-championship, especially when he had finished as the league's top scorer with 4-10 despite starting just three of Kilkenny's nine games.

*

In fairness to all concerned, it had been a scratchy old year for the Gowran man. Illness had ruled him out of the opening two matches, against Waterford and Galway. He scored a point as a substitute against Laois and then held his place for the last two fixtures in the first phase of the competition, hitting 1-1 against Clare and 1-6 against Dublin.

He was motoring well – better than many of his team-mates on the training field – but was nevertheless named on the bench for the league final, against Tipperary. He came on in that game and punched in for a highly productive, albeit brief, shift. Arguably, it was his vibrant cameo that rescued Kilkenny from the jaws of defeat and clinched the league title in an epic shootout.

But cracks had appeared in the relationship, and by the time the championship loomed no amount of whitewashing was going to conceal it. In his book *Triumph and Troubles*, Carter surmised that the slow fuse which eventually led to the burning of bridges between Cody and himself may have been lit away back on the night of the 1999 All-Ireland final, a poor enough game that Cork won. It was a game that Kilkenny had been red-hot favourites for, but incessant rain spoiled it as a contest and Cork finished the stronger to win by 0-13 to 0-12.

At the post-match banquet, Carter, as he recalled in his memoirs, gave Cody a piece of his mind for taking him off during the game.

By early June 2003, there was still widespread uncertainty over Carter's future. Kilkenny hammered Dublin by fifteen points in the Leinster championship, but the only sighting of Carter was of him bursting out the side door of the Nowlan Park dressing rooms before the rest of the team had even showered, evidently furious that he had seen no game time.

The national media milked the story for what it was worth, and locally it was the sole topic of debate. Two days after that game, with Carter now on the brink of retirement, a Radio Kilkenny poll revealed overwhelming support for the player, 80 per cent of respondents backing him and the other 20 per cent telling him to suck it up and live by the manager's decisions.

But polls didn't pick the Kilkenny team – Brian Cody did. And so Carter, only thirty-two, contacted the county board and relayed his decision to retire, notifying the county secretary, Pat Dunphy, before an announcement was later made on Radio Kilkenny.

As the summer passed, hurling fans being no exceptions to the general fickleness of human nature, sympathy for Carter waned. The feeling grew that he should have hung around and accepted his new role, and he would have got to lift the Liam MacCarthy Cup.

In his place, D. J. Carey, his Young Irelands clubmate, had the honour. Again, in another county such a turn-up might have led to serious local tensions. In Tipperary in 1988, there was civil unrest when Pa O'Neill lost the captaincy for the All-Ireland final and was replaced by Nicky English. The backlash was massive from Cappawhite, O'Neill's club, and English described it as one of the most stressful times in his life. But, as so often happened, Kilkenny hurling dealt with potential controversy by just getting on with it.

'I was sorry Charlie fell out,' Carey said, 'but I was representing the club and the responsibility fell to me. That's the only way I look at it. Looking back, a lot of big names went around then. Brian was possibly lucky in that he didn't have to deal with the public; he was a school principal and wasn't working on the road as a sales rep or in a bank. Then again he'd have hard enough skin to take the flak even if he was out and about. Because he certainly would have taken flak.

'Over the years, Brian let lads go and he did it with the view of what he thought was best for Kilkenny hurling – that's what he looked at. There was a drip feed of fellas going at one stage but the dressing room was fine; there was no real talk about what was happening because people were just fighting for their own positions.

'That's the thing about hurling – it's selfish. The dressing room carries on as if nothing ever happens. Guys are coming in for fellas who have walked or have been let go and the new lads want a jersey. It was the same with me. Things just moved on the day I left. You might like to think you left a big gap or whatever, but sure it all just carried on same as usual.'

The same evening that Radio Kilkenny dropped the Carter bombshell, news was communicated to Cody that his own club-mate Brian McEvoy was also calling time on his career. McEvoy was another class act, with two All-Irelands and an All Star on his sideboard. But, having gone from being among the best fifteen in the land to being a mere impact player with Kilkenny, he too felt his county career ebbing away.

The fact that he and Cody were James Stephens men was proving a complication, and so McEvoy decided against hanging around. His departure didn't cause the same fuss as Carter's, but it was something of a tragedy all the same to see such a lovely, natural hurler walk off into the sunset.

These controversies could have degenerated into a three-ring circus had they been handled less tactfully by those involved. Carter didn't reveal his innermost thoughts until he published his autobiography some years later, and by then wounds were healing. McEvoy held his counsel to the end, and so did nothing that might distract Kilkenny on their relentless way to winning that year's All-Ireland.

*

Around the time Carter and McEvoy bowed out, another high-profile but disaffected Kilkenny man, Denis Byrne, was drafted into the Tipperary panel for the visit of Galway to Semple Stadium. Byrne had captained Kilkenny in 1999 and 2001, both unsuccessful seasons. Like McEvoy, he was well decorated, with an All-Ireland and an All Star to his name.

Byrne had a passion for hurling, an insatiable appetite for training and an encyclopaedic knowledge of the game. Before official training started, he would be away on a back pitch hitting balls and practising frees. Having been the shining gem of the Kilkenny underage system, winning minor and under-21 All-Irelands, he was deeply hurt at failing to make the 2003 senior panel. His big fear was that he would never play intercounty again, so he made the wholly unprecedented and, in the eyes of many, unacceptable move of joining his native county's next-door neighbours and biggest rivals. It was like Gary Neville joining Liverpool.

Byrne moved to Mullinahone and was soon drafted into the Tipp camp, making an immediate impression with his dedication to training. The Tipp lads made no big deal of the transfer but it took Tommy Dunne to break the ice; one night at training he called the group into a huddle: 'Lads, from now on Denis is one of us. Treat him as such.'

Byrne bided his time and slotted into the Tipp team for the qualifiers, shooting six points from play against Laois at O'Moore Park. When Tipp qualified to make the All-Ireland semi-final against Kilkenny, Byrne had lost his starting place and remained on the bench as his adopted county exited the championship.

At the end, as the teams left the field, one Kilkenny player turned to the Tipp dugout and harangued Byrne, 'turncoat' being the gist of the abuse. That it didn't kick off there and then was a minor miracle.

From there, Byrne's short career with Tipp trailed off and following an illness in 2004 he wasn't called back into the set-up. He returned to his club, Graigue-Ballycallan, but never featured for Kilkenny thereafter.

Again, despite having been hugely upset at his abrupt departure from the Kilkenny squad, Byrne kept his sense of injustice to himself, and his silence saved the team another un-wanted sideshow as it continued on its merry way.

John Power believes that, as the team started to evolve, Cody tested its players. 'Brian had the ability to read contentment in a player,' he said. 'He would study closely and decide whether the player's energy and mindset were strong enough to last a full season. Would there be anything else to interfere with Kilkenny? If something was not right he would test that player to a degree and if that man failed the test he was no good to him.

'He would leave you off for a game just to see how you would react sometimes. Would you sit back and accept that you needed to work harder? If you did, you had some chance of a reprieve. If you didn't, you were gone. I would have loved if Charlie and Brian stayed on for a bit longer, and I understood the frustration Denis Byrne went through, but when you are in that situation it's hard to see everything clearly. You get so upset at missing out. And Brian is a great man to see just how far you want to put that throttle down.'

Philly Larkin was another scarcely heard from since he walked in 2004, after his game time was severely curtailed. Another clubmate of Cody's, Larkin was from a family steeped in Kilkenny lore, the third link in a family chain of Larkins to win All-Ireland medals – following in the studmarks of his grandfather, Paddy, and father, Fan. He made his call in April

2004, after not getting on the field in the league match with Offaly and sensed there was little hope of change for the better any time soon.

While it's debatable whether some of the aforementioned players walked away before their time or were simply usurped in the natural order of things by equally gifted but younger and fitter men, it would take an outrageous twisting of logic to argue that James 'Cha' Fitzpatrick had little more to give when he quit.

Cha, the game's unfettered spirit, retired in 2011, and while his form had dipped for a couple of seasons from its normally lofty heights, there was so much more left in the tank.

Fitzpatrick had made a swift transition from the county minors in 2004 to start in the All-Ireland senior final that same summer, and so meteoric was his rise and so sustained his brilliance, it was hardly credible the show could be over for him just seven years later.

By 1997, the name Cha was already in lights. He was chosen Player of the Tournament at that year's Féile na nGael, the premier all-Ireland under-14 competition, and a year later he was back to win the 'individual skills' title. By the age of twenty-six, when he called time on his career, he had five senior All-Irelands, three league titles and three All Stars and had captained Kilkenny to under-21 and senior titles.

So why did such a decorated player suddenly quit while still so young?

The answer was a lack of action, and the apparent move away from what Fitzpatrick perceived to be the traditional criterion for selection – training-ground form. One of the Kilkenny fundamentals had long been to pick teams based on what Cody and his selectors saw on the training field. And for at least six months before he hung up his hurley, Fitzpatrick reckoned he was producing the goods twice a week, every week, in Nowlan Park – but not getting recognition for it: 'I felt I was flying it in training but the team was sort of set from July onwards and if you weren't on it by then it was going to be hard. And I had no intention of spending 2012 sitting on a bench with my arse getting cold,' he smiles. 'Listen, Brian brought me on board in 2004, he trusted me and I won more than I could ever have dreamed of. I played with some of the best hurlers of all time and I really thrived when I moved to midfield, but in the 2010 All-Ireland final I was pushed off the pace a bit and taken off against Tipperary. I never really got back in. I felt that in 2011 my form on the training ground was as good as anyone's but I never got game time and that's what all of us want. I shut my mouth, bit my lip and trained my arse off. I was going nowhere so I moved on. No bitterness, no rows with anyone; I just had more to do with my life. It had been a short stint, I suppose, but it was one brilliant stint.'

He dialled Cody's phone number. The conversation lasted about half a minute.

'I said at the start of the year that I'd leave if I couldn't nail down a place. And that didn't happen,' he explained. 'You're supposed to be judged on form on the training ground but my personal opinion is that didn't happen this year.

'Brian just said that I seemed to have my mind made up, that he wasn't going to go down on his knees and beg me to stay. He thanked me and I thanked him. I could have had it out with him during that year but past experiences told me that wouldn't have been a wise move,' Fitzpatrick laughed. 'That's why there are no public controversies in Kilkenny – everyone saw what happened with Charlie, Brian and the lads over the years so lads just get on with it. Myself included!'

There was never going to be negotiation. Cody doesn't need

to make concessions and Cha has always been his own man – radically altering his career path from engineering to school-teaching, disc jockeying at weekends, playing golf, travelling the world; three pursuits he still enjoys immensely.

He was resolute in his decision. A sum total of eighteen minutes' championship action in 2011; the commute from Lucan, where he taught, to Kilkenny four times a week; being told three times to warm up during the 2011 All-Ireland final and yet not getting a sniff of action – they were among the reasons he walked away. He was convinced he still had much to offer but there was no point hanging around if Cody didn't agree. And he doesn't necessarily go chasing old comrades' company either.

'Life is short,' Fitzpatrick said. 'And there's more to mine than intercounty hurling. I don't miss it at all.'

For Eddie Brennan, however, there was no guarantee Fitzpatrick would have stayed on even if Cody had wanted him to.

'Cha is a great guy with a different personality and to be honest he never struck me as the type of fella who would play until he was thirty-five,' said Brennan. 'But I do feel the management should have told him to hang tough. They certainly could not force him to stay, nor should they, but no team can turn around and dispose of talent like his that quickly.

'His reading of games was second to none – he would see a pass a mile away. In 2011, he was playing unreal in training and to be honest I was lucky to get in the team ahead of him. It was only when Ricey [Michael Rice] went to midfield that I got in the starting fifteen, but Cha still had plenty to offer that Kilkenny team.'

No sooner was Fitzpatrick out the door, with lovers of the game nationwide lamenting his premature departure, than talk of him joining the Dublin set-up emerged. It wasn't idle talk –

the Dubs definitely had an interest and made moves to sign him up.

'Not a hope,' Fitzpatrick said. 'It would have been weird with a different shirt on my back. Never a chance of it.'

Eddie Brennan took a phone call in relation to a possible transfer of Fitzpatrick to the Dubs, but won't say who from. 'It was one of the Dublin lads looking for a meeting with Cha. I told them that if Dalo [Anthony Daly] persuaded Cha to hurl for him I would be more than impressed.

'I couldn't ever see him playing with Dublin. They train harder than us anyway and Cha had been through a punishing regime since 2004! He was more inclined to go off and play some golf rather than go through all that again with a different county.

'But I'm still very disappointed that he left when he did. We couldn't afford to let his talent go.'

Reflecting on the household names that left the party early, Brennan has acknowledged he could have been one himself had he not recharged his career in 2006 – and that in any other county the abrupt departure or culling at frequent intervals of such big names would likely have caused all hell to break loose.

'In Kilkenny, the moment you kicked up, someone else was waiting for the shirt. Looking back, I see it now as the natural evolution of a team.'

To lose so many big names so quickly? Natural selection?

'Well, people were saying to me that I left too early but I didn't – it was the right time. The show goes on without you in any case.

'Charlie Carter was proof of that. He was a huge figure here. Still is. He was back in training very early in 2003, doing the hard slog and putting a huge effort in. The previous year, there had been serious competition between us for the number thirteen shirt and one winter's night late in 2002 I just threw my arm around him and said, "Best of luck, Charlie, you're our captain next year and I'm hundred per cent behind you."

'I was kept in the team even though I wasn't going well and Charlie lost out. It was tough for both of us. I went out to his club for the homecoming when we won the All-Ireland. He had left the squad but he never blamed me, in fairness. If a lad has your position there's an inclination to be angry towards him but it wasn't personal with Charlie.

'Likewise, we didn't make much of it in the dressing room. It was like, he's gone now, but we'll manage. It was the same with D.J. Another county would be in mourning for years, but around here you just don't dwell on it.

'It's good too that no player leaks anything and few are inclined to take a pop at the manager. Sure how could they with all that he has won?'

After retiring, Brennan developed his career as a media pundit and found it affected his contacts with former team-mates. Not long after retiring, he went to Michael Rice's stag party, wary of the reception he would get, and was relieved when someone made a joke at his expense and the ice was broken. But as a Sunday newspaper columnist and prominent analyst for RTÉ he has been clearly on the other side of the fence.

His media role has left him vulnerable, whenever a story or rumour out of Kilkenny reaches the sports pages, to accusations or suspicions of being the source, whereas in reality he has never been. Like Fitzpatrick, he has had little contact with some of his old mates.

'You just move on. You're the best of pals three to four days a week for the bones of ten or eleven years and next thing it's nothing. Sometimes I feel strange texting the lads even though I was part of the group for so long. It's a bit like being in that film

Meet the Fockers, where a circle of trust is formed – I'm outside that now.'

Another player on the outside has been John Mulhall, who was dropped after the 2012 league. No reason was given but Mulhall hadn't helped himself some months earlier when he sang at the team homecoming in September 2011.

His stand-up cameo, intended in jest and for the most part hilarious, contained an impudent message for Kilkenny's beaten opponents: 'Tipperary, Póg mo thóin.'

It was all just tongue in cheek – but as the video went viral on YouTube you feared that, no matter what came next, Mulhall's Kilkenny career might be short-lived. And so it proved.

'We all do mad stuff,' said Brennan. 'As a county player you are watched a lot closer. I enjoyed myself on different nights in Kilkenny but there was never any real messing.

'Unfortunately, John could go down as having the shortest intercounty career of all time and that's a pity because Muller could do some mad stuff with the ball. The point he got against Tipp in the 2011 All-Ireland final, running away from the goal and over his shoulder, was serious.

'From a hurling point of view he could do anything, from the very best to the worst, but the thing about Brian Cody is that he wanted you to learn and progress and show that you were getting better in training. Maybe Muller just didn't kick on. At times he was hard to play with because you never knew what he was going to do from one minute to the next.'

And so Mulhall became another in a long line of Kilkenny casualties in the ceaseless pursuit of success. And yet, save for a few words from Carter in his book, no blood was spilt, and there was never a fear civil war would erupt.

Affirming that the county has known discipline problems like any other, Brendan Cummins said, 'The only difference is that in Kilkenny the same rule applies from top to bottom – if you put a foot out of line you're gone. With Cody, rules are rules and that's it. No one ever hears about what happens there anyway because the dressing room is so tight.

'His rules don't change. There's no leeway. He draws a line and you go left or right of that line and it's curtains. He doesn't need to preach either – they know the set-up.'

Liam Dunne of Wexford has concluded that Cody is greatly assisted by the personal quality of his players: 'If you want to meet a Kilkenny fella you nearly have to go to their gym, their local pitch or Nowlan Park. Other than that you won't meet them.

'I don't know how they ever got to meet their women or socialize. But they're a good bunch. They know there's a time and a place for everything. They have their few drinks but because they are so successful they only have a short gap between the close of the season and the start of a new one.

'For ten years they've more or less been going until September and getting ready to go back at it by the end of November. Whereas we usually have a six-month gap in Wexford, they only have November and December to keep their players right. That's a serious advantage. Lads can go off the rails totally with six months to kill.'

D. J. Carey would agree: 'One of the great advantages for Kilkenny is that they never go too long without winning an All-Ireland. They are heroes for a while and then it's back to their clubs the following week and back to square one again.

'I think with counties like Tipp, they went all over the world and were clapped on the back after their under-21s and seniors won in 2010. They were absolutely fantastic that year but hero status is something you have to deal with. They had it after winning just one title. They stopped Kilkenny winning the five-in-a-row and that was nearly good enough in itself.

'Clare will see it in 2014 – although they look to be a settled bunch. They'll be hit so hard though. When you're surrounded by medals, women and beer it's very easy to get carried away. Luckily, in Kilkenny we have lads who respect what goes on.'

Offaly's Brian Carroll experienced this first-hand during his time at St Kieran's: 'I haven't hurled in August yet with my county, and the thing about that is that we've been out of the championship in July, sometimes in June, over the past few years. Then a new manager comes in and we start back training in October or November. By the time the championship comes around the following year we have eight months' hard training done and lads are actually sick of it. It's a vicious circle.

'Them Kilkenny boys are on the go every year until September; then they go on team holidays with their wives and partners and most of them have had an All Star trip every second year as well. Their wives are happy, their girlfriends are happy and everyone is seeing the rewards for hurling as well as winning. That makes it easier. Sure, who's going to kick up a stink or a fuss in those circumstances? Fine, they've had a few big names leave but who has kicked up publicly? No one. And why would they?

'The funny thing is, people have this perception that they train harder than Offaly and other counties like ourselves. They don't. I would say we train harder and for longer. The problem is that our ratio of training to games is completely lopsided. Seven months' training and we had seven games in 2013 – five in the league and two in the championship. A game a month with four training sessions a week for that. That's where you get controversies. That's where players turn on each other – not in Kilkenny, where they can get on with things because they're winning and fair play to them.'

Single-mindedness can often be taken for selfishness, and certainly one big storm Kilkenny rode out was whipped up by their lack of cooperation with a militant Cork side over a planned GPA protest before the 2002 National League final. They were slated for their stance by the Cork players but it hardly bothered them.

In a team picture taken moments before the throw-in, Kilkenny's captain, Andy Comerford, is facing away from the camera, looking in a different direction from his team-mates.

A week before the game, an emergency meeting of the GPA, which was campaigning on player welfare, had proposed there would be no pre-match team photographs and the two sides would parade with socks down and shirts out. Cork were fighting their own battles with their county board and they wanted Kilkenny to show solidarity. Only Comerford did, though – and looking away from the camera was about as bold as his protest got.

Eight of the Kilkenny team had attended that GPA meeting, but only four were starting the final. D. J. Carey, Charlie Carter and Brian McEvoy – the other key GPA members – were either injured or dropped from the first fifteen. The young players that started instead were more concerned with claiming ownership of a shirt than with what was going down in Cork, or anywhere else.

At training a few days before the league game, Brian Cody had told Comerford and his team-mates that protest would not be tolerated. The captain responded with his view and decided he would make a symbolic gesture for the team picture but he was on his own.

Cody had buried the issue but, along with seven Cork players, Comerford marched the parade with his socks down and jersey out. He was the only one in black and amber to do so. The others turned a blind eye. In a way, the skipper was hung out to dry.

The Cork lads lost respect for their great rivals, and things soured further when some Rebels took offence at quotes from the Kilkenny centre-back, Peter Barry, about the importance of honouring the jersey. Barry always claimed his words were taken out of context and eventually, in November 2006, phoned Dónal Óg Cusack to clear up the matter.

From that league final there was bad blood between the counties and it festered in the years that followed, often spilling out in verbal digs and on All Star and interprovincial trips.

'The way I see that, it was a protest over players' rights but Cork were coming into it with their own gripes,' Brennan said. 'They had millions in the bank and they weren't happy with the way they were being looked after. The truth is we had no gripe whatsoever. It was hard enough to row in with a cause when you didn't have one.

'Cody is a GAA man through and through, and he had no issue with the Kilkenny county board. Neither had we. Even if Brian had a problem, he would have acted behind the scenes and there would have been no public stuff.

'Jesus, we had a young team, we were all fighting for the jersey and no one was dreaming of doing anything to rock the boat. Andy was the captain and more experienced and he felt he had to do something, which was fair enough. But the rest of us just didn't see it as our battle.'

That whole episode was seen as potentially damaging the Kilkenny jersey and brand. But yet again they rode out the storm. Despite the ocean being strewn with mines and icebergs, Kilkenny's hurlers have seldom been forced off course. They have managed with fierce singularity of purpose and rare clarity of thought to negotiate a safe passage, and thus kept on plundering booty and adding to the treasure trove year on year. That, more than anyone else, was down to their manager.

3

Alpha Male in a Pride of Lions

How one individual held sway among
so many big cats

Late in January 2008, as the green fields of Ireland turned to marshland under relentless rain, Antrim travelled south to Freshford, caught an unsuspecting Kilkenny with a sucker punch and knocked them out of the Walsh Cup.

It was a sensational upset – but little more than that: neither a fatal reverse for the team of the decade nor the launch of a glorious new era for one of the game's lesser powers.

Given the time of year, though, it was big news for a GAA media starved of appetizers. In their post-match chat with Brian Cody, reporters went probing and digging, seeking to unravel the mystery of why such superstars as Tommy Walsh, J. J. Delaney, Michael Kavanagh, Martin Comerford, Derek Lyng and James McGarry had all been bench-bound. Even as Kilkenny stared defeat in the face, not one of that crack squad – with twenty-six senior All-Ireland medals between them – was sent in to help his comrades. Instead, tyros like Eoin McGrath and Damien Fogarty were asked to plug the gaps.

Long-time followers of the game wondered if such bench-warming might not harm the long-term performances of these elite players – inevitably the names of such as Brian McEvoy, Denis Byrne and Charlie Carter sprang to mind, great hurlers whose careers, following similar demotion, had withered before their time.

When Cody was asked why he hadn't sent in the big guns to salvage the situation, his blunt response spoke volumes about his coaching philosophy: 'Who are the big guns?'

As the room went silent, his interrogators briefly lost for words, Cody continued: 'Places are up for grabs and lads are fighting for them.'

One message prevailed in the aftermath of that dreary Sunday afternoon in Freshford – the senior Kilkenny players had better not be basking in the glow of glittering trophy cabinets and past glories, because their manager was operating only in the present.

Around the same time, Cody was asked to address 770 coaches at the national coaching conference at Croke Park. Having landed five All-Ireland titles in the previous nine years, he was the keynote speaker on the day.

Cody was preceded on the platform by other managers who, lavishing anecdotes on an appreciative audience and offering insights behind dressing-room doors, all with the help of an array of multimedia presentation tools, revealed their own coaching philosophies and methodologies.

In contrast, however, to such high-spec, luxury service, Cody's was of the Ryanair variety – it got you to your destination but with absolutely no frills. It was straight to the point and devastatingly simple. There were no tales out of school, no family secrets revealed, no breaches of trust, no sly digs or scores settled. Speaking without notes, Cody mapped his fundamental philosophies of life and hurling and explained how he had learned from the lows to appreciate the highs.

'He ad-libbed for thirty-five minutes,' says the GAA's Director of Games, Pat Daly. 'He clearly had a sense of vision, where the team was going. Discipline was at the heart of it, but commitment and conviction too.'

Cody described the Kilkenny dressing room as 'a sacred place' and the training field in Nowlan Park as their 'centre of excellence'. He stressed the need for an indestructible spirit, a bond that should unite everyone from backroom team to number thirty-one on the panel.

'I hear people saying that a settled team is everything,' he said. 'But I'd prefer to have a settled spirit, settled backroom, settled unity of purpose where players take ownership.'

In six years, his message hadn't changed. Back in 2002, speaking at a Dublin hurling symposium, he had debunked the notion of any mystery in his method.

'The only thing that I feel I bring to the Kilkenny job is absolute enthusiasm,' he had said. 'There's no magic in this game, absolutely none. Certainly, if there is, I don't know any of it. It's about hard work, enthusiasm, passion for the game. And I certainly have those things. But I have no easy answers. Believe me, there are no geniuses of managers.'

That last assertion is highly debatable. Anyone who has ever taken charge of a group of thirty players, of whatever age or ability, would argue that there's much more to successful management than Cody admits. Besides which, to maintain the high standards and unity of purpose he describes, while routinely juggling squad resources – demoting and promoting great players seemingly on a whim – strikes many observers as almost miraculous.

Cody, though, has never dwelt on these things. Nor has he gone into detail about his methods. Hence very few outside that inner circle would ever profess to really know the man.

A fair chunk of his protégés may have won seven, eight or nine All-Irelands under his stewardship, but aside from Henry Shefflin, who has been closer to him than anyone else on the squad, none of the team would really claim to know him well.

Cody certainly hasn't been close to the players in the way Liam Sheedy was in Tipp, Liam Griffin in Wexford or Jimmy Barry-Murphy in Cork. Tender loving care and fatherly affection haven't been things clearly visible in the interaction between Kilkenny's backroom and squad; Cody has been simply a no-nonsense manager in the business of winning games and doing whatever it takes to make that happen.

Fellas may have arrived into the set-up with neon lights flashing signs of promise but all have been treated as equals: always playing for something, whether to break on to the team, to keep the jersey, or to reinvent themselves in adapting to an unfamiliar playing role. As long as players have known that, and honoured that, things have been fine. They've learned they don't have to share Sunday dinner or exchange birthday cards to be joined to the cause.

'We don't expect him to become friends with us,' J. J. Delaney said in 2008. 'He'll come over and chat away, but deep down, you know if you're not producing it, you're out. He has that reputation – it doesn't matter whether you're there six months or sixteen years, he'll have someone else in. He has to make those decisions; he's looking after Kilkenny. That's why he's so long there.'

Cody has usually talked freely in interviews but said little and tended to listen a lot. The exception to the rule used to be those emotional minutes when they had just landed another All-

Ireland title. These days, sadly, post-final conferences are a top-table event in a small auditorium underneath the Hogan Stand, which has robbed us hurling writers of a rare chance to get close to the great man in that small window of time when maybe the defences are lowered.

Before the change, Cody would speak to some journalists in the physio hub, adjacent to their dressing room. In these impromptu chats he would entirely loosen up, the big, ruddy face creased in a contented smile.

It was in that room and later with Brian Carthy on RTÉ Radio, in September 2007, that he gave Ger Loughnane, who had suggested Kilkenny were a dirty team, a good old lash, dismissing him as a 'lunatic from Clare talking rubbish'. He has always stuck by his players: evidence of the strong bond between them, even if that bond has been strictly professional.

Maybe there has had to be a gap. When you impose on players an intense and relentlessly challenging environment, tensions are inevitable.

In 2007, just before flying out on UN peacekeeping duty in Kosovo, Eoin Larkin was called aside by his manager and clubmate and told to come back in good shape. The implications were clear, the threat barely veiled, and so each day, when his soldiering ended, Larkin threw himself into a comprehensive training regime, determined to return, half a year on, finely tuned and match fit. That was Cody, 1,500 miles away, driving him on.

Then there's match-day Cody. Paradoxically, despite the deadpan interview style, he has always been something of an open book while watching his team. Most hurling managers stalk the white lines in a state of unsuspended animation, frustrated former hurlers itching to race in and draw a pull on the sliotar. John Allen and Jimmy Barry-Murphy would be two notable exceptions to that breed, but Cody was always one of the restless kind.

At the 2011 league game with Dublin, held under lights at Croke Park, he and Anthony Daly kept tabs on each other throughout. As the game edged towards a tense finale, Cody roared encouragement at John Mulhall. Then Daly let fly: 'Ah, Jesus Christ, Cody, will you leave him be! D'you want to go in and hurl for him and all?'

Cody spun round, replied with interest, and suddenly the two were head-to-head and nose-to-nose.

As the crowd strained its collective neck to see what happens when two of the game's giants eyeball each other, the adversaries broke apart. Paul Ryan went on to hit the equalizer and Daly went up the line pumping a fist with delight.

They could have gone at it again, but suddenly the tension burst, like a pin to a balloon. As the final whistle pierced the night air, angry stares turned to mild frowns before giving way to spontaneous laughter. The two warring chieftains then exchanged a firm handshake before retreating to their respective corners, already looking forward to the next battle.

With the 2004 Leinster semi-final approaching its conclusion, and Kilkenny treading water when everyone imagined they'd have been home and dried, Wexford's Mick Jacob blocked Peter Barry, ended up with the ball in his hand and went for the target.

The trajectory of Jacob's shot was a joy to behold. But not for Cody. Stationed at the far post, he watched in anguish as the sliotar spun straight and true, and when the net duly danced his legs betrayed him: he collapsed to his knees as if a bullet had taken him out – he'd probably have preferred to take a bullet than to go out of the Leinster championship.

It was a rare insight into the emotional side of Cody. An incredible picture. Lost in the business of hurling. Lost in the business of trying to win hurling games.

He has enjoyed heated encounters with Liam Sheedy and Anthony Cunningham in recent years but it's all part of the game. Men like that have a passion for hurling that courses in the veins. Hurling is a vocation to Cody; he doesn't see it as a chore or a job.

The Kilkenny county board has always struggled to get him to take expenses. Players have said the thought of submitting a phone bill or mileage sheet would not have entered his head. His indifference to monetary compensation eventually forced officials to calculate mileage from his house to various grounds so they could press a few euros on him.

In an age when most rival managers are handsomely compensated, Cody's commitment and generosity have been exemplary. Indeed, Kilkenny supporters probably need reminding from time to time of exactly who they've had in their midst and just how fruitless were the pre-Cody years.

They won four All-Irelands in the eighties and nineties combined. On his watch, they won seven in the noughties alone, nine in total. Add in twelve Leinster titles and seven league crowns and you see the impact he has had.

Eddie Brennan has never been in doubt about that impact: 'A lot of people would feel that they could manage Kilkenny to an All-Ireland title because the team has been collectively so strong over the years. That's just bullshit talk. Cody is just about the only one who could have done it.'

He is without doubt the best manager hurling has seen, even ahead of Cork's Jim 'Tough' Barry, who helped coach fourteen teams to All-Ireland titles between 1926 and 1954, and Kilkenny's Fr Tommy Maher, who trained seven All-Ireland-winning teams over twenty-one years.

You can almost trace the grain of victory in his face, but just who is Cody, the man with the red cheeks under the black Glanbia baseball cap?

His autobiography doesn't divulge any trade secrets. The main reason he collaborated on that project was the fear that someone else was about to publish a version, perhaps skewed, of life under his reign.

His countless media interviews have thrown little light on the subject either. Does he like to read, for instance, or listen to music, or smell the roses? Does he follow current affairs or support a soccer or rugby team? After all these years, we still don't know much, except that he's a Bruce Springsteen fan.

Instead, when you attempt to describe or explain him, all you come up with are the familiar categories: family man, school principal, understated, private, loyal, ruthless.

'I'd go as far as saying that only his wife, Elsie, and his children know the real Brian,' D. J. Carey said. 'He's just a private man who happens to be doing the Kilkenny job and doing a really excellent job at that.

'I remember having great chats with the lads and the selectors after training when we would have our meals in Langton's. Back then the selectors would sit with the players and mix. John Power was a great character and he, Brian and I would often sit down for a chat afterwards. John would give his opinion on a range of matters and some of the times they were far-out opinions. Brian would be there, listening away, but while he'd listen and laugh I didn't hear him give his opinion on many things.

'It's just the way he is. To this day, if I rang to wish him luck before a match I'd never dream of putting him on the spot by asking who was or wasn't playing.'

Carey learned from long experience that even the biggest of

names can be left off. Before that 2004 Leinster semi-final with Wexford, he himself got the treatment.

'I played in a golf pro-am in the K Club – I had committed to it months before. Tee-off times were delayed and I found myself in the thick of the hunt for prizes as the evening wore on. There was no way I would make training so I rang Brian to explain. He said, "Right so, D.J.", and there was no more about it.

'I finished up the golf, went along to training the following Friday night and found out I was dropped. I presume it was because I had missed training by playing the pro-am. I was absolutely raging, but Brian was right, one hundred per cent right, to drop me.

'I could have tried to take on someone else but no, Brian was spot on to do what he did. We lost that game and I often wonder, was I the cause of it? I felt I had let Brian down too.'

Maybe that comes with being a leader and commanding respect. Cody has always been a stickler for punctuality and discipline. And yet he hasn't been inflexible or lacked a sense of humour.

Early in his reign, John Power got bogged down with farm chores and slunk into Nowlan Park a little behind time.

'Mr Power, we start training at half seven,' the manager said, pointing to his watch.

'Mr Cody,' Power replied. 'If I had a handy schoolteaching job like you, I'd be here at half three!'

There were several nights after training at Langton's when Power, a farmer, would rush in and grab a bag of food prepared by Eamon Langton to eat on the way home. Power's day began at 6 a.m. and often ended up back on a tractor, or looking after calves or lambs, till midnight. During silage season, that could extend until 2 a.m. While punctuality was a core essence of the Cody era, Power says the manager never broke his balls on that score.

'I robbed more than I gave on that front,' Power said. 'Brian understood. He would sometimes say to me not to come to training if I was flat out on the farm. I appreciated that, but I always went and had craic with him too once it was all over. As I ran out the door with the food under my arms I would often say to Cody that he and Johnny Walsh, our old trainer, would both live to be a hundred. Both schoolteachers, I would remind them. Sure, they never worked a day in their lives!'

Cody would only smile. Perhaps he had a soft spot for Power because he didn't give many others the option of skipping sessions. Either way the John Lockes man has the manager up on a pedestal. Power, a two-time All Star, had been dropped in 1998 by Kevin Fennelly. A tall, wiry farmer with flowing locks of blond hair and hands like shovels, he was expected by everyone to get on with life but he carried that '98 season like a cross on his shoulders.

'The only two things in life that I'm interested in are farming and hurling,' Power says. 'I never drank or smoked, never watched soccer or got contentment from it. Hurling was what I did and farming then to clear my head if I had played a bad game. Let's just say I spent even more time on the farm in '98. That year was absolute heartache for me. I felt like someone was stabbing me with a knife all year long, every time I went to a game. I knew I was still good enough, but there was no place for me with Kevin.'

Fennelly didn't last long, though, and a year on his cousin, Cody, was at the helm. The call to Power was short but by God was it sweet. 'Come in and see if you have something to offer. If you don't, no harm done.'

That lifeline was grasped by Power. 'I had watched them lose the 1998 All-Ireland hurling final and within twenty minutes of that game people had told me how I could still do a job for them.

It took me a while to settle back into it, but I did. I never doubted my ability and Brian sprung me when the time was right.'

He returned to win two more All-Irelands, four Leinster titles, one National League. That was down to Cody.

'Thanks to Brian, I can look back on a second half of my career which gave me all the contentment I wanted. Okay, we lost the 1999 final and that was heartache. I had set my heart on going back to Kevin Fennelly and showing him the Celtic Cross that I had planned on pinning to my jacket. But that edge had gone by 2000 when we won. All I had then was utter contentment. I made no bones about thanking Brian for what he did for me.'

Not that the manager would have been too misty-eyed about Power's lifeline. As the 2002 final drew to a close, with Kilkenny well ahead, Cody had to be gently nudged by Henry Shefflin, who had Power's number eleven jersey by then, to give him a run late on.

'Brian treated me no differently to any other in that regard,' Power reasons. 'I was on the line wishing to get in and almost panicking, but Brian does what's best for his team and doesn't do emotion. I was lucky to get in at all and it was a nice way to end my career.'

Cody would have seen many admirable qualities in Power, but he didn't have to look too far for inspiration as he was a top hurler himself. His leadership qualities emerged early; he captained the 1972 All-Ireland-winning Kilkenny minors and in 1982 led the seniors.

He won four All-Ireland senior medals – 1974, '75, '82 and '83 – and two All Stars, and it's interesting to note that his All Stars came eight years apart, 1975 and '82, around the same time he won his two All-Ireland club medals. An illustration surely of his love for the club – when they were going well, he too was flying.

A teacher at St Patrick's De La Salle in Kilkenny, he took the county job when few others wanted it. It became vacant in late 1998 after Fennelly walked away. With virtually no track record outside his club, James Stephens, he wasn't an obvious choice, but he had intelligence, a passion for, and understanding of, the game that had delivered both good times and bad to his door.

Back in 1978, in an attempt to halt Cork's three-in-a-row march, the county's selectors experimented and played Cody at full-forward. The experiment didn't work, Kilkenny lost and he took more heat than anyone else. There have been reports of him being booed and jeered at the team's homecoming, though in his memoirs he wrote of having no recollection of that.

His own teams, though, have learned to be as graceful in defeat as in victory. When they were chasing the 'drive for five' and fell in 2010 to their fiercest rivals, Tipperary, it hurt the whole county, but there were no sour grapes. The team regrouped in a private room at the Citywest Hotel, where Cody gave a passionate oration that, according to Eddie Brennan, lifted them and helped salve the raw wounds of defeat. They left that room confident the good days would soon return.

'Brian said that we had won together and now that we had lost we would stick together. It was a great speech. He said every player from one to thirty was to fulfil the homecoming function back in Kilkenny city the following night. To a man, we were to be there. That was important. After that we could do what we liked.

'I don't know if he foresaw what was going to happen, but it was vital we were all there together because the vibe from the supporters was terrific. Everyone around the place sensed that particular homecoming was more important than all the triumphant ones put together. Thousands turned out and they gave us a right old lift. We were ready for 2011 again after that night.'

*

Down through the years, Brennan and Cody shared an interesting and complex dynamic. Brennan's introduction to centre-stage was both grand and glorious: he first pulled on the black and amber in their 2000 league meeting with Tipperary, walked on to the field a rookie but marched off it a hero, having dismantled the opposition by hitting 2-3.

By 2006, with three All-Irelands already to his name, he was recognized as one of the most lethal forwards around – when he was in the zone. Cody, though, kept demanding consistency, and by the time the 2006 league began, Brennan was fed up and close to calling it a day.

That league began with him on the fringes. He held his counsel in the hope of game time, but as spring unfolded, he was still only getting to break sweat at training sessions. On match days, Brennan would return home to Graigue-Ballycallan having taken no part, and with little or no feedback from Cody, would head to the local field to run off his frustration.

Brennan has recounted what he went through at the time: like Fitzpatrick, he felt that communication could have been better as he began to fall down the pecking order.

'I would be there at the club, running around in the pitch darkness for half an hour. It was just my way of keeping right. Going off and sulking because I wasn't playing was no good for anyone but still I was pissed off and angry. This was one way of getting rid of that anger. Fair enough, I was going poorly at the start of the year and there seemed to be no word coming from the top for a long time. So, I was very close to bringing it all to a close.

'One day in Thurles, Brian handed me the number twenty-eight shirt and my heart sank. Next time out I was number thirty. I knew I was down the pecking order but I didn't realize I was that low.

'I ran a few things by Dad and he wondered if I was better

off going back to the club because I didn't seem to be getting anywhere. My mother, to be fair, told me to hang in there and see out the year. I was so pissed off that I didn't want to let Brian and the selectors say that I had jacked it in. So out of stubbornness I stayed put.

'After we beat Westmeath we went training at Freshford and if I was looking for feedback I got it. We all got it, in fact. Brian fired shots at everyone that night, from top to bottom. Henry got it, Donnacha – his own son – got it, and I got it. But I got even more pissed off – how could I show improvement if I wasn't playing games? I was wondering by now if they were trying to push my buttons.'

The next day, Brennan and Cody met, and the player bluntly asked whether he featured in the manager's plans any more.

'No problem, if I wasn't, I said I would accept it. As a manager, Brian has to live or die by his decisions. But I felt they could have handled the whole thing better. Sometimes they had to see when lads were not going well and when lads needed a chat. Maybe Brian felt tough love was the way forward.'

If that's what Cody had in mind it worked a treat. Cody said, yes, Brennan still had a future, but that crumb of assurance arrived only when the player's simmering unease and uncertainty had boiled over into a raging determination to prove his worth – he was now ferociously determined to claw his way back into the team.

On the first night after the chat with Cody, he found himself marking Peter 'Chap' Cleere: 'We sawed the shit out of each other. Chap burst me and we were pulling on each other like mad. There was blood streaming off my forehead but no one came over to me. We tangled three or four times before Brian cut in and told us to play the ball. I was so thick and fired up I told him to go away from me.'

Given what had happened to other big names who fell from favour with Cody, it took serious cojones for Brennan to speak up for himself, but all he asked for was clarity as to where he stood.

With Michael Rice and Cha Fitzpatrick on top form, he had little chance of being a cog in the midfield engine room. The full-forward line, his natural habitat, was also well populated. Few guys of such talent, in their mid-twenties with three All-Irelands, have ever found themselves warming the bench for so long.

'Brian told me then that I had started to play better. And I was to mark J. J. Delaney for the next two nights in training.'

Brennan went back into the full-forward line, did well and broke even with Delaney amid more 'heavy skelping'. His reward for matching Delaney, a sublime defender, was hardly the stuff of dreams, however. It was a duel with possibly the greatest defender of all time.

'Brian said he was changing the goalposts again. "Let me guess," I said . . . "Tommy?" "Yeah," the boss replied.

'Tommy Walsh – an All Star each of the previous five years. I had to laugh. Everyone ran away to avoid marking him in training but I was now determined to go the whole hog. Brian said he might need a job to be done in the half-forward line and my challenge was to be a contender.'

To keep Walsh on his toes, Brennan made his stylish, often unplayable, opponent do what he hated most – chase a wing-forward around the field with no ball in clear view.

Reflecting on that pivotal time, Brennan said, 'At that stage if Brian had asked me to mark J.J. and Tommy together I would have done it. It was either dry dog or shite the licence. I was so driven I'd have had a cut off the two of them.

'There was no point in blaming Brian any more. Did I want to be a part of it? By fuck I did. I realized what hurling for Kilkenny meant to me.'

For Fast Eddie, every training session from then on became an All-Ireland final. He was wired to the moon. And he wasn't the only one. Is it any wonder they filleted so many teams that crossed their paths?

Whether intentionally or otherwise, Cody's handling of Brennan had transformed a hugely talented but easygoing corner-forward into a voracious, more rounded, lethal operator who used his new-found hunger to hunt down opponents, dispossess them and tear at them on the counterattack.

Before the 2006 Leinster final against Wexford the team gathered to hear the starting fifteen. Brennan felt like a Leaving Cert student about to discover his grades.

'From 2003 to 2005 the team had been settled enough, or at least I thought my place was, but I was there shaking like a leaf in the dressing room, wondering, would I start?

'Brian was holding the sheet in his hands and I was trying to look through it to see if my name was there. When I heard it called out, the sheer sense of relief took over – I let out a massive sigh. I had been on the bench with the younger lads all season long and I was sick of it. The field is where it was at.'

Brennan reckoned his difficulties during that 2006 season provided raw motivation for three years afterwards and is pretty sure Cody played him like the proverbial fiddle.

'Maybe he did, or maybe I just needed to get the finger out. Either way, what he did worked.'

Having flirted with retirement he tacked on another five All-Irelands, finishing 2006 on the steps of the Hogan Stand.

*

It's not just his own players that Cody manages to inspire. Donal O'Grady has described the aftermath of Kilkenny's seven-point hammering of Limerick in the 2007 All-Ireland final, when the Kilkenny boss walked into the devastated dressing room of Richie Bennis's team.

The Limerick players were streaked in sweat and tears, not to mention a share of blood, and racked with guilt and self-doubt, and on a day when, unfortunately for them, they had been blown away by a perfect storm of Kilkenny's hunger for excellence, the last thing they needed to hear was a string of hard-luck platitudes.

'A lot of managers come in and say the same old things and most of the time you don't even listen but Brian was different,' said O'Grady. 'Lads came out of the shower to listen to him and usually they wouldn't bother doing that.

'The first thing I noticed was the gold watch he was wearing. He was shaking it up and down on his wrist as he spoke. It was clear to me he was still playing the game in his own mind – even though they'd beaten us well – and his head was covered in beads of sweat.

'He told us to keep our heads up, that we were a young team on the right track. To be honest we were half afraid of him, I think. But he was desperate genuine.'

When Cody went to see the Galway team after they had beaten his men in the 2012 Leinster final it was a different man who spoke to the opposition. As he crossed beyond enemy lines he made no attempt to underplay the gravity of defeat for his team.

'He had a clear message for us,' said David Collins. 'We'll see ye in the All-Ireland.'

There's something about Galway that seems to raise Cody's dander. Three times in his reign they have been his chief tormentors: in 2001, 2005 and, especially, the 2012 Leinster final. They have usually managed to bring out all of his touchline repertoire: the thunderous scowls; the stalking back and forth; the undisguised frustration with refereeing calls, that angry index finger jabbing the air; the sense that at any moment he might grab a hurley and throw himself into the fray. Watching him take on Galway has always been fascinating.

Looking back on that historic 2012 victory and Cody's dressing-room visit, Collins said, 'You could almost see his thought process – he was thinking, "I'll get these lads again." I think he was nearly in to frighten us. None of us were carried away with the win anyway, because we knew what was coming down the tracks. And it came!'

It's one thing menacing the whitewash but there was always far more to Cody than match-day histrionics – including a devout knowledge of the game and a voracious appetite for monitoring new players and emerging talent; he has been regularly seen at games from under-12 upwards.

Wexford's Conor McDonald, for example, a bright young star in the making, was already on Cody's radar long before register-ing on the wider GAA consciousness, something Liam Griffin found, to his surprise.

'The phone rang one day and it was Cody asking about the centre-back on one of our minor teams. I told him the lad was Conor Devitt, and Brian replied that he was the best centre-back he had seen play minor. And then he said, "What about that McDonald lad? He's a fair hurler – by God, he'll be some handful in the years ahead!"

'Sure he knew more about our underage players than some hurling people in Wexford. Even at such an early stage in their development he had them flagged.'

For the record, young McDonald scored 3-4 against Kilkenny in the 2013 minor championship, having been introduced to that squad at just sixteen.

In 2008, after his team had clinched the coveted three-in-a-row, Cody was asked in a radio interview to name the highlight of his year. He could have plucked from a collection of golden memories and drama-filled moments, and in a way he did. But his answer caught everyone on the hop: again it was a nod to underage hurling – he listed his club, James Stephens, winning the All-Ireland under-14 Féile na nGael as his top moment that year.

After all that had happened that year, all the unforgettable victories, all the heroic cameos by superstars in heaving stadiums, what had most captivated him was the relatively unsung achievement and innocent joy of a bunch of young clubmates – the hope of the future of course.

Maybe the interviewer should not have been greatly surprised.

Kilkenny's spell of glorious dominance started with Cody and more than likely it will end with him. While these aristocrats will never dine too far away from hurling's top table, they will surely never again feast so long and so lavishly to the exclusion of others. Throughout their wonder years, Cody remained the driving force behind an unbreakable spirit.

Interestingly, he has never had an army of advisors around him. He was never into packing his backroom with gurus to make it look more professional. There were a few influences here and there but none that were immediately obvious – though John Mullane has conjectured that Cody's friendship with Mickey Harte changed the way Kilkenny approached the game.

'It's just a theory,' Mullane said. 'The two of them seemed close, and around the same time Kilkenny started swarming teams just as Tyrone had done in football. I remember playing against them in the 2008 All-Ireland final and though they were about twenty points up, there were three of them on top of me the second I touched the ball. I thought to myself straight away – Tyrone! There's definitely something in that.'

In 2006, while the team stayed at Monart, Enniscorthy, they brought in the hugely respected boxing coach Nicolas Cruz to chat to them. On a few other occasions they invited Gerry McEntee, the surgeon and former Meath footballer.

According to Eddie Brennan, 'Cha mentioned in an interview in 2008 that McEntee had been down with us and I don't think the boys were too happy with that one getting out. But Gerry started coming down to us in 2007 and maybe he might have a chat with us two or three weeks out from major matches, but it was not all that regular.

'We got a lot from his talks, though – some of them were un-believable. It's funny how the process of performance is similar in every sport, across the board. He didn't need to be a hurler to relate to us.'

When you have led your county to so much success, where is the need to go looking for outside help?

Richie Mulrooney, the former Kilkenny under-21 manager, has expressed it succinctly.

'Brian has been the greatest managerial appointment in the history of the game, it's as simple as that. Brian has kept those players coming back and has set the rules, parameters and discip-line standards that he lives his own life by. You can see by the way he talks to the players, the way he's respected, that they just don't cross the line at all.

'The set-up is Brian's set-up and no one else's. I had an in-teresting chat with him in 2013 regarding Cillian Buckley, who comes from the same club as me [Dicksboro]. Like the other lads, Cillian was doing all he could to get into the team. He was going to the gym trying to improve his strength and conditioning and there was a little concern in my head that he was overdoing it.

'I mentioned it to Brian and his reply was so straight: "I'll tell you what," he said. "Tell Cillian to work on his first touch – that's what he needs to work on."

'It was as basic as that and the conversation was brief as that, but it gave Cillian the information he needed. Brian is not one to talk around the issue.'

As the curtain came down on 2013, Cody had been sixteen years on the go. Keeping the show on the road on a journey where the good times just kept on coming. There were no signs he was considering passing the baton any time soon – in fact he returned to James Stephens as a selector in 2014. Asked about that possibility of Cody moving on in the near future, Mulrooney said, 'We are wary of that, because the next two to three years will see some of our greatest players step aside, Brian might go with them. I'd be praying that he has the energy and enthusiasm to stay going.

'He might point out too that although people claim we don't have the same quality emerging, some of the current players became legends when they were quite unheard of at minor and under-21. He regards the character of the player as key. That's always the yardstick he worked from, the key to everything. If the character is there you can work on everything else.'

No one could dispute the character was there. That, however, was as much as we got to know about that Kilkenny team. That and the fact that while they were serially high achievers all they wanted was to keep a low profile.

4

Men behind the Faceguards

Debunking Kilkenny's reputation
for soulless efficiency

A couple of weeks ahead of the 2000 All-Ireland hurling final, the national media packed briefcases and rucksacks with laptops, recorders, cameras and miscellaneous other digital paraphernalia and converged on Kilkenny for the hard sell. For all the welcome they got in the Marble City, they might as well have been chuggers knocking on the door of a young family at bedtime.

Early in Brian Cody's reign, Kilkenny press nights were struggling in the popularity stakes – slightly ahead of tooth extractions without anaesthetic but well behind watching paint dry. The two participating parties were coming from poles apart, and for a long while it seemed that never the twain might meet.

It was the job of a voracious and ever-expanding media – at one time you could choose your sports coverage from among sixteen Irish Sunday newspaper titles – to raise the temperature. Editors were on the hunt for exclusive content, hard news, high drama, all daubed with splashes of vivid colour to keep the reader enthralled.

But the Cody gang were looking at a different picture. They did everything possible to tone down the palette, to calm the viewer, to paint a scenario of idyllic peace and almost mind-boggling routine.

Very soon, both parties recognized the huge gulf separating them. From there a deep distrust was born, and as a result the greatest team to grace the game of hurling went about much of their business under a cloak of anonymity, with very little media profile and hardly any of the hype that normally attaches to sporting superstars.

The 2000 final build-up gave an early inkling of things to come. As a TV cameraman unpacked and started setting up his equipment, a sliotar whizzed past his head, uncomfortably close. Slightly shocked, he looked up and twenty-five yards away saw the guilty party, laughing but half turning away in a gesture of mock innocence.

The media pack know that if you cross battle lines at any pre-training puck-around you risk a clattering. Warm-ups are regarded as auditions for a weekend matinee role: players are out on the paddock earlier to impress the manager and steal a march on team-mates during in-house matches. And as you would expect from any Kilkenny hurler, this was a rasping, pinpoint delivery.

The cameraman was unsure how to react but instinctively masked his anger and, sharing the joke, flashed a conspiratorial smile in return. The player responded by waving his stick apologetically and the temperature, having briefly frozen, thawed slightly again.

It was a snapshot, though, that perfectly illustrated relations between the Cats of the early noughties and the press pack. The team won quite often and there was huge media fascination with what they were doing behind the scenes. But the players, or most of them, had no interest in putting themselves on a platform.

There were times when journalists had themselves to blame. On the same day that the cameraman narrowly avoided a sliotar to the head, two reporters persuaded another player to share 'a few quiet words' in a corner of Nowlan Park. Upon spotting an opportunity, seven other hacks rushed to the scene, thrusting dictaphones in the player's face, and a quiet chat became a media scrum. The defender, clearly uncomfortable, apologized and walked away.

That training session over, the players repaired to Langton's Hotel, and us journalists, assured we could wangle a few quotes in that more relaxed situation, eagerly followed. Cue more humiliation. As the unlucky D. J. Carey and John Power finished their apple tart and custard, reporters circled them like hyenas around two wounded buffalos.

Carey was box office and always cooperative. Power had a rasping honesty about him that cut through all flannel and flattery. It was just as well we cornered them that evening, for all their team-mates had scattered out a side door or back entrance.

Such was the hit-and-miss nature of Kilkenny press nights back then. Nowadays, sponsors and board officials organize sit-down events with a guaranteed number of players present. These contrived question-and-answer sessions, though tightly controlled and therefore somewhat anodyne, at least give reporters a minimum of quotes and some hope of a glimpse behind the scenes.

Soon it became a running joke among journalists that the almost annual foxtrot to Kilkenny was not so much about harvesting quotable quotes, more about digging into Langton's splendid sirloin steaks and ample desserts. As we wielded the knives and forks, the champions did likewise. Two or three fellas might talk, but the script was a familiar one, short on surprise and devoid of drama.

New stars emerged as Kilkenny began to amass the nine All-Ireland titles they would win between 2000 and 2012. As their dominance grew, most hurling neutrals, and a good few partisans, were crying out for change to a predictable plot, but apart from Cork and Tipperary finding temporary chinks in their armour, Kilkenny were never really in the mood to offer hope.

John Tennyson's reaction after the 2006 All-Ireland final offered a sense of the group ethos: 'We won the Walsh Cup, the league, the Leinster championship and now the All-Ireland,' Tennyson said as he recovered his breath. 'But I think if it was the Mickey Mouse Cup out there we'd have won that too. We want to win everything.'

Within minutes of claiming his first All-Ireland medal he was already targeting another. You just knew there and then you would be back to see him again at Nowlan Park the following August.

Each passing summer found them still driven by the sweet taste of success. As they kept on winning, their attitude towards the media improved, and even if still only the calmest of heads and safest of hands were wheeled out to talk, the tone of those media nights gradually became normalized.

In recent years, seven or eight of them, including two specific-ally assigned to Sunday papers, presented for media duty. Cody, as always, was accessible, as were selectors like Mick Dempsey and Martin Fogarty. It meant, among other things, that you could savour the steak and onions happy in the knowledge you'd get back to the office with at least a half-decent interview in the bag.

*

Not that the mist of distrust ever entirely dispersed. After the 2011 league final defeat to Dublin, Jackie Tyrrell arrived at Limerick Institute of Technology, where he had both hurled and studied, to attend a press event for Davy Fitzgerald. In an interview with the freelance journalist Jackie Cahill, Tyrrell, then twenty-eight, and one of the most honest and respected guys on the circuit, described the twelve-point defeat as the worst he had ever been involved in; he said he feared Kilkenny's work rate, intensity and discipline were slipping, and that in terms of 'physicality, speed, fitness and hurling' they had been blown off the field.

There was no suggestion of internal unrest, merely a highly motivated hurler putting a mirror to himself and the team, which, by the way, was enduring an injury-ravaged patch. Still, it was undoubtedly the most frank interview ever given by a Kilkenny player on Cody's watch, and it didn't go down well with the backroom.

Shortly after the quotes appeared in print, Cahill was in a phone exchange with one of the Kilkenny backroom team, the gist of which was that Cahill had failed to 'protect' the player and had thereby created a breach of trust between himself and the Kilkenny camp.

Cahill was flummoxed but argued his case, stating he didn't see what the fuss was about and that surely a 28-year-old man was entitled to offer an honest opinion. He added that since the press event was courtesy of LIT there had been no need to go through the usual channels, which would have meant emailing the backroom member to request the interview.

In any case – since Kilkenny went on to win the All-Ireland – Cahill could well argue that no structural damage had been done; it was just a highly driven player letting off steam.

So, though relations improved over the years, diplomatic incidents have never been a million miles away.

At a Croke Park press event early in 2012, Cillian Buckley, one of the young Turks introduced into the senior panel, was asked to give his early impressions of Brian Cody. It was a simple enough question, but Buckley, who in fairness was new to all this, froze in case he would divulge any of the team's trade secrets – he looked taken aback and couldn't answer. Genuinely bemused, but aware of his youth and inexperience, the journalists quickly moved on.

'Brian may have left certain lads out of media duties but usually he left it up to the players themselves to decide whether they want to talk to journalists,' said Eddie Brennan when his playing days were over.

'In all my time there I never heard him tell anyone they were not to talk. But for a long time there was mistrust between players and certain journalists, and I suppose that's why the public never really got to know this Kilkenny team. I have no doubt in my mind that I've had a higher profile – not that I'm looking for it – since I retired and started working as a hurling analyst.'

Brennan surely has developed a profile. But most of the team, with the exception of household names like Shefflin, Tommy Walsh and D.J., could stroll unremarked down most main streets in the land. A pity in a sense, but just the way it's been.

'J. J. Delaney could walk past Clara NS with all of his All-Ireland medals in a bag beside him and most of the students wouldn't recognize him,' said the school's headmaster, Richie Mulrooney. 'But that's how J.J. would like it – they're just a bunch of lads who are not interested in that side of the game.'

Brennan would not deny that people haven't really known the team.

'I suppose we were reluctant enough to be out there doing

media and maybe it was the same core of lads who were doing it all the time. As time went on, though, the likes of Tommy and Noel Hickey, who are very honest and forthright fellas, got used to it.'

Brennan had his own reasons for keeping to the background: he felt it was better to prepare for games with his head-space clear. The more he was reassured of that, the better he performed.

'It's an individual thing. I felt that when I did a few press interviews in 2003 it distracted me. For 2007, I just did a bit with RTÉ and told the management that was my lot. It worked out well for me and I didn't have silly little things about what I might have said in print playing on my mind. More often than not, I just kept to myself.

'I've gone full circle now and of course I understand and appreciate how the media works – but when I first started there was a small bit of distrust there, no point in saying otherwise.

'I can't recall the journo in question, but some lad rang me when I was based at Tallaght Garda station and I did a piece with him. I took him at face value and gave honest answers. I wasn't wise enough to cop that he had a certain angle in the offing. There was no major damage done, but the article appeared and certain things were lost in translation.

'That was one bad episode for me. The way it was, sometimes you would have a word with a lad you knew, but if you didn't know him you might pass. Maybe one or two of our lads got burned. As I got more experienced I would just say to the younger fellas to find out what the angle was before they agreed to anything.

'It wasn't out of badness that journalists were looking for a slant, just to make it more interesting, I suppose. But when you're trying to get, or keep, a place on the Kilkenny hurling team, you just don't need sideshows. It was hard enough to get selected in the first instance.'

D. J. Carey could explain better than anyone why team-mates were wary of the press.

'We won a lot and contrary to public opinion there were great characters and good craic along the way. But those guys that won seven and eight All-Ireland medals grew up scared of media because of the way I got hammered.

'Most of the present Kilkenny team were around when my private and business life were first taken apart under the public microscope. I got an awful hammering in 2002 and 2003 around the time my marriage ended and it wasn't the GAA media who were responsible, it was the Irish news media.'

D.J. could see that the sportswriters were not the ones to blame for what he endured, but, as he also observed, not all his team-mates made the distinction or saw past the headlines about his private life.

'That coverage would have frightened many of the youngsters. I was a public figure, I always helped sports journalists with interviews, I was always open because I felt I had to give something back – and yet on the front pages I was hammered time after time.

'I remember going to training sessions before the 2003 All-Ireland final and news reporters were outside my home, looking to talk to me about my private life. They were lurking. God, I was only a lad playing hurling to the best of my ability; I didn't know what it was all about.

'I even got a media roasting for helping out charities. We raised a lot of money for one particular project and some funds were seemingly left over. The organizers decided to use that money to help another project and I found myself being criticized for not helping further with the first project.

'I felt like walking away from all that until someone wondered aloud why I would give up doing good work because of what one or two people said. They were right. Those words always stuck with me. I had to remind myself that there was an awful lot more good out there than bad – it's just a pity the bad asses carry a lot of weight.

'I suppose at the end of the day the lads on the team saw all this and, even though I was able to get over it quite easily by not looking at the latest headline, maybe the others were taken aback.

'Brian was very protective of me – and still is – and he left me to deal with it once he was happy I was okay. I don't think Brian ever put a ban on players talking – that was just the lads them- selves. But, sure, could you blame them?'

Carey and Power soon became the go-to men for interviews. It was a real treat to sit around and listen to their views, share their company for a half-hour or so. But while the press depended on those two, many fans got the impression they were hogging the limelight. That view couldn't have been further from the truth.

Looking back, DJ could see the funny side: 'It used to be gas. I'd hear it back – "Carey had the media in the stand" or "Carey wrote this." Sometimes, it was as if I had called the journos up and asked to give them an interview. Jesus, I was the only one who'd talk at the time.

'If I wanted publicity and was hungry for it, I could get it every day of the week. The one thing I take out of the whole episode is that ten years on people still stop me on the streets and talk about how badly I was treated by news journalists. So if the public are saying that, you can bet the players still have it shelved at the back of their minds. The majority of the present Kilkenny team would remember all that.'

And so, despite stacking up the medals, the Kilkenny hurlers remained largely anonymous. Not quite 'us against the world' but the shutters mostly stayed down.

And soon the perception spread that this was a group of colourless or boring individuals – sublimely skilled and supremely fit but single-minded to the point of obsession, with little personality, no sense of humour and nothing of interest to say for themselves.

And as the siege mentality and mutual distrust took hold, what might be called the human-interest stories were left untold – which was a great pity, because of course there were countless such stories and no small drama behind the scenes.

Cha Fitzpatrick was one of their great characters. John Hoyne, who could take off every player and mentor in the set-up, and James Ryall, whose dry wit could cut the legs from under you in a flash, would join Fitzpatrick at the back of the bus and enjoy the craic on the way to games – even on All-Ireland final mornings. 'Those journeys are some of the best memories of my life,' Cha recalled. 'We were totally focused when we had to be, but we found that getting too worked up only drained us mentally.'

In the spring of 2002, Derek Lyng, then twenty-four and an unheralded club player, broke on to the Kilkenny team at around the same time that his day job as a sales rep was also on an upward curve. He had just landed a position that entailed a doubling of salary and a high-spec company car. But therewith came the rub.

At a three-week induction he learned he would be based in Galway – his hotel bill would be paid for six months until he got settled. He realized he was at a crossroads but decided to test the water, completed the induction and in the process missed several midweek training sessions at Nowlan Park.

It was time to explain his quandary to Cody, and when he laid his cards on the table the conversation was short and to the point.

'Do you want to be an intercounty hurler, Derek?'

'Yes, of course – more than anything.'

'Well, then, I'll leave it up to yourself so.'

Three days later, Lyng drove the Mondeo to Galway and gave his bosses the news. They reacted angrily, ushering him off the premises with instructions to return the car immediately to Dublin.

'They were raging,' said Lyng in a later interview. 'They didn't even invite me into the office in Dublin – I was told to leave the keys at the front desk. The mother had to come up from Kilkenny to collect me.'

Yet, the moment Lyng walked out of that door and towards his mother's car, he experienced a feeling of profound clarity. He had made his choice.

Martin Comerford, too, had other stuff going on before he made his name in the black and amber. With his hurling career about to take off, there was one afternoon when he played half a soccer match for the Kilkenny soccer outfit Freebooters before rushing off in a Garda car to play the second half of a hurling game with O'Loughlin Gaels, where Brian Cody would be in attendance to watch him and possibly invite him on to the county panel. Freebooters had been good to Comerford; he was one of their stars, and winning medals and playing in the FAI Junior Cup, but it didn't take him long to commit fully to Cody.

P. J. Ryan found himself at thirty-two breaking new ground by attending college for the first time. A bricklayer by trade, he had become a casualty of the recession and, with no day job to go to, heard about a new three-year degree course at Carlow IT – a Bachelor of Arts in Sport and Exercise (GAA) – and was one of the thirty students selected from five hundred applicants.

He gave them full commitment too. In February 2010, he

played two games within six hours, lining out for the college against Athlone IT in the Ryan Cup and later that evening togging out for Kilkenny against Thurles.

Eoin Larkin, too, went back to the books. As a youngster, Larkin had dropped out of school after doing the Junior Cert and had long regretted that decision. And so in September 2011 he took leave of absence from the Army and enrolled at Cork's College of Commerce to take English, Irish, maths, history and geography for the Leaving Cert. Larkin, the 2008 Hurler of the Year, based himself at Cork's Collins Barracks while attending school five days a week and sat his exams in May 2012.

Noel Hickey, Kilkenny's man of soil with a soul of iron, had five All-Ireland medals collected by his twenty-seventh birthday but remained largely unknown. He had been thrown into the lions' den at the tender age of sixteen, his first senior competitive club game the 1997 county final against Gowran, where he was handed the job of marking D. J. Carey.

The week before the 2005 All-Ireland quarter-final against Limerick, feeling weak and unwell, Noel phoned his sister, Catherine, a nurse, and described the symptoms. He wondered if he should take a few Panadol but she persuaded him to head straight for the hospital. Wisely, he took her advice.

It was discovered a potentially fatal virus had attacked the wall of his heart.

And though he was told he would miss the next six months, in the grand scheme of things, considering the tragic deaths of other elite sportsmen, he was blessed to survive.

Tommy Walsh may have quickly become the best young hurler on the planet when he first arrived upon the scene but remained totally unaffected by it all. When Walsh was picked on the Irish squad to travel to Scotland for a hurling/shinty international in 2012, he was by far their most decorated and high-profile panellist, but he mingled freely with the others and went for a three-mile jog through the streets of Edinburgh over the weekend.

'I got to know Mick Fennelly and Tommy Walsh through shinty,' said John Meyler, who was part of the Ireland management. 'They were already self-motivated but at the series they were first out on the field, warming up.

'They tore into the game as if it was a Kilkenny county final or an All-Ireland final. There was no standing back, no just being there for the weekend, no piss-up and no "I'm Tommy Walsh, I have eight All-Ireland medals."'

Those close to Walsh have described him as the most relaxed fellow you could meet, his only sore point being a vulnerability to slagging about having yet to win a county title with his club, Tullaroan.

'We all brought something different to the table and if we had a clash we left it on the training ground,' said Eddie Brennan. 'In 2010, John Dalton and I had one. I turned and pulled on him, accidentally got him on the forehead through the helmet. I pulled wrong and immediately said sorry. He walked off the field with me not long after it happened and there was no more about it.

'Lads might pull raw and clatter someone, but it never stopped us gelling as a bunch. There was always massive respect there and never any big rows at club level between various teams. That gave us a great chance – what hope have you if your players don't gel?

'Look at what happened in Galway over the years where players have been butchered and sent off. How can you stand in line with a lad and back him up on intercounty day if you don't have respect, if you hold contempt for him.

'We had lads to lighten the mood. John Hoyne was a fine hurler and an unreal character – a great man for impressions. We called him "Dougal" and he was as droll a character as you could get. Small things like you'd be stretching in a huddle with the team after training and maybe winding down after a tense night on the field and Dougal would let a big fart and we'd all explode laughing. Now that sounds harmless, and it was, but Brian Cody appreciated that we needed someone like that in our set-up. This was a serious business but you needed relaxed fellas too.

'Another night Johnny Walsh came into our dressing room looking for him and Dougal stood up right in front of him, with a jersey pulled over his head, and leaped right in front of him and still Johnny didn't cop it was him. Dougal more or less did a Riverdance in front of him but Johnny didn't know who it was and went off looking for him in another room.'

According to Brennan, there were plenty of characters in the group and a fair few jokers as well. And even though there were different personalities and often keen rivalries at club level, there was massive respect throughout, and they never failed to gel in the interests of the black and amber.

They stuck together in moments of sadness too. When James McGarry's wife, Vanessa, died tragically in a road accident in July 2007, the panel rowed in behind him, won the All-Ireland and dedicated the win to the McGarry family, Henry Shefflin asking James's young son, Darragh, to lift the Liam MacCarthy Cup with him high up in the Hogan Stand.

A year earlier, the team had gathered around a seven-year-old Jason Brennan, who was suffering with cancer, and made him an important part of the set-up – he was handed the number thirty-four shirt by Brian Cody and brought into the Croke Park dressing room before the All-Ireland semi-final victory against Clare. After the game Cody gave young Jason his renowned black Glanbia cap: another precious moment during Jason's final precious weeks.

In early September, the team captain, Jackie Tyrrell, dedicated the All-Ireland win to Jason in his victory speech, another highlight in his young life.

The brave youngster was laid to rest that November after losing his battle with the illness and as Jason's parents, Tommy and Esther, said goodbye to their young son at St Mary's Cathedral, Kilkenny, the team rallied around their little mascot. D. J. Carey, Brennan, Shefflin, Mick Kavanagh and Richie Mullally were among those present.

A pity then that many of the Kilkenny greats remained almost unknown throughout the wonder years, but maybe it was in keeping with a team certainly admired but not always loved across the hurling landscape.

'The most important thing to remember in all of this is that none of us really gave a shit about profile,' Brennan has said, perhaps explaining why many of these stories weren't widely circulated until the players involved had retired.

'These lads were a great bunch and maybe what made it special was that there were no egos around.'

No egos and no one standing back to admire himself. If there was any mirror-gazing in the Kilkenny dressing room it was simply a matter of players looking deep into their souls whenever adversity arrived.

5

When Push Came to Shove

Cynicism, the dark arts and a
constant scrutiny

During fifteen years straddling the noughties, Kilkenny grew accustomed to hitting the ground at full stride, surprising opponents by dint of speed off the mark and ruthlessness of execution. With every victory they honed the skill of putting teams away good and early in games. It made for many a satisfying run to the tape.

'We would go after teams early – that was a given,' said Eddie Brennan.

Their physicality and tempo soon led to accusations of going over the top, a remarkable sea change given that around the turn of the Millennium they were criticized for being 'soft'.

Cork brushed them aside with a late charge to win the 1999 All-Ireland final. Galway rolled them over in the 2001 All-Ireland semi-final. By then Cody was three years into the job and fully expected the Tribesmen to flex their muscles, but he was convinced Kilkenny could fight fire and fury with speed and skill – and he instructed his players to turn the other cheek if push came to thump.

'Those were specific orders,' said John Power. 'But not everyone heeded them. I was on Liam Hodgins and he was giving it to me from the start. At first I did nothing. But then I looked over and saw Richie Murray tearing into Brian McEvoy and Andy Comerford. Brian hit the ground, and though we'd been told not to retaliate I had to do something.'

In what would be his last championship start for Kilkenny, Power decided to 'politely chastise' Hodgins, the Galway centreback. The John Lockes man had a brand new hurl, custom-built especially for the game, but it had broken in two before the ball was even thrown in.

In the crowd, a nun called Sister Aileen Tynan was looking on. When Power's mother passed away in 1999, Sister Aileen, her first cousin, had stayed with the family for six months, helping them cope with bereavement, and then flown back to Perth, where she worked at an addiction centre. She returned for that 2001 semi-final, but as her young relative ran to grab a replacement stick, she must have been inclined to block her ears.

'As I threw the hurl away the Galway lads got out of their seats and called me every name under the sun,' said Power. 'The whole litany. Poor Sister Aileen had to listen to that.

'I think some Kilkenny supporter home from Chicago got the hurl, repaired it and stuck it up in his bar in the States. I don't know how impressed Aileen was, though.'

Despite Power's breaking ranks, most of his team-mates obeyed the manager's non-aggression edict, but for once their staying on message was a mistake. They lost 1-13 to 2-15, but more embarrassing was how they were pushed around even before the first whistle and bullied from pillar to post after it.

*

Cody knew things would have to change. And the template had been duly tweaked by the time they re-emerged ravenous in 2002 and won the next two All-Ireland titles. Suddenly they had become the ones setting the physical agenda – one they adapted as they saw fit.

When in 2007 they were grinding out results and running opponents ragged, Ger Loughnane, then Galway manager, said they were a 'dirty' team. And in an interview with RTÉ Radio ahead of the All-Ireland quarter-final, he didn't so much stoke the fire as douse it with petrol.

In a specific reference to the Kilkenny defence, he said, 'We must be prepared for hurling savagery,' and went on to give reasons.

'We hear of this skelping and belting that's going on down in their training sessions. It's harder now than ever before. Let no one underestimate in any way the kind of savagery they will come out with next Sunday to try and down us right from the start.

'They're so physical – they choke you and then when you get the ball they're constantly flicking at your hands and wrists. By the time the game is over your wrists are hardly able to move. They are really expert at that.

'We don't know how good we are in the hard, physical stakes but we will find out on Sunday. I hope it's an open game and that whoever is refereeing it will give some chance to us so we won't get this ferocious barracking a forward gets from a Kilkenny defender when he has the ball and this belting across the wrists.'

It was typical Loughnane jousting, much of it surely tongue in cheek, looking for the psychological edge, and few took it seriously.

But when he beat the drum again on radio before the final, it infuriated Cody, who waited the few weeks until they had won the All-Ireland before retaliating, dismissing Loughnane as a 'lunatic'.

Cody had cause to react. Loughnane's rant, however much intended as a wind-up, had struck a chord with many followers of the game who felt Kilkenny were indeed turning into a gang of hit merchants. The spotlight was now firmly on them.

'After 2001 is when Brian really got a handle for the job,' said D. J. Carey. 'He became legendary after that. The team was transformed, the players toughened up, worked hard in the gym and hit hard too, but to say they were dirty is just ludicrous.'

Cody did strip down the team, though, and reshape it with Peter Barry at its spine. Nobody had ever regarded Barry as a centre-back, but that's exactly where Cody positioned him, to give them steel and backbone. He was understated and smart, athletic and aggressive. He wasn't an out-and-out stylist but he was the bedrock on which Kilkenny would compete over the next seven years until he retired.

The likes of Noel Hickey, Tommy Walsh, Jackie Tyrrell and J. J. Delaney gave the back unit added strength. More than once they were accused of going beyond the bounds of fair play. But maybe that came with the territory of appearing in so many high-profile games.

'There's an old saying that success breeds contempt,' John Power said. 'People started seeing them succeed so often that eventually less and less of the country wanted to see them win – they'd wish the underdog would cause a shock.

'That said, I'd be disappointed if the calibre of player we had was ever held up as being anything but ambassadors for the game. Christy Ring carved up men when he had to, because they carved him up. He poleaxed lads and was often poleaxed himself, but his fame, skill and determination were never questioned.'

*

Still, the critics were now on the alert, and soon there was a new charge on the rap sheet – Kilkenny were allegedly aping the so-called Tyrone football template. Columnists cited their employment of smother tactics, crowding opponents, sly tugging of a marker's free hand, grabbing hurleys – in short, a whole catalogue of negative ploys, foul as well as fair, calculated to frustrate the opposition.

Whatever their style, it was a blur of right and wrong that became notoriously hard for referees to police in such a fast-moving game. There was little blatant fouling, but the harrying and hassling of opponents proved highly effective. It most likely migrated from the Nowlan Park training ground, where night after night thirty players fought tooth and nail for a jersey.

As for Tyrone's footballers, Cody undoubtedly admired them. In 2008, he met with Mickey Harte's squad in Dublin, two weeks after their Ulster championship defeat to Down, and delivered a motivational speech their midfield general, Seán Cavanagh, described as 'one of the biggest turning points of the year'. Tyrone went on to win six qualifier games on the trot and stormed to a third title in that decade.

Cavanagh raved about Cody's half-hour talk: 'He spoke about Kilkenny copying Tyrone's work rate and things like that, and you sit back and realize that they actually copied us and look what they're doing now. They're winning All-Irelands for fun and they're so mentally strong. They never let anything get to them, they are just very, very efficient. He spoke with great energy and everyone took something out of it.'

It took other hurling counties a while to cop on to this style but eventually most did. Meanwhile Kilkenny, who for good measure boasted many of the country's most technically proficient hurlers, had sprinted far off into the distance in terms of aerial ability, tracking, work rate and core conditioning.

The manager's attitude on the training field had changed too following 2001. Among other things, he swallowed the whistle when it came to internal practice matches.

He may also have felt 2002 was make or break for his team so he tried a whole new generation of unproven talents such as J. J. Delaney, Eddie Brennan, Martin Comerford and Derek Lyng.

When they went on to win the National League title, pundits commented they had done so with their B team, but Cody didn't see it like that. A plethora of big names watched from the sidelines during that campaign but as far as the manager was concerned they would be staying there.

People were now seeing a new, highly tuned, souped-up Kilkenny team. Their first big test came early in that 2002 league campaign when they met their old friends from the west. This time they would boss the exchanges.

'Brian was possessed,' Carey said. 'I think he got involved in a row with Noel Lane, the Galway manager. But he was fit to row with anyone who came near him that day. He hadn't liked the fact that Galway had beaten us both physically and hurling-wise a few months beforehand. That was never going to happen again. He was a man wired up that afternoon.'

Carey has admitted that despite all their technical skill and finesse over the next decade, the charge of rough-house tactics was repeatedly thrown at them, full-frontal tackles and flick-backs of the hurley being provided as evidence. He felt they were no different from other teams.

'Hurling is hard and it should be hard and leave it there,' Carey argued. 'Dirt shouldn't happen in a game. In the 2013 league final, for example, I thought it looked awful that Lar Corbett and J. J. Delaney were involved in a skirmish. Who was right and who was wrong? I don't know. But how many other high-profile, poor incidents have there been involving Kilkenny teams? I would say very few.

'Yes, the Kilkenny–Tipp All-Ireland finals between 2009 and 2011 were just ferocious but they didn't really spill over. I think analysts look back to some instances years ago when there were frontal charges and maybe a loose swing of the hurley from Kilkenny players. That's fair enough and at the time I came out publicly and said I didn't like that. It was wrong.

'I have great respect for the Kilkenny lads but if you hit a dirty blow and get away with it, that doesn't make it right. But the same applies to any team out there. A dirty belt is a dirty belt.

'People harp on about mistimed tackles but we all know what they are. Frontal hits, flick-backs, throwing hurleys and running into the back of players are things I don't want to see. A player should be either booked or sent off.

'Funny enough, I'm not against the professional foul, like pulling an opponent down as he bears down on goal – a fella has to do that – but I'm against the pull across the chest.

'I would say to people who say Kilkenny are over the top to look a little deeper. It's always Tommy Walsh and Jackie Tyrrell who get highlighted but look closer at it. Tommy got a roasting for a few years from referees and it was totally unnecessary. Any sub that ever came into a game seemed to run at him and try to get him to lose his temper by giving him a clip. They hadn't even hit a ball. Tommy would retaliate and the cameras would pick him up hitting back.

'I've heard awful stuff talked about him but it's off the wall. The same fella got a terrible belt in the 2009 All-Ireland final but got up straight away and walked on. That's a mark of the man.'

It has been pointed out that Walsh's loose strike, which cut the face of the referee, Brian Gavin, in the 2011 All-Ireland final, constituted dangerous use of the hurl, but Kilkenny players themselves have been on the receiving end.

In the 2012 All-Ireland semi-final against Tipperary, Michael Rice suffered a blow that shattered several fingers. In August 2004, Henry Shefflin needed surgery to repair a tear duct after a heated clash with Clare. T. J. Reid was left with a dislocated kneecap after a whack from a Galway player in the 2012 All-Ireland final replay.

It may have taken time, but as referees began to let games flow, which suited Kilkenny, opponents adapted, realizing the best way to match Kilkenny was to plough back into them and take their chances. Their closest rivals hit the weights room with gusto, and as players bulked up, ground hurling disappeared because the stakes were too high to risk losing possession. Battles were fought in the air and players sought tackles and confrontation. From 2008, especially, tactics from Gaelic football coaching manuals were more evident, and not only crowding – turnovers became almost as important as scores.

And so the game evolved and it's true that Kilkenny were the driving force of that evolution – which explains why, when sparks flew, they were often seen as the villains. Skill may have crowned them, but raw power defined them, and that trait was never likely to wane on Cody's watch.

The manic passion with which they played often erupted internally, never mind on match days. On a team-bonding trip to Wexford in the mid-noughties, two of their superstars clashed in a tackle and went to ground to sort it out. As the training match continued around them, the two wrestled furiously, then got up, dusted themselves down and went back about their business.

A Wexfordman present described another incident: 'Martin

Comerford came running through with the ball and was hit with a high tackle that nearly took his head off. Still, there was shock when Cody actually blew the whistle for a free.'

To the further astonishment of the neutral observer, the free was given against Comerford for over-carrying.

In July 2008, the GAA's director of hurling, Paudie Butler, went to see them train at St Kieran's College. They played twenty-five minutes a side and the sliotar was in play for forty-nine of those fifty minutes. No ball went out of play, there were no frees and no wides. The pitch heaved with relentless concentration. Such was the spirit in which they prepared for most games.

As the '08 All-Ireland semi-final against Cork loomed, and minds and hearts were concentrated, two former county hurlers watched them train and both predicted they would win by at least eight points (they won by nine).

That night at St Kieran's they hurled without boundaries but, according to our two witnesses, they were stopped three times in their tracks and called into the centre by Cody, who raged that if they were prepared to give team-mates two inches of space on the training field, they might as well go home – those crucial fractions of space were just not acceptable.

Of course, much of what they produced on the field wasn't acceptable to the analysts either. In May 2012, Offaly's former All-Ireland winner Daithí Regan said that while he didn't want to take away from Kilkenny's success, he felt hurling referees were too liberal in applying the rules and such liberality helped Kilkenny more than most.

'Simple things like a little tug on the arm to slow a guy down and then a second player coming in. It means ball is not being cleared as readily as it would have been. It's not dirty, but it's illegal or bordering on illegal and refs are letting it go because we've all lauded the last three All-Ireland finals, which were outstanding.

'I think Kilkenny make no bones that they bring a huge physicality to the game and I think Brian Cody is influencing referees, in a subtle kind of way, to keep doing what they're doing.

'Human nature being what it is, the stronger the team you are, the stronger in character you are, and the more successful you are as a manager, the more will be thought of what you say.'

When asked if Kilkenny's legacy would be tarnished, John Power smiled: 'Do you honestly think that, when people look back on what Tommy Walsh, Henry Shefflin, J. J. Delaney and Jackie Tyrrell did while they hurled at the top, the word "dirty" will be mentioned? Not a hope.

'These guys and what they achieved will stand the test of time. They'll only be remembered for what they were best at – hurling. Little bits and pieces have been said but that will not interfere with them over time. Their legacy will be about one thing only and that's success.'

Brendan Cummins sums it up nicely. 'They were some formidable team,' he said. 'They didn't open their mouths, nothing distracted them. They never said anything to us on the pitch – ever. If you hit them a clip they would look at you; they might clip back but not a word from them. People can say they went over the rules, behind the rules, whatever. I think it was just the case they went to play their game.'

Two

A GREAT STIRRING IN THE LAND

6

What the Others Did Next

How the dispossessed mobilized to
wrest a share of power

Hurling was by no means flagging, but after the great revolution of the 1990s it had become wholly predictable again. From 1999 until 2013, not one county outside the Big Three managed to gatecrash the party. Staleness was setting in.

Even within that elite circle, Cork and Tipp had made only two or three telling raids apiece on what had become Kilkenny's territory but they could not sustain their incursions. Instead, like the rest, they looked on in envy as the Cats surfed a big and beautiful wave, winning every title bar four over thirteen years.

As the mid-1990s exploits of Clare, Offaly and Wexford faded into the mists of memory, and the Cody era kicked off in earnest, it was Cork who initially looked best placed to uncouple Kilkenny's chain of success. With their slick power running and sublime stickwork, they left Kilkenny perplexed on a number of occasions. But their momentum was stalled three times by bouts of picketing by players against the county board, all of which set the senior team back years and, more worryingly, cost them a generation of young blood. After losing the 2006 All-Ireland final they had to wait seven years to reach another September showdown.

Still, they emerged once more in 2013, in Jimmy Barry-Murphy's second coming as manager, and plucked youthful talent from third-level academies to form a new-look team. With most of the household names that had taken on the county board now absent, Cork caught Kilkenny in an All-Ireland quarter-final. This time the Cats had little left in the tank and, unlike in former times, had no obvious gripe with their opponents.

Previously, it had been easy for the Noresiders to raise the dander against the Leesiders; a succession of disagreements had driven a wedge between the counties. On Railway Cup and All Stars trips, they avoided each other like the plague. When they clashed in the league in April 2009, Cork were not long over their third domestic stand-off. Kilkenny may not have shouted it from the rooftops but they clearly disapproved of the Cork team's stance. And a twenty-seven-point destruction of their bitter foes roared out a thunderous rebuke.

Of the strained relations with Cork, Eddie Brennan said, 'I could see what they were trying to do with their protests but I felt that when they stood down a third time and refused to play for Gerald McCarthy it was a bridge too far. That man is an icon, not just in Cork, but all over the country.

'As hurlers, though, we respected them. We had always gone for aerial strength, winning our own puck-outs and being strong in the air, but they devised a plan to counteract that and we had to shape up and come back at them. A lot of teams were just pucking ball out on top of us, but Dónal Óg Cusack changed the game for everyone. After we got back on top in 2006 they started to fade. But thanks to them, other teams were getting closer to us – Cork had us analysed to the hilt.

'We changed our own game over the years and in fairness Cork were responsible for that because they found ways to attack us. Dónal Óg could put the ball on a sixpence and so their half-back line became our key target because with Cusack feeding them they could create havoc. We looked to nip their tactics at source. We were content to let Pat Mulcahy and Brian Murphy have possession in the full-back line. They could lord it down to our half-backs, which suited us. Once that was done we pulled away from them again.'

Tipperary had dropped hints that they could stack a few titles together during the noughties, but they stuttered too. In 2001, every drive they hit split the fairway; they made all their putts and walked off the eighteenth green with the cup in hand. But in 2002 they seemed to have tinkered with their swing. They never followed through from the success of the previous season; while there were no ugly shanks, their approach play was hesitant and unconvincing.

It cost them. An All-Ireland-winning team broke up without adding another major title and Tipp drifted between managers before regrouping and stopping Kilkenny's historic drive-for-five in 2010.

Under Liam Sheedy they identified how Kilkenny could be caught by pulling their backs out of position, exploiting the space and varying deliveries into their own forward line. But first, as Brendan Cummins said, they had to bulk up: 'Cian O'Neill, our physical trainer, ensured that, for the first time in my career, we were able to match Kilkenny physically. He turned our boys into animals.'

O'Neill, now coach–selector with the Kerry footballers,

reckoned he had no choice: 'Kilkenny were different gravy. They changed the game for everyone. In hurling guys are slow to change – they want to let the stick do the work – and when I went to Tipp, athleticism wasn't top of the list. I did tests at the start and we were way behind in terms of flexibility, speed endurance and squats. It was just a matter of working on that, linking into what game plan Liam and coach Eamon O'Shea had in mind and trying to build up a team to beat Kilkenny.'

In the 2009 All-Ireland final, Tipp cleaned their neighbours in the puck-out battles, winning twenty-three out of twenty-eight on the Kilkenny hand. But they also missed three goal chances, had Benny Dunne red carded, and looked on in disbelief as P. J. Ryan performed miracle after miracle in the Kilkenny goal. Interestingly, though the following year they lost eleven of Kilkenny's twenty-seven puck-outs, Tipp finally broke through by manipulating and isolating the Cats' full-back line.

In 2011 Tipp won nine of seventeen opposition puck-outs – more than enough to prevail – but still lost another final. The first two deciders, especially, were gladiatorial in their thunderous physicality and raw drama – especially the first. Tipp had their age-old foes gasping for breath and could have won both. But they didn't.

'It was so disappointing,' said Cummins. 'We should have beaten them more than once. We didn't give them as much respect as other teams did.'

Back came Kilkenny to win the 2011 and 2012 championships. It was the same old same old. Neutral hurling fans felt like holidaymakers doomed to read the same airport novel every year.

While Tipp and Cork underachieved in not winning more titles, they at least turned up to do battle. Others were beaten before they left the trenches. They had so much respect for Kilkenny there was little left for themselves.

At various junctures Galway looked like they were about to inject life and freshness into the game but ultimately they turned out to be – well, Galway: capable of anything but consistency. Kilkenny had always struggled to get a handle on them, and nearly fell by their sword in 2012. Inexplicably, though, just a season later, the Tribesmen played like a second-tier county.

As for Waterford, they had always shown a remarkable ability to bounce back from adversity, and with such frequent commotion in their ranks they got plenty of practice. They pulled the rug from under Justin McCarthy in 2008, though he had brought them no little glory. Davy Fitzgerald, too, left the hot seat with feelings running high. And in 2013 the players took more heat when Michael Ryan was jettisoned just weeks after they had almost pulled off a famous coup against Kilkenny in the qualifiers. Another season ended on a sour note.

Limerick lacked the artillery and teamwork to win the big prize and to make matters worse lost a season or two after their players downed tools on Justin McCarthy's watch in late 2009. Mind you, they had seen much talent wasted before McCarthy went near the place, the majority of the under-21s that won three All-Irelands never fulfilling their vast potential.

Wexford's players forced John Meyler out and it split the camp for a couple of years. They tried other managers with little reward. Nor did it help that their club championship became staggered and fragmented.

Clare navigated a route out of their term of unrest. Mike McNamara left the job in 2009 in controversial circumstances after a falling-out with a group of players. That was the last thing they needed after the discord accruing from Davy Fitzgerald's axing by Tony Considine in 2007 – discord played out in the full glare of the national media.

Offaly shipped some woeful hammerings and found themselves languishing near the basement of the second-tier counties.

Antrim at times couldn't even be sure of getting their best fifteen on the field.

Dublin's development, meanwhile, was only in its infancy and their gradual progress wasn't enough to rattle Cody's side until the end of the noughties.

All Kilkenny had to do was remain stable, keep their heads down, train hard and hurl like nothing else mattered. The rest were too busy either tripping themselves up or rebuilding to mount a sustained challenge to the throne.

Eventually, though, the also-rans started to shape up. It happened in 2012 and 2013 – when Galway and Dublin beat Kilkenny in successive provincial series. Chinks were appearing in the Cats' protective armour. If proof were needed, Cork beat them in the 2013 All-Ireland quarter-final.

Galway found those gaps with ruthless effect in the first half of the 2012 Leinster final, as John Power admitted: 'For thirty-five minutes that day Galway looked like the best team to ever play the game – they destroyed us.'

To their eternal credit Kilkenny regrouped and recovered. By the season's end they had clearly learned from the provincial final, putting the Westerners away in the All-Ireland final replay.

The Dubs, too, after years on the scent, looked to have finally hunted the Cats down. They should have put them away first time around in the 2013 Leinster semi-final and eventually did so in the rematch. As far back as 2006 Cody had referenced Dublin's evolution into a serious hurling force.

Initially, just as the Dubs began making serious inroads,

Kilkenny kept bashing them right down the pecking order, putting them back in their box in the 2009, 2010 and 2011 championships and absolutely wiping them out, 2-21 to 0-9, in the 2012 series. Publicly they may have lavished praise on Dublin but there was little sign of admiration on the pitch. As Michael 'Babs' Keating might say, a pat on the back is only ever inches away from a kick in the arse.

But the Dubs persisted. They learned from each defeat, shored up their defence and refined their attack. When they beat Kilkenny quite handily in the 2011 league final it was a milestone win. They drove home the stake in that 2013 Leinster championship mini-series.

'We should have won the drawn game in 2013 and doubts over us once again surfaced,' said Niall Corcoran. 'But there were no doubts in our dressing room; we knew we had the measure of them. We learned from previous experience. The year before, we were talking ourselves up but it was front; the truth was we were mentally weak. The only way you can beat teams like Kilkenny is to keep playing them and learning from them. That's what happened to us.'

In the summer of 2013 Kilkenny were finally looking like just another team. Apart from Dublin beating them, Offaly fired four goals past them, and Cork trusted young, fresh legs to run them ragged.

Paradoxically, even though they lost an enthralling qualifier, Tipp were the ones to really flag Kilkenny's decline, according to John Power, who detected an unfamiliar vulnerability in his former comrades – one he intuited could spell the end of an era.

'In Nowlan Park that evening we pulled off a famous win but we were under pressure,' Power said. 'James Woodlock wasn't a regular on the Tipp team by any means and yet he took us apart that night with direct runs through the heart of our defence. He carved us up like a tin opener on a can of beans. We couldn't match him for pace. I was fearful then that if we met a running team at any stage in the future we'd be in trouble.'

Kilkenny survived that night but almost fell in Thurles in their next qualifier, against Waterford. In a frantic finale they surrendered a lead when victory looked almost assured. From bouncing around the ring with a swagger they suddenly looked like a punchdrunk old slugger, clinging to the ropes for survival.

'Kevin Moran gave one of the greatest exhibitions in modern hurling,' said Power. 'One more body blow might have put us down for a long time, but it never came. We stayed on our feet. Waterford didn't kill us. When full time blew we were still alive.

'I said to the chap beside me that we'd blow them away in extra time, that the streetfighter in us would get a second wind. Sure enough we skinned them. That's the pride those lads have. Their era was on the line but they weren't just going to roll over.'

Yet, towards the business end of an exhilarating championship, Kilkenny were left looking on as the action reached white heat. Soon after they withstood Waterford's onslaught, they had rings run around them by Cork. And by the time Cork took on Clare in the All-Ireland final and subsequent replay, the style of modern-day hurling had undergone a veritable metamorphosis – pace, precision and speed had replaced high catching and brute force.

Kilkenny had made their name on winning aerial possession and breaking down opponents with power and pure goal hunger, but how things changed!

The conclusion could only be that the game of hurling was in a great place – possibly the best place it had ever been in. This hadn't come about overnight. Some counties had gone through tortuous soul searching. Others had lost their bearings, ripped up the roadmap, reset the satnav and started again on the way to rejuvenation.

Every county had a different journey to take. Some routes were more or less direct, some wild and scenic. But all were interesting.

7

Blues Brothers Blowing Hot

The rocky road to Dublin's extraordinary evolution

In November 2008, as Anthony Daly concluded an interview with a hurling reporter, he casually enquired if anything was happening with the Dublin job.

Word on the street was that the Dublin county board were struggling to get the right man to replace Tommy Naughton; Nicky English had been their dream target but had made it clear he wasn't interested. As the weeks passed and players grew impatient, the board were under increasing pressure. Dublin hurling may have been bursting with promise but it seemed the potential wasn't clearly visible to the outside world.

When the interviewer reassured Daly that, as far as he knew, the position was still wide open, the Clareman wondered aloud if he himself might meet the job spec. Within minutes the journalist had phoned the Dublin chairman, Gerry Harrington, informing him of Daly's interest, and received a wholly enthusiastic response.

Harrington could hardly believe that the man who had

stepped down two years earlier from managing his native county and lived more than two hours away in west Clare would be keen on the position. The reporter assured Harrington he was.

Two days later Daly met with Harrington and colleagues and agreed in principle to take the job. An announcement was made that week, courtesy of the reporter who, thanks to being in the right place at the right time, had been able to play a part in mediating the move. Everyone was happy.

After the initial getting-to-know-you process was complete Daly brought the squad for a weekend of deep personal exploration – or, to put it more plainly, physical and mental torture. The players had never experienced such duress.

You could say that from Friday till Sunday the section of the Geneva Convention relating to the treatment of prisoners was stretched to breaking point. No one was allowed shut-eye for more than two hours at a time, and when lads nodded off, soldiers would burst in and drag them from their bunks for a stint of night-time orienteering.

'They were trying to break you down,' midfielder Johnny McCaffrey said, with more than a hint of understatement. 'Trying to get you tired, make you confused. Dalo and the lads wanted to see who would wilt but they couldn't break us. It was one of the most testing weekends of my life; nothing could compare to it in terms of suffering so it actually made the rest of the season easier. No game could ever be as tough.'

McCaffrey and his team-mates had been told to bring only two home comforts with them – a pair of pyjamas and a tin of baked beans. At four o'clock on the Saturday morning they were roused by Army officers and ordered to stand by their bunks for inspection. Everyone brought PJs but only one, Alan Nolan, brought beans. And so the players were accused of letting the team down and were savagely ridiculed for it.

'Dalo wanted to dampen a growing expectation around the team and he wanted to see who his leaders were as well,' McCaffrey maintained. 'This weekend was make or break for a lot of lads and it nearly broke the lot of us. On the Friday night we were running from 8 p.m. to midnight. From then on we were given different tasks before going to bed at 3 a.m. At 3.30 a.m. the Army lads woke us and put us into a different room. We slept till 4 a.m. We were punished for not bringing beans by having to do hundreds of press-ups at 4.30 a.m. and at 6.30 a.m. we ran for another hour and a half. We wondered would it ever end.'

They were set mental and psychological tasks on Saturday and that night they were brought orienteering from 10 p.m. to midnight. They were sent back to their rooms and told to prepare for the next task when the soldiers burst into the room.

'They walked in and we wondered what was next,' McCaffrey recalled. 'Then they said, "Lads, we can't break ye." Not one lad had shirked throughout the whole weekend. A new team had formed under Dalo and he saw what we were made of that weekend even though we were in the depths of despair.'

Their respect for each other grew too. Players had stepped up to the mark and carried struggling team-mates – and it was noted that some of those who took command were the quieter, the less likely, of the group. Leaders followed other leaders. That was the weekend Daly's revolution began in earnest.

When telling the story of Dublin's resurgence, their transformation from whipping boys to All-Ireland contenders in the space of a decade, you could easily devote chapter after chapter to Daly and his ways. And yet this extraordinary tale is about much more than one individual.

In 2001, Michael O'Grady and a dedicated review group drew up a blueprint for Dublin hurling. If Daly led a momentous crusade, O'Grady and his like-minded colleagues were the ones that assembled the foot soldiers and put the supply lines in place.

The blueprint was simple but ambitious. At the top of page two the main target was spelt out: hurling to be the number one sport in Dublin by 2010. The dream was that, within the decade, Gaelic football and Leinster rugby would look enviously to hurling as the pacesetter and role model in the capital.

It didn't quite work out within the hoped-for timeframe, but by aiming for the stars, O'Grady and company managed to hit the moon. They wanted to be consistently in the top six; under Daly they would win a league and Leinster title and figure repeatedly in the shake-up to be a top-four team.

Long before the Clare man came to town, however, a Kilkenny man, Diarmuid Healy, had the spadework done. Healy, who managed Offaly to two All-Ireland titles, was appointed Dublin Director of Hurling in 2001 as part of the blueprint and it was a position he held for eighteen months. In that time development squads were formed, prioritized and run as strict meritocracies, with dropped players continually encouraged to keep improving with the prospect of being recalled at the next stage. Healy coached the coaches, put in structures and addressed the tiniest of issues, like instructing clubs how to cut the grass on their pitches to make it suitable for hurling. At that stage the hurlers were only slowly getting to parity with the footballers but still there was some resentment from certain quarters.

At a county board meeting the executive was taken to task for not appointing a director of football first. One speaker maintained that their most marketable product, the footballers, were losing out because of the fuss over hurling. That undercurrent of begrudgery was still there when some of the 2005 dual minor hurling and football fraternity were placed under huge pressure to choose football. One player asked for twenty-four hours to make a final call on his future. When his mentor rang back and asked for a decision, the player chose hurling. The line instantly went dead.

Five years later, in July 2010, that antipathy towards hurling was still obvious when the senior football management withdrew Rory O'Carroll from the Leinster under-21 hurling final in case he jeopardized his chances of featuring against Armagh in their senior football qualifier three days later. O'Carroll, left with an almost impossible call, opted out of the under-21 showdown against Wexford. Anthony Daly was baffled. 'I think it's unbelievable,' he said at the time. 'He's a twenty-year-old, fit young fella. It's rubbish. It just seems to me some people in Dublin football are more worried about Dublin hurling than Armagh.'

Around the same time, after successfully introducing hurling to its students, one north county school asked a local club to form an underage team. They were ignored.

Nonetheless, despite the considerable associated costs of playing the game, including the provision of helmets, hurleys and sliotars, constant efforts were made by the likes of Humphrey Kelleher, Jimmy Boggan, Tom Ryan and Tom Fitzpatrick to put a hurley in every kid's hand.

All the time they chased a goal. With the bar raised so high, however, tumbles were inevitable, and they took one in 2004, when Dublin suffered a fifteen-point hammering by Offaly in the Leinster championship and drew Kilkenny in the qualifiers.

A web designer by trade, Kevin Flynn had a work contract lined up in the USA, and so, having weighed his options, he decided to pull up stakes and go west. Flynn knew he was leaving the team in the lurch but his design business, iCreative, needed attention and he felt he had little choice but to move away. Vice-captain Liam Ryan also pulled out of the squad.

When Flynn explained his situation to Humphrey Kelleher, the Dublin manager, he seemed okay with it, even if the county board took a dim view. Flynn's team-mates, acutely conscious of his efforts for the cause, stayed quiet on the matter, but his family took heat and he was peppered with flak. Kilkenny beat the Dubs by twenty-six points in the qualifiers, on a day when the Cats were so rampant that even ten Kevin Flynns would hardly have made a difference.

Consistent with the county board's wishes, Flynn was omitted from the Dublin panel the following year, and without him they lost all six of their Division 1A games, by an average of fourteen points. Halfway through the season, Kelleher was removed and Tommy Naughton, the under-21 manager, was proposed for the senior job. He intimated that one of his first moves would be to recall the Prodigal Son.

The board took that about as well as an end-of-year tax bill, and a bitter stalemate ensued. An interim management – including the county chairman, John Bailey – was installed, but the hurlers refused to recognize it.

In late July, Bailey, Tom Ryan, Mick O'Riordan and Mickey Whelan presented themselves in Parnell Park to oversee a training session that never took place. The players claimed Bailey was trying to insert himself in the manager's seat, something they weren't having, and declined to cooperate. And though Bailey insisted he was merely acting as 'facilitator', the players stood firm and said they would train away without his help.

Both parties went to war in the sports pages and news bulletins. Players accused the board of intimidation, claiming among other things that Bailey had threatened to scupper their careers – and when Bailey strenuously denied the charge, thirty players signed a document backing their argument. The Gaelic Players Association got involved, releasing a statement on behalf of the squad.

Eventually, Naughton was named manager for the remainder of the 2005 season and that brought a temporary end to hostilities. That ceasefire became permanent when Bailey's five-year term as chairman ended in December of that year. Remarkably, he decided to stand as vice-chairman and was emphatically outvoted – 129 to 69 – by St Sylvester's Danny O'Connor. Clearly, the preceding period of turbulence contributed to his heavy defeat.

Meanwhile, through all the sorry mess, a gifted amateur sportsman who had left a leaky ship to provide for himself had seen his character and motives impugned. And the irony of it all was that Flynn had been the one carrying the team through difficult times. The O'Toole's man had established himself as a consistently excellent forward, and through all the county's travails he had been trying to raise standards. It was often a thankless job.

One Sunday afternoon in 1998, Dublin suffered a heavy league defeat to Clare at Parnell Park. Flynn had played well but as he walked off the paddock he heard Ger Loughnane tell a journalist that, rather than travelling, he and his team would have been better off with a good training session back home in Clare. Flynn was deeply hurt by the comment. The fact, though, that several years later some of his own people, board officers in the main, had turned against him hurt a hell of a lot more.

It was hard to see an end to the debacle. It wasn't as if life as a Dublin hurler had hitherto been a bed of shamrocks. They used to train at Trinity College's sportsground in Santry, eating sandwiches prepared by the groundsman's wife. The groundsman, incidentally, was the father of the Ireland, and later England, cricketer Ed Joyce. They also did some training at O'Toole Park – they had little or no access to Dublin City University at the time. The Kilkenny hurler Denis Byrne took some of those sessions at O'Toole Park and later described an intercounty team training in an environment barely fit for junior B club hurlers. At night, the only significant illumination came courtesy of the glare from Ben Dunne's nearby gym. Some of the sliotars were long past their puck-by date. There were no goalposts. At times the grass was so high it would have yielded a decent cut of silage. Before training and matches, players would load up on puddings and sausages and were then pitched against teams of Division 1 standard.

Byrne recalled a team that did everything he asked of them, but he said the set-up, the preparations and the general environment were disastrous. The stand-off over Flynn and the interim management was merely the straw that broke the camel's back.

In June 2005, news reached the squad that Kevin Heffernan, a Dublin football icon – and a good hurling man too, it must be said – was ready to make a dramatic return to management with the hurlers. Heffernan, the man who ignited Gaelic football in the capital in the 1970s, was prepared to enter a management team with the former dual star Mick Holden and ex-manager Marty Morris – provided the board agreed to it. But the board didn't agree – they objected to Morris, who in 2003 had quit as manager in a row over lack of financial support for the team. Thus, the sensational return of a true GAA legend was scuppered and a glorious chance to reunite the troops was missed. Towards the end of 2005, another living legend turned down the opportunity. Seán Boylan, who had resigned after twenty-three years in charge of the Meath footballers, was informally approached about the Dublin job but said he was taking a sabbatical from Gaelic games.

With Bailey no longer in administration, the stakeholders of Dublin hurling were running out of people to blame for their never-ending slump. It had been forty-four years since they narrowly lost an All-Ireland final to Tipperary. Quality hurlers were being produced only sporadically and when they did emerge they were treated like second-class citizens. Did anyone care? It didn't appear so. Dublin were damned by indifference.

By now, honest and talented players like David Curtin, Carl Meehan, Aodán de Paor and Tomás McGrane had grown weary of their lot. Ten others had cried off the panel. The rest, instead of preparing for upcoming games and a possible qualifier run in the 2005 championship, had been arming themselves with mission statements to lobby county board delegates entering bouncer-patrolled meetings.

What most infuriated them was to be accused of lacking commitment. They responded by training away manically on their own, determined to shut the cynics up. In the month of January alone they met twenty times. It was a recipe for disaster – and burnout.

Naughton took over and applied some balm to the wounds but the healing process took time. They lost to Westmeath by two points in the first round of the 2006 Leinster championship on a day so rain-sodden that racing was postponed at the Curragh. They wouldn't let horses race but the Dublin hurlers were sent out to hurl. For the record, the Dubs played into the shallow end in the first half. And so, a bright new beginning for kids like

John McCaffrey, Tomás Brady and Keith Dunne got bogged down in a Portlaoise monsoon.

Both McCaffrey and Brady were sought after by the footballers, who had just entered an era of provincial dominance. In 2005, McCaffrey was captain of both the county minor hurling and football teams while Brady was considered Na Fianna's best footballer. The senior hurlers, in the meantime, had lost fifteen games on the trot so it was a watershed moment when both youngsters chose the small ball and forged a path for others to follow.

'The hurlers were the first to call me, simple as that,' McCaffrey says. 'We had been going well at minor level and being from Lucan I always had a dream to play senior hurling for Dublin so off I went.'

Most of the current team is the product of the era that started with Brady and McCaffrey. Once those two nailed their colours to the mast, others found it easier to follow. Danny Sutcliffe, for instance, was another great football prospect but played three years with the county minor hurling team before winning an All Star in 2013.

So, while they were disappointed to lose to Westmeath, the players nonetheless recognized that their manager was honest and industrious and that Gary Maguire, Stephen Hiney, Michael Carton and seventeen-year-old Alan McCrabbe were all keen for more responsibility. Maguire and McCrabbe were two other prodigies who turned into leaders and would later become All Stars.

Progress was slow at first. In 2007, after a fine league run, they were pipped by Wexford in Nowlan Park before losing three qualifier games against top-tier sides. A year later they ran Wexford to a replay in Leinster and pushed Cork hard in the qualifiers.

*

For all the rumblings of negativity in those years, the Dubs' underage foundations were clearly being reinforced. In 2005 they landed their first Leinster minor title since 1983 and won another in 2007. They reached provincial under-21 finals in 2005 and 2006, landed the crown in 2007, regained it in 2010 and retained it in 2011. Remarkably, they figured in eight of the eleven Leinster under-21 finals between 2003 and 2013.

In 2006, Dublin Colleges won an All-Ireland A title. Further down the age scale, four of the nine Division 1 Féile na nGael (under-14) hurling All-Irelands from 2005 to 2013 were won by Dublin clubs – Kilmacud Crokes (2005), Castleknock (2007), St Brigid's (2012) and Ballyboden St Enda's (2013).

What was now different with youngsters graduating to the Dublin seniors was that the likes of Sutcliffe and Liam Rushe had been introduced to hurling at an early age – by the time they turned six or seven, the requisite skills were becoming second nature to them.

Naughton, meanwhile, didn't have his managerial term extended beyond 2008 but he left a side speckled with potential. 'He took us from rock bottom and got lads interested again,' McCaffrey said. 'We had a great league run in 2007, drawing with Kilkenny and beating Galway and Limerick, and that was the first sign of what was to come. Tommy was a genuine man.'

History would unkindly overlook Naughton's role in building a structure from the rubble of what went before, but he walked away surely happy to know that, after almost fifteen years of having its wings clipped, Dublin hurling was finally ready to take flight again. Few could have guessed just how high it would soar with Anthony Daly.

*

A master motivator, Daly forced the players to look in the mirror as well as at the opposition and, while not doubting themselves, to recognize the size of the challenges they faced. To do that, though, much work was needed; there was a cockiness in the group that wasn't justified. There were fault lines too.

Niall Corcoran, a product of the Galway underage system, moved to Dublin in 2005 and spent two years commuting to play with his club, Meelick–Eyrecourt. He was on the Galway senior squad for a while but had been cut by Ger Loughnane. The M4 wasn't as navigable then as it would become, and despite all the to-ing and fro-ing Corcoran felt he was going in only one direction: backwards. He decided to join Kilmacud Crokes, where he was employed as a games promotion officer, reasoning that if it didn't work out he could always go home.

He had played just two league games with Crokes when Damien Byrne, one of Tommy Naughton's selectors, asked him to join the Dublin squad. Two other non-Dubs, Maurice O'Brien and Declan Qualter, were already in the set-up at this stage and Corcoran also agreed to join; he hadn't been deemed good enough for Galway, and though he arrived for his first night of Dublin training knowing no one but his clubmate Ross O'Carroll, he was ready for a new adventure.

'I had barely sat down when Kevin Flynn came over and said, "You're sitting in my seat",' Corcoran recalled. 'He wasn't joking either. Listen, I could understand. At the time there were issues with lads coming in from the outside and playing for the Dubs. Kevin probably thought it was more important that they develop their own players – he was right too. But from my perspective I had another opportunity to make it at intercounty, and I soon got a feel for it.'

Before long, Daly found out that, despite recent progress in several areas, the general standard of hurling in the county was patchy. As Corcoran himself put it, only two or three senior teams were up to scratch and many of the others would have been considered junior standard back in his home county: 'It was obvious that had to change pretty quickly. It didn't matter if Dalo or Our Lord himself took over – the quality of players coming through had to improve.'

Corcoran admitted, however, that even if the club scene wasn't hectic, the atmosphere and support services around the Dublin camp were excellent. He learned to train smart and worked harder on his touch and speed of striking – and yet when he made his championship debut against Wexford he found he needed to work even harder: 'I was way off the pace – at a completely different level. Rory Jacob cleaned me out.'

Dublin drew Cork in the qualifiers and Corcoran made a promise to himself: he'd been knocking on the door long enough and now it was time to blow the bloody thing down. He marked Joe Deane, as crafty a forward as ever gave a defender night-mares, and made his name as the underdogs pushed Cork all the way: 'After that game I just said if I can do that imagine what I can do if I get a whole year's training behind me.'

Although they were beaten, the whole Dublin team took heart from their performance.

Daly went to work on the mechanics of the squad: strength-ened the team bond, upped the intensity and made them commit to the lifestyle required.

'There were a few lines of demarcation in the squad before he came,' Corcoran recalled. 'Lads would have gone out after games but there wouldn't necessarily be an invite there for you. I would have been with Ross all that year and to be honest I wouldn't really have belonged anywhere else.'

Fortunately, Daly treated Corcoran the same as the rest and gradually they accepted him.

'The team moved on in personnel and the lads I'm playing with now are my best mates,' Corcoran said in 2013. 'I get on with them more than I would with some of the lads from back home. But the only way to get to that stage was to prove myself – show that I had come here to contribute the best I could. I wanted to help myself but I wanted to help Dublin hurling too, and Anthony helped facilitate that. The landscape changed. Lads just became a lot closer.'

Certain issues still existed early in Daly's tenure, however. As Corcoran recalled, not everyone bought into the entire culture of intercounty hurling.

'The one thing I felt Dublin were missing was that, while lads would train like diehards, they weren't fully prepared to put in the effort when it came to lifestyle and diet. Besides that, myself and others weren't always doing the right sort of training. We lacked a bit of tradition and belief too, and often those are enough just to get past games.

'But Anthony improved all those areas in his few years here – he just cut out excuses. In the past, lads could blame the facilities and say they weren't conducive to training. Tommy Naughton was great, but over the years lads could always blame managers or claim that certain aspects of training were just not good enough. We always had a reason for why we didn't play well. Dalo cut out all those excuses one by one.'

Eventually, the hurling set-up would rival that of the Dublin footballers. The county board invested heavily in them, as did the GAA administration in general, and in time they lacked for nothing. The days of overgrown training pitches were long gone.

Of course, it took years of effort and persuasion to get there. Even Daly, a born leader, had to be patient. He worked on their bodies, pumped them up, broke them down again, and refined their hurling skills and tactical nous. While admitting that flaws persisted, he always backed his players in public. Nor did he neglect their heads: he brought in psychologists like Liam Moggan and Declan Coyle to work their magic.

The transformation after 2005 was steady. In 2009 they beat Antrim and Wexford before losing by six points to Kilkenny in the Leinster final. Second-season syndrome struck in 2010, and they were dreadful – destroyed by Kilkenny in the provincial semi-final and knocked out of the All-Ireland series by Antrim.

Perhaps they got too far ahead of themselves. And maybe the huge turnover of personnel – fourteen players within eighteen months – was a factor. Either way, they came back revitalized and chomping at the bit in 2011, winning the league and reaching the All-Ireland semi-final. That league title was a significant milestone; it was their first spring crown since 1939.

'Consistency was what Dublin hurling needed at that time, and the more consistent we were, the more the public reacted,' Corcoran reflected. 'And there were immediate effects. You were getting recognized around the city. Even guys from down the country were telling you how they followed the team.

'It was weird because it had never happened before. But on the morning of that league final, sitting in the bus as we left the Spawell Hotel in Templeogue, there was huge belief there. We were playing Kilkenny but for once we weren't worried about the opposition. That took huge pressure off. Lads just went for it. Kilkenny were missing key players but it was a serious milestone for us.'

As for that year's All-Ireland semi-final, they could claim in hindsight they could have beaten Tipperary. They were unfortunate in that Lar Corbett was then turning water into strong porter with his every touch of the sliotar and had rattled a goal and a point before the Dubs drew breath. But from there they matched Tipp blow for blow and threatened one of the biggest upsets in hurling history. They went down fighting, but they still went down – by three points in the end.

'We played with three midfielders that day and two inside,' Corcoran recalled. 'Don't forget where the two teams were coming from. We were getting gradually stronger but they had just put seven goals past Waterford in the Munster final and could you blame us for being wary of that?

'Peter Kelly set the tone for us that day. Lar got those early touches but Peter went to a different level after that – he was unreal. At full-back he's wasted because he's such an athlete, but he won every ball in the air and really inspired us. We came up just short.'

Despite that end to the season, there was huge satisfaction that talented youngsters like Shane Durkin, Eamon Dillon and Mark Schutte had made the grade. As the team developed, so too did the reserves. They now had serious options off the bench. Conal Keaney, whose best days with the footballers were over, still caused a stir when rejoining the hurlers. Shane Ryan, likewise, put a decade of elite football service behind him and linked up, injecting for the short time he was involved a welcome dose of attitude and energy.

This all pointed to a sea-change in the perennial tug of love between the two codes; Dublin's dual players would no longer automatically choose football – though such prodigies as Ciarán Kilkenny, Cormac Costello and Eric Lowndes did. There was another seismic shift. When the Boys in Blue had last won the hurling All-Ireland, in 1938, only one native Dub, Jim Byrne, made the team. Now, with the exception of Corcoran, Tipperary's

Ryan O'Dwyer and Limerick's Maurice O'Brien, they were all locals.

The 2001 revolution had worked. By the late noughties, every Saturday and Sunday morning, from Na Fianna in Glasnevin to Ballyboden to Cuala in Dalkey, kids were out with their hurleys, pucking around as they walked to training. A Martian touching down in suburban Dublin might have thought he had landed by mistake in Kilkenny. It was a seismic shift in attitude.

Only five years earlier, the likes of Kevin Flynn, well-versed in the history of obscurity, had seen the set-up at an all-time low. Now Liam Rushe, an unlikely hero from the football heartland of St Pat's, Palmerstown, was steaming through the system. With underage hurling picking up in untypical areas like Castleknock, Swords and Balbriggan, others were hot on his heels.

When he arrived from Cashel in 2010, Ryan O'Dwyer found a team he could finally belong in. With the exception of minor hurling, O'Dwyer represented Tipp at every level in football as well as hurling, but his senior career had stalled; he was going nowhere.

A bustling centre-forward, O'Dwyer was always likely to struggle for promotion in a county where the silky skills of Nicky English, Eoin Kelly and Lar Corbett were the benchmark. His unglamorous job spec, whenever he got selected, was simply to nullify the opposing centre-back. It was only when he arrived in the big city – and found Daly – that he finally made the grade as an intercounty regular.

Before then, he had been jinking in and out of Tipp squads with dizzying irregularity. Shortly after the obliteration by Cork in the 2010 Munster championship, he received yet another call to arms; Liam Sheedy wanted him back in Semple Stadium. O'Dwyer had planned to go to Boston for the summer but turned up for a training match and ruffled feathers by throwing himself about.

He was on the Tipp football team as well and was in decent shape, but the hurlers had trained since January and he didn't feel he could make the required impact, certainly not in the fringe role he was likely to be given. He was tempted to hang around with the footballers – but they had drawn Laois in the qualifiers and would have faced Dublin had they won that, so after weighing everything up, he proceeded with his plan to head Stateside.

Nine weeks later he was back – and looking on as Tipp smashed Kilkenny's drive-for-five by winning the 2010 All-Ireland final. Standing on Hill 16, he had never felt as weird in all his life.

'Bittersweet,' he said. 'No point in saying otherwise. I remember everything about the day down to the fact that I was wearing a red hoodie. I was delighted the lads won and at the same time wondering why I had gone to the US – I could have had an All-Ireland medal. But sure I wasn't even officially on the panel. And if I didn't go to Boston I might not be with the Dublin set-up now and ultimately that's what has me where I am.'

After that All-Ireland, O'Dwyer started a teaching job at St MacDara's CC in Templeogue. One evening after work his phone rang. Richie Stakelum, another Tipp stalwart but also a Dublin selector, was on the line, wanting to know if Ryan would like to link up with the county squad.

Meanwhile, back home O'Dwyer's club, Cashel, had a Crosco Cup final looming, and so, not needing to be distracted, he asked for the proverbial raincheck. Cashel won that final and O'Dwyer then agreed to chat with Stakelum and Daly. Within minutes of meeting them he had agreed to become an honorary Dub.

Some thirteen years earlier O'Dwyer had walked into Daly's sports shop in Ennis and asked the man himself to sign a Clare jersey. Now the two were united in a single cause. As for Dublin, they had found themselves a combative centre-forward, one who, for better, for worse, would weave himself into the fabric of their story.

Unlike Corcoran, O'Dwyer never noticed any resentment among the natives. He threw himself into the city way of life and fast became a back-of-the-bus merchant when travelling to and from games.

'He was instantly a popular man,' Corcoran smiled. 'Cracking jokes, big personality, I suppose. I was more reserved, which didn't help things either, but Ryan is a different kettle of fish – the lads took to him straight off. They also trusted that Dalo knew what he was at, bringing him in.'

O'Dwyer would later wince when recalling the first meeting with his new team-mates; he couldn't put a name to any of the faces: 'We met at the Castleknock Hotel in late 2010 and I walked upstairs, literally not knowing where to go from there. It was the team's first get-together and I was quite nervous. Hedgo [the selector Ciarán Hetherton] came over to me but I didn't have a bull's notion who he was. Next over was Chris Thompson, who said he was the doctor.'

Fortunately for the new boy, he was put in a group with Dave Treacy, Shane Stapleton, David 'Dotsy' O'Callaghan and Dave Curtin: 'As soon as Dotsy knew I was living in Tallaght we just clicked because he said he wouldn't have to drive to training any more. He wasn't joking either. That broke the ice.'

For good measure, Thompson invited O'Dwyer to his annual New Year's Day party. As it transpired, O'Dwyer was too nervous to attend, but wouldn't miss the gig thereafter.

According to O'Dwyer, it was only when he arrived in Dublin that he was given a licence to play hurling: 'In Tipp I was a stopper, but Richie Stakelum said it to me one day: "This is your chance to re-establish yourself as a hurler. No one here knows what to expect – you go and do what you like."'

O'Dwyer needed no further encouragement. He worked hard on his finishing, won a league medal in 2011, his first full season, and a few months later ended his first championship narrowly losing an All-Ireland semi-final against his native county, with a personal tally of 3-6 from four games. With every passing season, as Tipp struggled for grit and ball winners in their forward division, their fans wondered why O'Dwyer had been let go.

'No confidence back home,' he said. 'If someone says something about you long enough you start to believe it. I was thinking, "I'm the stopper." Then when I came to Dublin I'm a hurler again.'

Much like O'Dwyer's own trajectory, though, the following season, 2012, would prove a rollercoaster for the Dubs. Throughout the winter they talked themselves up, spoke of how they visualized being applauded on to pitches countrywide in 2013 as All-Ireland champions. They beat Laois and were pulverized by Kilkenny before being dumped from the qualifiers by Clare in Cusack Park. For a while the spark of revolution was dimmed.

In fact, the eighteen-point loss to Kilkenny in Portlaoise hit them like the collapse of an edifice three years in the building, bricks and timbers tumbling down around them.

'All the praise went out the window and suddenly we were being painted as gym monkeys who couldn't hurl,' said O'Dwyer. 'That was some hit to the confidence, a serious kick in the teeth. Embarrassing.'

Corcoran described it as one of the worst days: 'We learned a lot from 2012 in how we hadn't progressed. We had talked a lot of bullshit and it backfired so it was back to basics. In the six weeks leading up to Christmas 2012 we focused a lot more on the traditional type of training.'

Traditional was a euphemism. What Corcoran meant was that sports science was put on hold and they ran in the muck and wind and rain of O'Toole Park until they threw up or seized up. It was as raw a six weeks as Corcoran ever put in: 'Dalo felt we were mentally weak so he said, "Let's get the work done and see who really wants this."'

The manager called several players aside and told them to shape up – or else. Careers were on the line. They rolled up sleeves and targeted the 2013 Walsh Cup the way other teams target early September. And they won it.

O'Dwyer, for his part, reckoned the 'gym monkeys' jibe was near enough the mark – he had focused too much on brute strength in 2012 and was feeling muscle-bound and heavy-legged. On Mondays he would take in a wall session at Thomas Davis or St Jude's, whipping out the camera phone for a selfie to show he was there, hard at work. Later that evening there would be a pitch or gym session; on Wednesdays another gym session; on Thursdays two more sessions; on Fridays yet more weights; the week rounded off with a match on Saturday or Sunday.

When they played Galway in the league in February 2012, O'Dwyer was jumping out of his skin. But shortly thereafter, during a training session near Dublin Airport, his legs turned to lead and he would eventually conclude, with the benefit of hindsight, that he never fully recovered that season.

He gained seven kilos of pure muscle and didn't allow himself sufficient rest after sessions. The increased bulk caught up with him. He felt at times he was running against a gale.

Early-morning sessions were held, at least once a week, under lights in Bray. O'Dwyer would go to bed in his Under Armour shirt, shorts, togs and socks, hurley to hand, ready to hop up when the alarm sounded at 4.45 a.m., but so anxious to be there on time that often he would sleep only fitfully. After training he would wolf down bacon and eggs and join rush-hour traffic, landing at school around 8.15.

To a man, everyone was at those sessions. Sometimes they would meet up again the same evening. They put in all the work required to win an All-Ireland. They maybe put in too much work, because their results graph quickly went south.

'Mentally we thought things were just going to happen,' O'Dwyer admitted. 'It was, "Look what we did last year – even if we lose a game we'll get back to the All-Ireland series." We were looking at the mountaintop rather than getting over the first hill. We were beaten in a few league games by a point and with that a few cracks came and ate away at my confidence.

'But the attitude – "Sure this won't matter when we win the All-Ireland" – I hold my hand up; I was the biggest culprit for talking us up and I regret that so much. I had to relook at that and I did – in 2013 I kept away from interviews as much as possible.'

Meanwhile, Daly wanted to find out how keen the squad were for him to stay on and so he asked them to convene a team meeting and get back to him. The answer was they were extremely keen – but all concerned were agreed that certain things had to change, including the translation of training-ground form on to the pitch on match day.

They met, reviewed the year, and agreed to go again. Despite getting a few frights and robbing Limerick in the final, they won Division 1B of the league. Wary of 'same voice syndrome' Daly introduced Tony Griffin as a quasi-life coach and a number of players took particular benefit from his unfailing positivity. Griffin spoke to the squad the night before their 2013 championship opener with Wexford and had no problem getting their attention; they had witnessed how much he had helped Dotsy O'Callaghan, who had lost his dad the year before but went on to enjoy a brilliant hurling season.

'Tony spoke and we took up the momentum from him,' Corcoran recalled. 'The gist was that we relied too heavily on Anthony and Richie – and maybe a couple of players – to take control. We had to develop a few more leaders. Tony is doing that for us and he's absolutely super, just so honest. You know what he's saying is totally genuine and when the players ring him they know he's one hundred per cent behind them. Lads saw that this guy has done something extra with his life.'

Tommy Dunne took fifteen sessions throughout 2013 and so impressed were the management and players with him that he was given a permanent role. On the night of his first session, he saw O'Dwyer experimenting with twenty-metre frees and called him to order.

'Do you take twenty-metre frees in matches?'

'No.'

'Well then, stop messing around!'

Message received and understood. O'Dwyer loved it, as he explained: 'The intensity went up another level when he came in. We did simple drills – strike the ball into a lad's hand from seven yards – but under pressure and on the run. He pulled us up on that because we weren't doing it consistently, and we had to work on our touch with everything going at a hundred miles an hour.'

What a year they had! Getting out of Wexford Park with a draw by the skin of their jerseys but winning the replay comprehensively. Beating Kilkenny up and down the field in the Leinster semi-final but again only getting a draw before finally taking Brian Cody's side in the replay. As the players waltzed with each other in sheer delight, they heard a chant normally reserved for the footballers, one they had never previously heard sung at a hurling match: 'Come on, you Boys in Blue!'

'There was a lot of hurt there, built up over the years,' Corcoran said of their history with the Cats. 'Everyone reckoned our chance to beat them had gone, but we didn't have one serious training session between the draw and the replay and it kept us fresh. Actually, the games had started to stack up at this stage and it was great.

'Our dressing room went nuts for a while. Dalo did too for about ten seconds, but then he roared at us to come back down to earth and we refocused quickly. He just said, "Lads, fucking nothing is won. No one will remember this at end of year unless we win something."'

The key to beating Kilkenny was that they stayed calm until the end. And throughout those busy four weeks they had kept the ship on course even when some of their main men had dipped in form. Liam Rushe and Dotsy O'Callaghan were taken off in their first game against Wexford, so too were Conal Keaney and Danny Sutcliffe in the drawn Kilkenny match, and apart from their All Star full-back Peter Kelly and goalkeeper Gary Maguire everyone had either been moved or substituted.

It would have been no surprise had they failed to raise the intensity one more time when they played Galway the following week, but they did it – and with ease. Facing his native county meant little to Corcoran; he had played them on several occasions. He got a few verbals, but nothing too slanderous, as the Tribesmen were swatted aside.

'It was tough but I had played against them so often that it was nearly just another game. Fergal Moore, David Collins and Damien Hayes were about the only three lads left that I had played with anyway.'

As Corcoran noted, the switching of colours was more

problematic for his family, friends and cousins from back home – loyalties could hardly be undivided: 'They were in Croker wearing Galway shirts but still wishing us [Dublin] the best of luck. But if I had overbuilt it I wouldn't have got the best from myself.'

Dublin played Cork for the right to contest the All-Ireland final and appeared set fair for a big September date. That was before O'Dwyer incurred a second yellow card for what the referee James Owens deemed an illegal shoulder charge on Lorcán McLoughlin and Cork went on to win.

The first yellow card was harsh and O'Dwyer reacted with disbelief when the ref ordered him off, and though some of his team-mates, assuming his guilt, were initially furious with him, they changed their minds when they saw the replay of both incidents and felt that he should not have been sent off at all.

The player was understandably devastated: 'I let down my family. My mother, Bernie, was getting chemotherapy at the time; she had just had an operation to get a breast removed. I talk to her on the phone every night and you'd always know how proud she is. But there I was, walking off the field in an All-Ireland semi-final and the only thing I had in my mind, that I was after letting down my mother.

'In the Leinster final, with the game in the bag, I had a picture taken of me in the dugout and there were tears in my eyes. I started crying thinking of my mother. So you can imagine what I felt like being sent off.

'I had trained so hard to get back right after a poor 2012. I had recovered from surgery to get my shoulder right and had done every little thing I was supposed to. All I wanted was to make my parents proud and it was taken away from me by that man. Well, he had his day in the sun. All I can say is hurling is a man's game – there is something unique about it. It's a warrior's game – you give and take it.

'You need to be half-mental to play hurling. I get leathered and take it – I don't mind getting the shit beaten out of me. If it means the team wins I will gladly take a hiding. But when you do the slightest thing and get a red card? I asked him was he taking the piss when he showed it to me, said he couldn't be serious.

'"Get off," was his reply.

'In that dressing room after the Cork match I was as low as I've ever felt. I apologized to Dalo but he told me to shut the fuck up, that I had nothing to apologize for. I suppose I'm learning all the time, hitting the lows and using them as motivation for the next year.

'We're good enough, we know that, but if we do the same things again we might not get to where we want to. We need to evolve and I hope we have that ability. There are good lads coming through the ranks. Cian McGowan was in goal for the Dublin minors in 2012 and he's already at wing-back for Kilmacud Crokes seniors. He's as good as anyone I've seen. But the great thing is nearly every lad on the Dublin team knows of some young kid coming through the ranks.'

McCaffrey admitted that they are still learning lessons: 'It's taking a lot of hard work to get over the finishing line and we've had setbacks like Westmeath in 2007 and losing to Antrim in 2010. But we know we can get over the finishing line; the dream is becoming more real all the time, it definitely is. I only have a few more years left but we could be handing the baton on to a team that wins everything for years and years. I'm not getting carried away either. We are close. The provincial title, the league title, even the Walsh Cup – hopefully they were just landmarks along the way.

'But hurling is so cut-throat. We know there are no guarantees. We need to get on a roll and stay on it. Kilkenny will be stronger after the hurt. Clare will fear no one. We are only one of the chasing pack.

'We have Dalo, though, and we'd stay listening to him all year long. He still has the dressing room in the palm of his hand and the players can see that this man just loves Dublin. Every year he has managed to bring in ideas to freshen it up and it's never become one bit stale.'

And just as it was before Daly took over, the Dublin underage scene has been purring nicely – they appeared in the All-Ireland minor finals of 2011 and 2012, although they lost both, after bringing Tipperary to a replay in 2012. Development squads are up and running from under-13 onwards, both north and south county. It has meant sufficient coaching for any kid half decent at hurling – even in clubs more orientated to football. Which is hugely important where traditionally only the same four or five clubs could realistically challenge for a county title.

Each year, the Irish Sports Council has given almost €1m for Dublin GAA projects, and the county board's lucrative deal with AIG has meant great financial security. Some have talked of money being thrown at Dublin hurling – and maybe so – but crucially the investment has borne remarkable fruit; between 2010 and 2013 the number of teams from under-8 to under-16 jumped from 546 to 602.

Taking hurling and football in tandem, the county enjoyed tremendous growth right through the noughties. In 2003, counting football teams from under-9 up and hurling teams from under-11 up, the total was 620. By 2010, with the starting point at under-8, the ballpark figure was 1,359. By then almost every club had pitches, changing rooms and gyms the likes of which former generations could hardly have dreamed of.

As Dublin hurling emerged from the shadow of football it has seemed more and more likely to win over dual players like Ciarán Kilkenny, but as Corcoran admitted, that will always be something for individual players to decide: 'Whether they come back, or not, is up to themselves; we can't worry about guys who don't want to – or can't – play.

'The only thing we worry about is letting all this slip. Too many people have put in endless hours of work and it's crazy difficult to quantify just what they do. But maybe we are coming to a place where we can't go backwards now, and the only way is forward.

'Kids are going to Croke Park to see the hurling team and are turning up at summer camps in the most unlikely of areas saying they want to be hurlers. That's some shift in mindset from when I first came up here.'

It's not that long since one Dublin hurler recalled stories of hurleymakers keeping aside rough cuts and warped wood to send their worst sticks up to the capital where no one would ever care to challenge them. Those days are well behind them. A dim and distant memory.

8

Calm after the Storm

How Limerick put a turbulent decade behind them

Relentless, determined sheets of rain battered the roof of Donal O'Grady's supermarket in Ballingarry, overflowing gutters and gushing from downpipes. A typical late summer in Ireland: pockets of intense heat one minute, storm-blown showers the next.

O'Grady smiled when it was put to him that the vagaries of the weather might well provide an apt metaphor for Limerick hurling. It was not meant as a dig, merely a reflection of the countless highs and lows they had endured over the previous ten years.

At the end of July 2013, O'Grady led the team on to Croke Park for their All-Ireland semi-final with Clare. Of the 63,000 watching in the stadium, it was estimated that nearly 40,000 hailed from Limerick. O'Grady had been part of the 2007 All-Ireland final team and when he ran out beyond the tunnel on to Croke Park that day, a wall of noise and light engulfed him and sucked life from his legs. It did much the same to his team-mates;

they were dead and buried within about seventeen minutes of the sliotar being thrown in for that final.

This time, though, as he led the team out to play Clare in the last four of the most open hurling championship in history, a surge of adrenaline coursed through his limbs. The sight of the team strip seemed to do the same for the Limerick supporters – the stands and terraces erupted in a forest of green. In 2007, many of those same fans had travelled to support a team with little chance of winning. The class of 2013, however, had moved to a different place in their consciousness. They felt confident they could go all the way. They were, after all, the first Limerick team since 1996 to bring home a Munster title.

A month earlier, in June, they had beaten Cork in the Munster final and on that occasion the supporters simply could not be restrained. They broke the GAA code of conduct by invading the pitch and turning the Gaelic Grounds into a heaving frenzy of celebration. O'Grady stood on the presentation platform and showed the fans the Munster Cup. In the city where rugby had dominated for years, hurling, like O'Grady on the winners' platform, was back on top.

Little had been expected of Limerick at the start of 2013 – they had failed to win the Division 1B league final against Dublin – but with just two games left between them and an All-Ireland they were now right up there. And so the faithful could dream the ultimate dream: with Kilkenny and Tipp out of the reckoning there was a growing belief that the Shannonsiders could win their first senior All-Ireland in forty years.

They endured a five-week gap between the provincial decider and the Clare game and in that time the hype grew. Players tried to remain unaffected but gradually it all spiralled out of control. Sadly for the team, that excitement somehow manifested itself on the pitch and nerves seemed to grip players from the start.

They snatched at shots on goal, their touch was clumsy and their marking slack. Spells of frenetic effort were punctuated by bouts of apparent numbness, and though they rallied and pushed themselves back into the game they lost by seven points to the eventual All-Ireland champions.

Afterwards O'Grady was barely consolable. And while the year had been a success in general the mood around the county slumped, moving from carnival fever to crushing disappointment and then to outright anger.

Some fans – a tiny and unrepresentative minority, it must be said – reacted with venom. For a couple of weeks O'Grady received letters and emails that don't bear reprinting. He's not the hardest man in the world to track down – he runs the Spar shop in Ballingarry.

'I couldn't believe it really,' he said. 'It had been a good season for us and I think we're really well placed for the next few years. We were probably favourites against Clare and maybe that didn't suit us but the letters were just full of crazy stuff. I wouldn't call the people who wrote them Limerick people anyway, no matter what they called themselves. Some were signed, some were not. The gist of them was that we needed to learn from our "mistakes". They were the polite ones.'

The less polite ones directed personal criticism at O'Grady, one of the county's most dependable lieutenants, questioning his role and suitability to captain the team.

'I showed the most personal stuff to my wife, Catherine, and no one else,' he said. 'I read them to her to get her opinion and as I did I threw them in the fire because Catherine would be the type to try and find out who these people were. It was disappointing, but life goes on. Sure I did as much as I could.'

He certainly did. Young Declan Hannon put down a nightmare innings against Clare, missing frees he would normally convert in his sleep. He was disconsolate after the game, though at nineteen the pressure on his broad but youthful shoulders had been ridiculous, as O'Grady recognized: 'He'll bounce back. He's a natural leader but it's a lot to have the weight of a county on your back at his age. We have to mind these lads. Declan's expectation of himself is so high.

'I went down to his house on the Tuesday after the game and he was destroyed. I'd say he was destroyed for a good while after. He had a trial for the Super 11 series [a hurling exhibition staged at Notre Dame University in the winter of 2013] but he wouldn't go because he couldn't face other intercounty players.

'I'd admire him though. He missed two frees against Clare and then we got a sixty-five, which he could have shirked but he came out with the ball on his hurl and walked to take it. Gavin [O'Mahony] asked did he want him to take it instead but Declan said, "Nah, you're fine." And he put it over. He proved to me that afternoon that he will never shy away – he was still looking for the ball.'

Another one of O'Grady's house calls in the wake of the Clare match was to Séamus Hickey, who tore a cruciate ligament in the game. Not that O'Grady had any long-term worries about the team's ultimate athlete and fitness freak.

In truth, O'Grady played the captain's role long after the season ended, liaising with the county board and the independent committee formed to appoint a new manager when John Allen stepped down at the end of the campaign. Hard to understand why he was subjected to abuse.

'Whatever about me, John had been getting two or three letters per week all season long.' O'Grady laughed. 'Lads were actually picking the team for him. I know people are hurling fanatics – I get that.'

*

That semi-final ended Allen's journey with the team. He had his mind made up at the start of the year that he would hang up the bib no matter what. And even if the season ended in disappointment, that Munster title win was a fine way to bow out.

The panel wanted the Cork native to stay around – he had that priceless ability to always appear in control of things and they had huge time for him. They knew he was interested in their personal, as well as hurling, development and they appreciated how he treated them as humans and not commodities. They accepted too that Allen's easygoing demeanour was misleading. He may have spoken softly but he carried a stick at the same time. And they respected that.

The team bus crawled down the N7 that Sunday evening of the semi-final, and when it finally pulled into Limerick city, O'Grady and Allen stepped off at the same time. The manager had given no Braveheart speech in the dressing room and wasn't likely to either.

'I'll ring you in a couple of days,' O'Grady said.

'Right so,' Allen replied.

But the captain knew any phonecall would be a worthless exercise and, as he later admitted, he was devastated: 'I knew that was him gone. He was never going to make a big scene; it was in his nature to let things settle gently. Even if we'd won the All-Ireland he would have left. Sure, on the night of the Munster title win he toddled off on his own, out to the Woodlands Hotel or somewhere, while the rest of us joined the whole city and went mad. We slagged him later that he had gone there to hear Crystal Swing – they were playing in the Woodlands that night.

'Getting our gear, I shook his hand and said, "Who's to say who'll be here next year? I know you well enough not to plámás you, but the lads have great time for you and it would be great to see you back." He just said, "Thanks, we'll keep in touch."'

They didn't, though. And that's the nature of intercounty hurling these days: fast-moving, pragmatic and sometimes short on sentiment.

For his part, Allen had found much to his liking in Limerick, a county that had brought colour and high drama to the game during the mid-1990s. And now the challenge for the man who both preceded and replaced him as head coach, Donal O'Grady – by rare coincidence a full namesake of the captain – would be to see if they could go all the way.

Despite their huge contributions to the game, Limerick of the nineties were set apart from Clare, Offaly and Wexford by one demoralizing statistic – they never won an All-Ireland. A collapse lasting four minutes and fourteen seconds turned a healthy five-point lead into the two-goal defeat by Offaly that cost them the 1994 title. Two years later they lost by two points to fourteen-man Wexford. Over the years they had suffered repeated disappointment. That happens when you have won just one All-Ireland since 1940.

Allen felt pressure to deliver something for the people when he took charge. He was not long retired from teaching, and the pressure of management – or more accurately the demands of the job – weighed heavily on the shoulders of a man with lots of interests and passions outside the game: hill rambling, cycling, reading, guitar playing, to mention just four.

He had worked his way up the ladder in Cork hurling, from massage therapist to selector to All-Ireland-winning manager, and at the end of his Cork tenure he promised himself he would never again step into the intercounty spotlight. When Limerick came calling, however, he forgot his resolution.

'Within hours I was wondering aloud had I lost my marbles,' he smiled. 'It totally consumed me from day one.'

After a satisfactory first season Limerick had work to do to keep him for 2013, because even though he retired from the day job, he had found himself with less leisure time than ever before. Mornings were spent emailing or phoning selectors, players, doctors, physios, club officials. On training days he left Cork at four in the afternoon and got home at eleven. Managing the team had turned into a full working day.

'The travel was the big one for me,' he said. 'Cork and Limerick are not far apart but the road is not great. And I felt the expectation straight away. Not pressure to win, but pressure to do something because Limerick hadn't won in so long.

'I was an outside manager too, and I was aware of that. Every second club in Ireland has an outside manager and many counties have too. If you're a local and you fail, people will say, "Ah well, sure he invested all his own time, fair play to him." They're forgiving. But managers from outside don't have that.

'I was thinking of the Limerick job every second of every day; it took up every moment of my life while the season was on. Why wouldn't it? You were managing forty people and they all had their own issues, the players particularly. They were starting college, or starting work, or planning to get married.

'I wanted to get to know fellas and make sure that I could come into their "quality circle" as a manager. By that I mean I wanted to be rated as someone they could trust. Inside any quality circle there are very few people. Who can you completely trust? Getting their trust was essential. There had to be a line obviously. But being a man who could be approached helped me make a personal connection. I didn't know many of the players before I went in so that helped me greatly.'

Allen presented the players with a professional template they easily warmed to. They secured an ambitious young coach in Donach O'Donnell, who had led Nenagh CBS to their first-ever All-Ireland Colleges A title. Allen also surrounded himself with strength and conditioning coaches from the Munster rugby set-up. Catherine Norton, a highly rated nutritionist and sports psychologist, made herself available whenever needed. Allen leaned heavily on Joe Hannon, Declan's father, as a link between the team and the county board and that dynamic worked perfectly.

In short, the manager did almost everything for the players – but not quite everything. In conversations with Declan Kidney, the former Munster and Ireland rugby coach advised Allen against handing everything on a plate to the players – don't wash their gear, for example.

The squad bought into Allen's ways, and he was able to tap into the excellent development work being done by city clubs like Na Piarsaigh and promising underage Limerick squads. His tenure was – like O'Grady's – a period of stability after almost seven years of chaos and turmoil.

The strike of 2010 was the lowest point. In 2013, O'Grady the player had been eleven years in the Limerick set-up and had played under six different managers and alongside an enormous cast of midfield partners. The likes of himself, T. J. Ryan, Niall Moran, Brian Geary, Donie Ryan and Mike O'Brien kept the fabric of the team knitted together when all looked threadbare. But they were only a five-out-of-ten team compared to what they could have been.

'Inconsistent and frustrating – that's what we were,' said O'Grady. 'It wasn't that we weren't trying. But, Jesus, the Limerick supporters were going to games not knowing what to expect from their team and that was hard on them. Did we know what to expect from ourselves? No.'

It was indeed heavy going for the long-suffering supporters, who watched their team lose eight championship games by a point during the noughties. When they reached the 2007 All-Ireland final, promise scented the air again, but the ruthless hammering by Kilkenny was the start of a rot. And what followed over the next few seasons left nothing but a bad odour.

'The worst time for me was between 2008 and 2009,' O'Grady admitted. 'We had reached the final the year before and there was good unity. Richie Bennis was over the team and everyone was in tow; we expected to drive on. Then we played Clare in 2008 and they beat us in Thurles. I was never as low. We were like, "Clare are an ageing team – we have these." But we didn't. We thought we'd regroup but then Offaly beat us by ten points. Cleaned us.'

At half-time in that qualifier with Offaly, O'Grady walked down the tunnel, only looking up when he heard a commotion. Above him, a frustrated Limerick fan had emptied a cup of tea down on the players: 'There was hot tea everywhere, but you could nearly understand the anger. Sure it was back to the same old. The players needed to take full responsibility. We totally underestimated the challenges that lay ahead in 2008 and our surprise element was gone. We thought we'd be all right, but we weren't.'

Bennis stepped down and Justin McCarthy took over – their sixth manager in nine years. It was yet more upheaval. They reached the 2009 All-Ireland semi-final but then waved a white flag to a Tipperary team that was going places. They regressed further the following season and if you looked close enough you could detect falling pebbles prefacing the avalanche.

Late in 2009 McCarthy decided to omit twelve players for 2010 without so much as a puff of white smoke to indicate what was coming. It was the manner of their omission that caused a huge stir – none of the players – bar two-time All Star Mark Foley – had been forewarned about their axing; they found out through media channels. In solidarity with fallen team-mates, others refused to join the panel, which meant twenty-four of Limerick's best hurlers didn't tog out in 2010. As civil war ensued, McCarthy persisted with a second- and third-string team and the year became one prolonged embarrassment.

O'Grady stood among a group of experienced players who wanted to take a stand: 'The only regret I have is that we weren't men enough to sit down and not leave the room until it was sorted out for the good of Limerick hurling – as opposed to the good of individuals. I was so frustrated. The head was wrecked. In the middle of it all I rang my father and said, "Look, I'm going to withdraw from the panel in support of the lads," and he said, "Just stick together."'

The Ballingarry man did that, and along with others sacrificed a year in the jersey. This team seemed condemned by the fates at every hand's turn. But sympathy for the players was lacking on the streets. The reaction was poisonous.

'Look, we are the best county in Ireland when things are going well,' O'Grady reflected. 'But when things are not well . . . here in Limerick if a lad goes out for one pint it almost hits the papers.

'Justin could have dropped whoever he wished; he was the manager. All we wanted was that he contact the players he was leaving go. He didn't do that. Instead he mentioned that the group had discipline issues. The likes of Shocks [Andrew O'Shaughnessy] didn't have discipline issues, I can tell you that.

'When my namesake, Donal O'Grady, replaced Justin as manager for 2011 every player received a letter telling him whether he was in or out and that solved everything.'

O'Grady the hurler revealed that before any 'strike' was called, or before any player decided to pull out, the panel went to the county board but their thunder didn't clear the air.

'In one meeting Damien Reale challenged Justin on what he had said about our discipline, but Justin replied, "Damien, you're not your brother's keeper." So then Damien pulled the plug. We lost another great lad.'

Any residual confidence in McCarthy's fledglings dissipated when they leaked 6-30 to Dublin in the final round of the National League and were duly relegated to Division 2. The county board also lost €75,000 in gate receipts, the fans staying away in droves as Limerick fielded scratch teams when hosting Galway, Kilkenny, Tipperary and Cork in the NHL. The usually productive Supporters' Club also suffered, revenue plummeting from €72,997 in 2009 to just €32,308. The Dublin branch of the Supporters' Club also endured a fall, from €45,764 to €20,895.

Diehard fans lost their way for a while too and revenue from the Mackey Stand Draw, an ongoing earner for the county board, fell by more than €100,000 as the 2010 season petered out.

Against that backdrop, Donal O'Grady the manager took the reins and from there the curve was largely upward. He ensured among other things that there was no lingering resentment towards those youngsters that had stepped into the breach for McCarthy – the likes of Thomas O'Brien, Kieran O'Rourke, David Breen and Nicky Quaid. O'Grady asked for concentration on hurling only and he was met by a squad eager to do nothing but hurl their hearts out. For good measure, the players soon noticed the county board was more organized too.

'Expectations were so low when we came back that the whole saga didn't really set us back a whole pile,' O'Grady the player reasoned. 'Everyone had his own take on it – some swayed towards the board, and others to Justin. Some to us. But our biggest problem was that we had won nothing for fifteen years at that stage. Things couldn't have got any worse.'

The players' reputations needed rebuilding. The last conflict had bequeathed a costly legacy and the perception was out there that team members were responsible for getting rid of six of the previous seven Limerick managers. There were even suggestions the group had become unmanageable. But the players were an easy enough target. It's important to remember, for instance, that at the start of the noughties the county board pursued an unwieldy system employing five selectors – a surefire recipe for division and acrimony. Remember too that it was the county board that submitted the notorious twenty questions (investigating why they had not beaten Wexford) to Tom Ryan when he failed to bring home the 1996 All-Ireland.

Then there was an urban myth that the players got rid of Ryan's replacement, Eamon Cregan, but Cregan was five years at the helm and many of the issues he had were with his own backroom team. In 2001, senior hurlers actually put their heads above the parapet to defend him over the issue of dual players.

They were, admittedly, instrumental in the removal of Pat Joe Whelahan in 2005, even if the Banagher native officially walked of his own volition after two years in charge.

Dave Keane had guided the county to three consecutive under-21 titles and, given that he had moulded so many young players, was an obvious choice when appointed to lead the side in 2002. Unfortunately, the senior and emerging stars didn't always get on. And to complicate matters, Keane had differences with Mark Foley, one of the marquee players. Keane should have been given way more time at the helm but ongoing turbulence prompted the county board to put his future in the hands of the clubs and they voted him out.

Joe McKenna took over from Whelahan in 2005 and struck up a decent relationship with the players, but after a loss to Clare the following year he walked away.

Richie Bennis was held in great affection by the players. They would have seen him as old-fashioned in his ways, but they also recognized his honesty and passion and the fact he had several good men around him. Bennis went for re-election in 2008 but the board and its delegates decided to go with McCarthy.

There may have been a few dodgy apples in the mix but from the outside it seemed like the whole set-up was a basket case. Lurid tales of players drinking and clubbing flew from mouth to mouth – in such a fraught climate, exaggeration was cheap. The sad irony is that the county was blessed with youngsters long on ability but maybe short on desire and discipline. Yet nearly the entire panel was tarred with the one brush. Following Niall Moran's retirement in 2013, O'Grady was the only one from those three all-conquering under-21 teams of the early noughties still playing senior for the county. A damning statistic.

Even more worrying was that of Limerick's ten All Star nominees in 2007 only two were still playing six years on: O'Grady and Séamus Hickey.

'There's definitely a lost generation there,' O'Grady acknowledged. 'We produced three serious under-21 teams – I was playing out of my skin in my final year and still couldn't get a game – but we've lost so many from those teams and the oldest those lads would be now is mid-thirties. I suppose intercounty hurling is about fifty per cent ability and fifty per cent out-and-out commitment to the cause and physically being in shape.'

When those youngsters stepped up to the senior ranks they found a different world awaiting them. A medley of kids taken from those three vibrant teams went from hero to zero in jig time. The Limerick captain explained why: 'If you won and had a drink, you could drink twenty pints and not a word would be said. If you lost and went for one drink, the public had you down as an alcoholic. Things went nuts around the place in terms of stories about players socializing when those lads left the under-21 grade for senior, and people seemed to turn against the team. It happens in every county; the difference is that other counties seem to keep their problems in-house. We couldn't.

'But where was the guidance for those young lads twelve and thirteen years ago? That was the biggest reason they fell away – the lack of a guiding hand. There was no one there to mind them. They were kids, caught up in it all, and how could you blame them?

'In 2001, after we beat Wexford in the All-Ireland under-21 final, there was a crowd of over twenty thousand there to greet us on O'Connell Street. Out of all those people, though, there was no one to mind those young lads.'

In hindsight, you might say they could have done with Donal O'Grady the manager a long time before he finally took charge late in 2010. The new boss quickly restored order, leading Limerick to the top of the Division 1B league only to lose out on promotion in a league reshuffle. In the championship they were pipped by Dublin in the 2011 All-Ireland quarter final, 3-13 to 0-18.

O'Grady's first term lasted only one year but they had their discipline back and O'Grady's fellow Corkonian Allen was then lined up to replace him. In terms of style and strategy, the two managers had much in common, so some continuity was maintained.

Meanwhile, off the field, the revolution was moving apace too. The Limerick board had developed an excellent training hub at Mick Neville Park, Rathkeale, including a new synthetic pitch, fully floodlit. They moved seven full-time coaches and back-room staff to the University of Limerick. Two senior hurlers, Gavin O'Mahony and James Ryan, were appointed to the coaching staff.

The former All Star goalkeeper Joe Quaid was part of an underage drive that netted two national titles. He was later appointed coaching and development officer to target those between the ages of ten and twenty-one, the aim to drive hurling in a city where the oval ball is almost a symbol of veneration.

In the seven years up to 2013, participation in hurling at primary schools almost doubled.

'At underage the challenge was to change a mindset among players, coaches and administrators,' said Éibhear O'Dea, one of the driving forces behind the resurgence. 'Shane Fitzgibbon, the former Limerick hurler, was a huge change agent. When Shane took on the under-14s he, along with many other dedicated coaches, devised a plan that greatly improved structures.'

By the close of 2013, a progressive academy was in situ and some of the coaching structures were the envy of other counties. The Limerick underage hurling project was being part funded by Gerry McManus, brother of the legendary entrepreneur and racehorse owner J. P., which was offering a competitive advantage over several other counties.

For all the good work, there remained occasional glitches in the machinery. Quaid took over a group of hurlers when they were under-14 and led them to those national titles, including their first All-Ireland under-16 title in 2012. It was widely expected he would get the chance to bring those players to minor level. Instead, the county board went back to Eamon Cregan, with Brian Ryan in tandem. Jerry Wallace was added as coach.

The minors went on to enjoy provincial success for the first time in twenty-nine years and only bowed out of the All-Ireland series following a Hawkeye error in the semi-final with Galway. Thus the board's decision to give the job to Cregan and Ryan was ultimately vindicated, but who is to say Quaid, who had put in four years of spadework with those players, would not have achieved similar success?

Still, the heroics of the minors and the Munster success of the seniors in 2013 served as serious tonics for Limerick hurling. It had been eight years since their minors last reached an All-Ireland final – they got in through the back door in 2005 – but they were now producing fine young talent with serious regularity. In 2011, the under-21s ended a nine-year run without contesting a provincial final and won that year's Munster championship.

'The great thing about that,' said O'Dea, 'is that Leo O'Connor was in charge of that under-21 Munster-winning team. It was a huge shot in the arm for the seniors but Leo came straight back into the system afterwards to work again with the under-14s in 2012 and 2013.'

Out of those 2005 minor and 2011 under-21 teams, the bedrock of the 2013 senior team was formed in the persons of Hannon, Dowling, O'Mahony, Tom Condon, James Ryan, Conor Allis, Graeme Mulcahy, Séamus Hickey and Kevin Downes.

The schools had also been churning out the goods. Dowling, Downes and Hannon were products of the Ardscoil Rís academy, a rugby stronghold but latterly just as adept at producing hurling talent. They have lost two All-Ireland finals to St Kieran's of Kilkenny and those setbacks were heartbreaking and partly self-inflicted, but it was still significant progress from where they were a decade earlier. Limerick could also now boast four schools in the Harty Cup, the competition that feeds players into county minor panels and third-level colleges.

*

Traditionally, Limerick have shown what can be done when they get their act together and put collective shoulders to the wheel. When they set up a five-year development plan in 1995, for example, it paved the way for a senior football progression in the noughties and also set the tone for the under-21 hurlers' run of success. But they are sick of talking about that era, just as the 1973 team grew weary of being wheeled out to have their stories retold. They need fresh role models.

When Allen was replaced in late 2013, the appointments of Donal O'Grady (his second stint) and T. J. Ryan as joint managers were the best possible in the circumstances. The saga of replacing Allen dragged out and was messy and at times threatened to undo years of good work. A Limerick presence at the helm was desired, and they got that in Ryan. And soon O'Grady had them motoring again.

'The 2014 championship is wide open now and I think it's a great time to be a Limerick hurler,' John Allen concluded.

They must take the positives from 2013 – they have lived too long in the past. The GAA is in thrall to reminiscing, but Limerick are sick to the teeth of nostalgia; it has soured with too much serving. As 2014 dawned, the future looked a lot tastier.

9

No Country for Old Men

Why Waterford can look with confidence
to the youthful guard

When Michael Ryan lost the post of Waterford senior hurling manager in August 2013, you didn't need to be a visionary to see that the role to be filled was an enticing one for potential candidates.

While the teams built by Gerald McCarthy, nurtured by Justin McCarthy and tactically stabilized by Davy Fitzgerald were adorned with big personalities and swashbuckling stickmen capable of running amok on any given day, the fact remained that they never won an All-Ireland title. They won everything else, mind, and along the way classy talents like John Mullane claimed an impressive five All Stars.

The late nineties and early noughties proved a decent era but records of their feats around that time come with an asterisk attached. Everything is layered with a coating of frustration. They could and maybe should have won the Liam MacCarthy

Cup in 1998 and again in 2006. There are those who feel they just weren't good enough, but most would say they underachieved.

A pantheon of household names subsequently retired and moved on but the irony has been that expectations have risen rather than dropped. For all their failures in not getting to climb the steps of the Hogan Stand, the teams the two McCarthys refined had inspired a new generation. And by the close of 2013 there was a major transfusion of new blood. They looked ready to go places.

The young men steaming through had been schooled in how to win national titles. De La Salle landed Harty Cups and All-Ireland A colleges titles in 2007 and 2008. Dungarvan Colleges won back-to-back Harty Cups in 2012 and 2013, and in 2013 also managed an All-Ireland title. Blackwater CS joined the party with All-Ireland B and Dean Ryan Cup successes. But undoubtedly the biggest coup for the county was winning an All-Ireland minor title in 2013, their first at that grade since 1948.

It was an unexpected win – they lost two championship games en route to the final – but it made the choice of the next Waterford senior manager all the more vital. After six years of development work a bunch of promising hurlers was mushrooming, near-ready for senior level.

Derek McGrath was the early leader in the race to replace Michael Ryan. He had coached De La Salle to those college successes and also led his club of the same name to the 2012 county senior title. And so it was no shock when he got the nod. A brother-in-law of Mullane, McGrath immediately checked in with the recently retired firebrand to determine if there was any hope of a comeback. There wasn't.

McGrath now looked to players he had mentored on the colleges scene – the likes of Noel Connors, Stephen Daniels,

Jake Dillon, Stephen O'Keeffe and the Mahonys, Pauric and Philip – to push the team on.

The outlook was bright but there remained huge challenges for McGrath, including relegation from Division 1A in his first season. Managerial doors tend to revolve quickly in the south-east, and security of tenure is far from a given. When Ryan got the chop it was the second time in five years a Waterford hurling boss had been ushered to the exit by disaffected players. Well before Ryan got the heave-ho, Justin McCarthy had suffered the same treatment despite guiding the Déise to their first Munster title in thirty-nine years. Davy Fitzgerald took over a team in transition and led them to an All-Ireland final and a Munster title two years later, but even at that there were tensions between himself and some players by the time he left.

Outsiders could be forgiven for assuming these Waterford lads have been hard to manage – that maybe some lost the run of themselves over the years. Forcing McCarthy and Ryan out certainly reflected poorly on the relevant panels.

Páraic Fanning, a former GAA officer at Waterford IT, has been involved with four Fitzgibbon Cup wins for the college. He served as selector under Davy Fitzgerald and was considered an early contender to replace Ryan. Acknowledging that the unseemly dismissals of McCarthy and Ryan contributed to a common view of the panels as unruly, he would nevertheless argue that the perception was far from accurate: 'It was more the way the thing was handled with Michael Ryan. The players got the blame for the whole thing. All I can say is that those present hurlers – and the lads of the last ten years – would train night and day for you. They have an excellent attitude and I would consider them very easy to work with.'

In fairness to the panellists, while the county board indicated

Ryan would get another year, it seems some officers were happy enough, when push came to shove, to accommodate the players' desire for change. They were made aware the squad wanted more coaching expertise brought in and they allowed the players to make the call.

Justin McCarthy might take a different view that the players were easy to deal with. He oversaw some huge occasions for the county, including three Munster titles and a National League crown. Seven years is a long time to be talking to the same dressing room, however, and he stayed put too long. In the wake of their heavy Munster championship defeat to Clare in 2008 the players met and it was clear they had lost faith in their Cork coach. After a four-hour meeting at the Majestic Hotel in Tramore McCarthy's fate was officially sealed, the squad carrying by twenty to four a vote of no confidence in him. For Planet Hurling at large it was a seismic move, and reaction was divided when it hit the public domain.

John Mullane was part of the squad that voted to get rid of the Corkman. He wasn't to meet McCarthy in the following five years and remained unsure how he would react if he did. Emotions continued to run high in the county over the ditching of arguably their most successful ever manager. Years later Mullane could still get worked up recalling what happened.

'It was the hardest time I ever put down over all my years hurling. When we did sit down to take a vote it was clear that we were looking for change. But they were a rotten three to four days and I couldn't sleep over what was happening. Justin had done an awful lot for my game and obviously for Waterford hurling too.

'If I'm being honest Justin was the best hurling coach I ever trained under. Everything we did was with the ball. His trainer,

Gerry Fitzpatrick, would work with us for fifteen minutes before and after training and in between Justin would take us for an hour. That hour flew.'

McCarthy took heed of the vote and walked away. The team were left with lots to prove and plenty of detractors – although those critics had their powder dampened if not saturated by what transpired in the following two months as Davy Fitzgerald took over a side bereft of confidence and sharpness, freshened their ranks and brought them to Croke Park and the All-Ireland final.

'The game was moving on,' Mullane reflected. 'If we'd had Davy and Justin together at the one time we would have had the ultimate coaching team. Whereas Justin was a top-class hurling coach, Davy had so many new ideas. We had never experienced half of the stuff he brought in – from video analysis to tactical awareness to hydration. Previously we had just relied on our hurling ability under Justin's guidance to get us through games.'

Mullane tells a story of Fitzgerald's manic intensity and exhaustive preparation for games. Shortly after he took over, routine tests revealed that every one of the players was more or less dehydrated. The new manager became obsessed with the problem. Insisting they drink two and a half litres of water daily and record their intake in a diary, he instituted frequent checks and took it as a personal slight if any of them flunked the test. So determined was he in this regard that players feared being dropped if test results failed to corroborate diary entries.

In the heat of the 2008 championship, Mullane's day job took him to Dublin and he spent the long summer's day driving around the city, forgetting, in his dedication to the work in hand, to grab a bite of lunch, never mind a sip of water. As bad luck would have it, his phone beeped en route to training – a group text from the manager about a hydration test later that evening. Mullane knew he had about as much chance as a desert castaway of making the grade.

In the dressing room his worst fears were realized; the sample he produced was a fright to behold: 'I started peeing into the jar with my name on it and it wasn't good – my wee was an orange colour, like the contents of a bottle of Lucozade. I knew I was in trouble.'

With the rest of the panel already on the paddock, Mullane took his bottle of purest vitamin C to its designated place on the shelf; he was ready to accept his fate. But as he placed the jar on the shelf he noticed looking back at him a sample as limpid and sparkling as a Comeragh mountain spring. The name on the label: Jamie Nagle.

'When it comes to hurling, Jamie lives his life like a choirboy,' Mullane explained. 'He does everything by the book. He would have been drinking three litres a day – at least.'

Mullane yielded to temptation, peeled off the J. Nagle sticker, placed it across his own jar of contaminated effluent and slapped the J. Mullane logo on to the prizewinning exhibit. Then he went off to hurl.

Ninety minutes later, as the team showered and changed, Fitzgerald blew a gasket in the dressing room. No way was he fooled by the false labelling.

'Whose is it?' he demanded.

Mullane couldn't tell a lie to save himself. He's as open as a twenty-four-hour chapel in Las Vegas. The cheeks reddened in admission of guilt.

'Feckin' Mullane!' roared the manager as the De La Salle man tried but failed to hold in the laughter. All Fitzgerald could do was laugh back.

*

Fitzgerald did much for Waterford. His influence was a great tableau of little things; he brought huge attention to detail with a massive backroom, the cost of which received criticism when it came to totting up end-of-year accounts.

Reaching the 2008 All-Ireland final was a fine achievement; they got a decent qualifier draw and took advantage. They arrived at the showdown confident they could beat Kilkenny but that optimism was grossly misplaced. Kilkenny had scored eleven goals and ninety-eight points in just four games that summer. They hammered Waterford 3-30 to 1-13 in what was among the most one-sided All-Ireland finals ever. Even in the warm-up the Waterford men looked off-colour, dropping and fumbling the sliotar and fluffing their rehearsal lines. Apart from Mullane, who hit 0-3 and was the only forward to point from play that afternoon, no player in blue and white reached any sort of acceptable standard.

The game was well over by the break. Waterford trailed by seventeen points and as players sat with heads drooped, thoroughly demoralized, they were addressed by Bernard Dunne, who had been brought in that year to motivate the team. For all that they respected the former world boxing champion, the players did not want to listen. Humbled and dejected, they had ears for nobody.

Afterwards Mullane waited on the pitch until every Kilkenny player had climbed the Hogan Stand. Countless supporters wearing the black and amber approached him but not one sly dig was given. Mullane just folded his arms, soaked up the pain and watched the greatest team in history raise Liam MacCarthy aloft one more time.

'We got to the final at the same time Kilkenny hit their peak,' he recalled. 'They were beating teams by cricket scores. It was our first time in an All-Ireland since 1963 and we really didn't realize what was involved. We gave ourselves a chance, no doubt about that – they were just another team to us – but we weren't prepared for an onslaught and that's what it was. We were in a daze.'

A look at the Kilkenny bench that day would support Mullane's perception of a dream team and squad operating at optimum level. Michael Rice, Mick Fennelly, Willie O'Dwyer, Richie Mullally, John Dalton, P. J. Delaney, James Ryall, James McGarry, John Tennyson, Richie Hogan and T. J. Reid were all held in reserve. That's an All Star eleven in itself, never mind another county's first choice.

For many of the Waterford boys it ranked as their worst day ever, but not for Mullane. For him the 7-19 to 0-19 drubbing by Tipperary in the 2011 Munster final was the nadir. Again the game was well over by the interval, 5-10 to 0-8. After the punishment beating ended, Mullane came out and apologized to the fans. Waterford hurling had been laid bare, stripped of its soul. He felt others should have said sorry too.

'The management should have apologized. Whatever about playing Kilkenny, we weren't expected to win, but Tipp should never have thrashed us the way they did. Two lads I felt especially sorry for were Jerome Maher and Eoin McGrath.

'Jerome was making his debut and was put on Lar Corbett, the best hurler in the country at that stage. Eoin was picked to play, but more or less told to do nothing except stop Paudie Maher from hurling. In other words he was on the pitch but not really meant to hit a ball. I felt really sorry for Eoin. We had what was called a dead zone that day. If we had possession, the ball was not to go anywhere near Paudie Maher. So Eoin didn't get a touch. We were almost playing with fourteen men.

'That game didn't do Tipp any favours either – they got a false sense of optimism out of it. In fairness to Davy, he would usually have his tactics spot on, but we got it wrong that day. We were an embarrassment to the people of Waterford and as a camp we should all have apologized to them.

'Why? We had Brick [Michael Walsh], the best centre-back in Ireland, playing at full-back and Liam Lawlor, a very good full-back, on the bench. Poor Jerome had some debut on Larry, who scored 4-4 in the end – not all off Jerome in fairness. The only other time I saw a guy in a similar scenario was when Denis Coffey was told to track Eoin Kelly on his debut in 2006. Eoin came out with 2-3 from play. Sure it wasn't fair on Denis at all.'

To give Fitzgerald his due, those disasters were the exception. Of his eighteen championship games with the county, they won ten, drew two and lost six. There was that 2008 All-Ireland final appearance and a Munster title in 2010 – highly impressive considering the marked turnover in personnel and change of style during his tenure.

'Davy came in during the end of an era really,' Mullane said. 'To be fair to him players were moving on and the game was changing. Teams were crowding defences and corner-forwards were tracking back the field chasing lost ball. Davy put an awful lot into planning how to counteract teams like Kilkenny and Tipp and he brought more organization.

'People moaned that we had twelve men behind the ball but again Davy was right – we had probably been too positive, too attacking, in the past. And too open, which definitely cost us games. Maybe that's why we didn't win an All-Ireland. Davy brought in tackling and defence and it shaped the way the team played for the next few years.'

*

Páraic Fanning, Fitzgerald's right-hand man at that time, would say the Clareman treated everyone fairly and handed a good many young players their opportunity.

'He did a fantastic job, because we were losing some greats like Ken [McGrath] and Dan [Shanahan] and he had to blood a lot of young lads. But that was one of his strengths. Even after we shipped seven goals against Tipp we came back two weeks later to beat Galway by ten points in Thurles.

'I think he proved himself as a manager with us. He had five different options and plans for every game and he was about three things really: closing down space at the back, making sure the defenders lifted their heads coming out with the ball to deliver proper ball to the forwards, and ensuring there was space in the forwards for our fast lads. It wasn't too dissimilar to the way Kilkenny played.

'Had he been there a few years earlier we would have had great ball winners in the air to work with, but they were absent so I think Davy did a great job.'

Until he took over, the team wouldn't have had a tradition of playing smart, but apart from those two horrible beatings, Fitzgerald got them playing in a more organized, compact way at the back.

When Fitzgerald stepped down and took over back home in Clare, the Waterford board looked locally for his successor. With money scarce, it was always going to be an internal appointment. They gave the job to Michael Ryan, a gentleman of the county's GAA scene and a coach who had made his name on the ladies' football circuit, winning fifteen All-Irelands between club and county. He had served alongside Justin McCarthy as a selector but little did he know that just two seasons later – and not long after they had run Kilkenny to three points in the

2013 qualifiers – the players would give him the heave.

Forcing Kilkenny to extra time and keeping the result in doubt right up to the ninetieth minute was a more than respectable swansong, but the feeling among the players was that if one or two switches had been made earlier they would have won that game. As alluded to earlier, few outside the loop – and not many inside it – could be quite sure how the county board felt about the manner of Ryan's departure. But they certainly made no great attempt to stop the players from moving him on.

Ryan didn't have the easiest of passages, it must be said. Mullane, who had retired in January 2013 at the age of thirty-two, was a massive loss to the side. Eoin Kelly retired on Ryan's watch too, following Eoin McGrath. Stephen Daniels had been a revelation in 2012 but picked up a season-ending knee injury in a challenge against Offaly earlier in the year. Philip Mahony emigrated and Stephen Molumphy was posted overseas on a military tour of duty. All in all, Ryan's options were greatly reduced.

After five months and three successive 2012 league defeats – to Cork, Kilkenny and Tipperary – Ryan's selectors Nicky Cashin and Br Philip Ryan stepped down. Ken McGrath and Seán Cullinane stepped in, but McGrath moved on at the end of that season. There was a lot of traffic in both directions and it was unsettling. They were tipped for relegation in 2012 and 2013 but Ryan kept them up both times.

He had already begun looking for a coach from outside to assist with preparations in 2014; reportedly Ger Cunningham, the former Newtownshandrum manager, was lined up, but that collaboration was never to happen.

The Waterford squad met at the Ramada Hotel on the same day the county minors played an All-Ireland semi-final. At half-time of that game came the statement that Ryan's term was up.

The players received huge flak for the timing of that announcement but it's understood they felt under pressure to make an immediate call on the matter. A few players, including Kevin Moran and Noel Connors, would be unfairly singled out as 'ringleaders' but that was mainly because they were captain and vice-captain.

Only eleven players turned up to the meeting, and the decision was ultimately reached by a show of hands and text vote that ran eighteen to ten against Ryan. While the minors battled to reach a first All-Ireland final in twenty-one years the press release hit the public domain. The timing was awful and it took the sheen and focus off the youngsters' heroics.

Noel Connors was left with the unenviable job of informing the manager on that Sunday at 1 p.m. that he had lost a vote of confidence among the players.

As for Ryan, who soon returned to club management with St Mary's in Tipperary, he had deserved a whole lot better. But even after the smoke and sulphur cleared, he would still – had he pursued the matter – have looked in vain for a straight answer as to exactly who wanted him out.

In many ways, the subsequent All-Ireland minor semi-final and final took the heat off the county board and senior players. Instead of the spotlight lingering on the controversy it was shone on the emerging generation.

Although the eleven years from 2002 yielded more for Waterford hurling than the previous fifty-four – including four Munster senior titles and twenty All Star awards – the truth is that the emerging kids, weaned on those All-Ireland Colleges and Harty Cup triumphs and that All-Ireland minor win, were shaping to achieve even more than the preceding generation.

Darragh Duggan, who led Dungarvan Colleges to their

national A title, expressed certainty that those coming off the production line were mature enough to cope with the lofty expectations: 'They don't panic. Those minors lost to Tipp in the first round of the 2013 Munster championship and lost to Limerick in the final, but look how they kept it together to win when it counted most.

'There were eight Dungarvan Colleges players on that minor team and in fairness they were handled well. One team's success almost led to another's. The schools championship was definitely a good experience for them as our lads had beaten two Kilkenny teams along the way to the title, and for Waterford hurling, mentally, that was a big step.

'So the outlook has to be different for Waterford now. I definitely think there's an All-Ireland senior title in the making. The only thing I'll say is it will take time and I'm not sure the people of Waterford realize that.

'I was reading Nicky English's book where he spoke of the 1980 minor-winning team he was part of and how they didn't make the senior breakthrough until 1989. Philip Mahony, Paudie Mahony and these guys have all been spoken about at underage level for years but at senior they are only just making it now. The 2013 minors will not transform the 2014 seniors.'

One revolution that has spread like wildfire in the county is the broadening of hurling beyond the traditional hotbeds of Waterford city and its immediate hinterland and out into the west of the county, into places like Ballinameela, Ardmore and Clashmore, traditionally football heartlands. Player numbers in those parts have grown exponentially.

Duggan talked of leafing through a match programme for a Tipp–Waterford minor championship clash from the early 1990s and finding only four players from West Waterford listed on the squad. In 2013 eleven clubs were represented on the corresponding panel.

They have to look after those youngsters. Waterford is a great county for awards and more awards and ceremonies. They honour someone every weekend by the looks of it: club awards, sports stars of the month, sports stars of the year. They seem to reward their athletes far more than other counties.

As De La Salle and the combined colleges paved the way to All-Ireland glory a huge following attended their games. The crowds came out in force for the minors too. Suddenly lads from small football clubs that hitherto had no exposure to hurling began appearing in newspapers and on TV, hurling in national finals. The residents of small parishes saw their young neighbours beat St Kieran's in an All-Ireland Colleges final. It had a snowball effect; the hype became huge, the interest in those youngsters massive.

In the past Waterford senior teams had failed to win All-Ireland titles because they were too exposed at the back, had too many individuals on their books at the one time, and possibly were too happy to celebrate provincial titles. Growing up, however, those earlier generations never had to deal with anticipation and expectation the classes of 2014 and beyond must cope with. How this is handled is crucial to the county's prospects.

'What happened with these lads is a huge boost,' said Mullane in 2013. 'Anyone born the year we last won a major title is on a pension now, but for all the hype I think we'd quickly like to target an under-21 title and see where we go from there. We should follow Clare hurling – they got to a minor in 2011 and then had a couple of under-21 successes. Only if we do that can we think of doing it at senior.'

Mullane never stood out at underage level and looking back from the vantage point of retirement he was delighted he didn't. The minors of 2013 won't be allowed to enjoy such anonymity.

'There was no attention on me, and no expectation that I would ever make it, so it gave me a chance to work on things like my weak right side. When I first broke into the senior team in October 2000 people within my own county were wondering what I was doing on the panel. People doubted me but I loved proving them wrong – it drove me on. Those young lads won't have that but if they employ the three As – attendance, application and attitude – they'll develop even more.

'But we all have to watch out for them. I'm mindful of that. They could get sucked up with hype and we have to guard them. Patrick Curran, Stephen Bennett and Austin Gleeson go into every game with people expecting them to lead. I didn't have that until I got my first All Star in 2003 – that's when pressure really came on for me. Then when the big-name players like Ken and Paul Flynn retired I put even more pressure on myself. It can eat you up. You feel like you can never have a bad day. So apart from the hype and the backslapping, the boys must be prepared for that scrutiny too.'

Páraic Fanning, however, has said he senses a maturity about the emerging group and feels that as Derek McGrath is a teacher used to dealing with students there will be no gaps in communication: 'Those lads are further down the line than people think and I wouldn't say we're in much of a transition at all. We have a lovely blend – all these guys to blend in with Stephen Molumphy, Noel Connors, Kevin Moran, Brian O'Halloran, Darragh Fives and Maurice Shanahan. It's great.

'We cannot let them go the way of previous teams who have disappeared after being built up. Derek is working with youngsters on a daily basis in school, and his assistant, Willie Maher, managed the Tipp minors so they'll be well looked after. I can't see any more than one or two making it in the immediate future but bring them in for the strength and conditioning and let them get a feel for it. They are grounded enough and have yet to prove themselves at under-21. Don't forget that they did lose two games en route to that minor title as well so we are no world beaters just yet.'

Looking towards 2014 and beyond, Fanning said he could not bear thinking the breakthrough might not happen. He still looked back on the teams Waterford boasted in the nineties and noughties and wondered how they didn't make the summit.

'Maybe those lads found it hard to deal with the hype. Belief was possibly a reason too. We lost narrowly to teams that ended up winning the All-Ireland and maybe we needed a willingness that we didn't get from one or two lads to buy into things. There were a lot of strong characters on those teams and maybe one or two of them took their eyes off the ball in terms of how they played against what we wanted them to do.'

It was time to look in the mirror for answers. From 1998 right through to the epic qualifier against Kilkenny in the summer of 2013 opportunity had knocked on Waterford hurling's door. 'How did we not beat Kilkenny that night?' asked Mullane, who watched in retirement from the stands. 'They were caught for quality on the bench – they just didn't have the players. Brian Cody brought off a player [Walter Walsh] and brought him back in again? When did you ever see that?'

As for his own playing days, Mullane expressed no regrets – not even about the sending off in the 2004 Munster final, which led to his suspension for the All-Ireland semi-final against Kilkenny. Had he lodged an appeal, or a temporary injunction –

as every other suspended player was doing – he would have had his ban overturned. But Mullane had no time for High Courts or technical loopholes.

Money was put on the table to pay for that appeal but he just accepted his punishment. For that principled stand he became a popular idol, and as much as he would miss match days – and the fact his brother-in-law was over the team – there wasn't a hope in purgatory of him coming out of retirement.

'I won't lie – I did miss it more on match days than I thought in 2013. I wondered had I made the right call. But it was when I watched the Dublin–Cork All-Ireland semi-final in 2013 that I knew I had. It's a young man's game now; I wouldn't last in that any more.

'Even in my last year I dreaded the thought of going training. I often sat in the car park in Carriganore before training wondering if I would turn the car around and go home. And that's not me. I couldn't switch off from hurling – it had to be a hundred per cent or nothing, so I stepped aside. It's up to the young lads now. They come into the senior squad with medals and belief. They have beaten teams from all over Ireland. They know how to get over the line.'

If they do break the tape in years to come, those young men will, symbolically at least, drag a former generation of Waterford players over the line with them.

10

Marooned by Western Shores

How Galway's golden generations have
struggled to reach the fair land

The Galway Races are a festival for everyone. Well, almost
everyone. It's a time of relaxation and self-indulgence; a time
to rub shoulders with the great and the good – and a few of the
not-so-good; a week to let the hair down and sink a few sherbets.

David Collins, though, detests race week. If he's there it means
Galway are out of the All-Ireland hurling championship. Again.
It also means he'll have his ears bashed by people who hold the
answers to Galway's ongoing struggle: the battle to end an All-
Ireland famine stretching back almost three decades.

Collins knows it's a hard-knock life following his team –
between 1990 and 2012 they contested five All-Ireland finals
and lost every one – but he doesn't need constant reminding of
it. Nor does he need a commentary on their inconsistencies as
reflected in those All-Ireland finals and the gaps of three, eight,
four and seven years between them.

Losing five finals was bad enough, but worse was that they

could never trot out the old chestnut of 'not having the players'. They've always produced plenty of young hurling talent. Between 1999 and 2011 they won six All-Ireland minor titles; between 1991 and 2011 six under-21 crowns. Lack of raw materials was never a hindrance to the production process.

Galway players have long excelled in the Fitzgibbon Cup. As for All-Ireland senior club titles, Portumna, Clarinbridge, Athenry and Sarsfields have between them garnered ten since 1992. In every hurling category, except the one that counts most, Galway have enjoyed a golden era, one in which their seniors should have established themselves as Kilkenny's main rivals. But for almost three decades their dream of winning a senior title has always run ahead of them.

Consequently, Collins has found himself watching the races in Ballybrit more often than he would like, mingling with other punters and wistfully raising a glass to another championship gone south. He could hardly tell one end of a thoroughbred from the other, but Race Week offers a chance to keep the Galway hurlers together for a few days longer, to dissect what went wrong.

'You do not want to be out of the championship in July and you do not want to listen to criticism,' he said. 'But after spending your whole year – well your whole life really – not socializing, the races are an outlet. Every year I say I'll avoid it but I've been there on and off since 2004, often listening to shite – the Galway hurlers are useless, stuff like that. People putting down my team-mates. It's not always our own supporters either. The problem is the younger lads start to believe what they're told. I have a simple response to that: fuck everyone else outside the forty hurlers in our group.'

With every passing season, however, the case for the defence of Galway's seniors has weakened. While the youngsters continued to prosper, their elders – and all those behind the scenes – maintained an extended run of sheer frustration. Along the way they bade farewell to the era of Eugene Cloonan, Kevin Broderick, Joe Rabbitte and Ollie Canning – just four of a galaxy of sublime talents to retire without an All-Ireland senior medal. The fear has been that the next wave – the likes of Damien Hayes and the even younger Joe Canning – could be fated to one day walk off without that coveted Celtic Cross and end up as names to check in those perennial barstool debates about the best hurlers never to win an All-Ireland.

Despite taking a scalp here and there, Galway have lurched from setback to setback. After beating Tipperary in 1993, they failed to achieve a meaningful championship win over top-tier opposition for seven years – until they beat Tipp again in 2000.

It's that post-All-Ireland final record, though, that most intrigues and baffles observers. Not only in hurling but also in other codes, teams frequently bounce back from a final defeat to win the next season but with Galway the response has been quite the opposite.

In 2001 they qualified for the September showdown by outgunning Kilkenny in the semi-final, and though in the final they suffered a narrow defeat to Tipperary their campaign had brimmed with so much promise they looked sure to push upward and onward. And yet what followed was serial let-down.

In 2002 they were beaten by Clare in the All-Ireland quarter-final. Their 2003 season started in June with another loss to Clare and ended in July when Tipp knocked them out of the qualifiers. They fared little better in 2004, sent packing by Kilkenny in round two of the qualifiers as their public stock continued to plummet.

They rallied under Conor Hayes to reach the 2005 All-Ireland final – having thrillingly overturned Kilkenny in a sensational semi-final – but then flopped in the final against Cork.

'We tried to emulate what we did against Kilkenny but it didn't happen,' recalled Collins, who was named Young Hurler of the Year that season. 'Cork put aside their running game and played directly against us. And after his hat-trick against Kilkenny we put Niall Healy, a 21-year-old, in on top of Diarmuid O'Sullivan. The Rock absolutely roasted Niall physically, but what did we expect? He had just scored three goals, but to put a young lad in on a fifteen-stone, battle-hardened 27-year-old full-back – I wouldn't fancy it myself. Hindsight is twenty-twenty vision, but Chunky [Kevin] Hayes would have been the ideal man to put in.'

As 2006 dawned, fans and pundits readied themselves for a sequel with either Kilkenny or Cork, and Galway duly started well by thumping Laois and Westmeath before losing to Waterford. It was obvious that the hammer jammed and the trigger locked when the big guns came to town. Kilkenny gained revenge for the previous year by plugging them full of holes in July.

Seasons came and went but fulfilment eluded them. They seemed to have the beating of Clare (2007), Cork (2008) and Waterford (2009), but managed to lose each time. They would deem the narrow loss to Tipp in the 2010 All-Ireland quarter-final as the most tantalizing one that got away, but if they needed to prove a point in 2011 they failed to do so – Waterford hosed them by ten points in the All-Ireland quarter-final.

As for 2013, so disastrous was it for Galway that everyone in the game wondered how they had brought Kilkenny to an All-Ireland final replay the year before. Patience was wearing thin out west and the salt air was pungent with cordite. Change was demanded and even the Galway hurling board, convening at year's end, levied criticism on Anthony Cunningham and his players.

'People were calling for the board to get rid of Anthony, but what does that achieve?' Collins asked. 'It just leaves us with no belief or consistency. Yeah, a new man will come in and there might be a new intensity but the existing manager would have been able to achieve that anyway. Look at Brian Cody and how long he has been with Kilkenny. There needs to be a settled team and a settled management structure here too. People have been quick to compare 2013 to 2012, and yes, we had a few low days, but the low days make the good ones all the sweeter.'

In Collins's view, life is a succession of lessons that must be lived to be understood. And yet bearing in mind Galway's steady flow of underage talent, the question has to be asked as to why all that early promise has failed to yield mature fruit.

Collins won't deny that Galway's most recent appearances in finals were followed by seasons of woeful anticlimax: 'The last few times we reached an All-Ireland final we disappeared for a while afterwards. No one is more aware of it than the players. The 2002, 2006 and 2013 seasons were extremely poor years and that represents a huge challenge for us.'

No hurling county has broken the hearts of its supporters quite so often and so painfully. Perhaps only the Mayo footballers come close in the matter of cruel and unusual punishment inflicted on fans. And yet Galway have shown that when in the mood they can win on any day and against any opposition. Maybe that's why the toughest censure has emanated from within the camp.

In June 2011, on the day of their championship match against Dublin, the former players and managers Noel Lane and Conor Hayes and the former player and selector Brendan Lynskey were interviewed by the *Irish Independent*. They used the opportunity to castigate the players.

Lynskey was most scathing: 'Galway win an All-Ireland minor and all of a sudden these lads' heads become as big as buckets. They're on Galway Bay FM, they're down in Supermacs, they're opening up this, opening up that, signing jerseys. There's too much made of them.

'We're making superstars out of middling hurlers, blowing up bad hurlers as good. And they end up putting on the jersey as if they're entitled to it. They're not entitled to it. In fact, my honest opinion is that three or four of the lads on the current senior team are not entitled to be wearing a maroon-and-white jersey at all.

'Why are we afraid to put up our hand to catch the ball? God almighty, fine, you might get a few broken nails or broken fingers – we got them and played on with them. Are we taking the easy options now? I'm trying to be as mild as I can but I just cry with vexation at what's happening.'

Managers, meanwhile, were being turned over like ruck ball in a schools rugby junior development league match. While Mattie Murphy continued through 2013 to oversee the underage academy with purpose and huge success, Lane, Hayes, John McIntyre, Ger Loughnane and Anthony Cunningham had all tried but failed to take Liam MacCarthy west of the Shannon.

Cunningham, at least, guided them to their first-ever Leinster title in 2012, en route to defeat in that All-Ireland final replay. Hayes, for his part, looked to be on the verge of something big during his time at the helm. In the 2005 All-Ireland semi-final, one of the most spectacular championship games ever seen, his team fired an incredible 5-18 past Kilkenny. But they never again looked like reaching those heights, as he himself admitted: 'What we built up in 2005 just all drifted away again. They [the players] couldn't be spoken to. They knew it all, had everything sussed. They were the next Kilkenny. The next Cork. The attitude was, yeah, this is it, we've made it!'

Loughnane, a household name, was expected to bring success to a county coming down with stylish hurlers. It never happened. It didn't help that he suspected half the county board and several of the panel didn't want him in the job. There were nights he arrived at Salthill for training and found the gates to Pearse Stadium locked.

'Ger was a fantastic manager who didn't get a buy-in from his own management team and not enough from the players either,' said Collins, who was made captain under Loughnane. 'We just didn't have the commitment across the board. There was a lot of pressure on his back but had he stayed put, with the right back-room he would have done something massive for Galway. He's a dictator as well and he wanted to clean out the set-up but he never got the chance.'

John McIntyre took over and worked hard on the team's development, but he didn't get much luck either. As his team travelled to Tullamore to play Dublin in the 2011 championship, the contents of the aforementioned newspaper piece were relayed to the team. Damien Hayes, long-serving forward and three-time All Star, said he simply chose to ignore them: 'People are entitled to their opinion, but I was totally focused on the game at hand and it didn't have any effect on me. Sure people would cut you down all the time – you can't listen to it.'

Collins, like Hayes, turned a deaf ear but felt younger team-mates were affected: 'At the level we're at we should be able to block this sort of stuff out. But players are under pressure from everyone, and reading this craic from former players? I just wanted to take it and shove it up their arses. It could have left the younger lads half rattled or taken the wind out of their sails, but most of us are used to it. We have got massive amounts of criticism over the years.'

That is down to inconsistency. Each time expectations increased the team had failed to measure up, especially after they let Kilkenny off the hook in the 2012 All-Ireland final. From there they went into freefall, losing six of their next ten competitive matches. A dismal 2013 season ensued as, plagued by staleness, changing formations and perhaps a loss of manic desire, they blew up before the championship proper even started.

'I have no explanation for what happened in 2013,' said Damien Hayes. 'We trained as hard as ever – if not harder – but for one reason or another we just went backwards.'

Nor could Collins offer definitive reasons: 'There were seven St Thomas players away from the panel until the end of March and maybe we missed them while they were club-tied. That has been the case several times in Galway when our teams go well in the All-Ireland series; lads are away for ages and then they come back and take someone else's place.

'The intensity of hurling at club level here is another factor – our championship is so intense and everyone throws themselves into it. There have been differences of opinion between a few clubs over the years and maybe that has been a factor, although I'm not so sure it applies to the current set-up. Personally, I don't think that's a big deal now. I think we are all united with Galway.'

According to Hayes, people have to expect passions will run high while players are on club duty: 'When I play or train with Portumna I bring my blue-and-gold gearbag and wear the club colours. When I play or train with Galway I wear my Galway gear and bring a maroon gearbag. Players will clash at club level, but I don't know if our championship is any less hectic than in other counties. The thing is we should all be able to leave things on the field, shake hands at the end of a game and move on.'

Another problem has been the deployment of Joe Canning – Galway's talisman cut an isolated figure throughout 2013. Canning has been their undoubted leader but the team would need to realize that the chain is no stronger than its weakest link. Other players have relied too much on the Portumna prodigy.

The selectors must pick Canning in his best position, undoubtedly at full-forward, and leave him there. In the past, with no supply of ball coming to him, he has ended up retreating, much to the joy of opponents, to his own half-back line and pumping the sliotar into where he himself should be. In 2013, though, it wasn't just Canning who ended up playing out of position; the whole team lacked shape.

The pity was that we had seen a glimpse of Galway steel as well as skill in 2012. When Cunningham took over he went about hardening bodies and minds with a hellish training regime. He aimed to find out who could handle the pressure, and who couldn't.

He arrived with a three-year master plan and they hit the ground running in November 2011. With the winter training ban still in force, they assembled in fours and fives, pumping iron in different gyms. Players reckoned they did more training from there to February 2012 than they had done in their whole lives. As Collins explained, 'Kilkenny had won eight All-Irelands and we wanted to be the team that stopped their run.'

Cunningham turned the screw and wielded the axe; out went ten established players, some of whom had backboned the previous three years, including two former captains, Shane Kavanagh and Damien Joyce. Ger Farragher, Adrian Cullinane, Joe Gantley, one of their most impressive forwards in 2011, and John Lee, once likened to Clare's iconic centre-back Seánie

McMahon, were omitted, as were Alan Kerins and Eoin Forde.

Meanwhile, in keeping with the 'out with the old and in with the new' mantra, feeder and development squads were restructured. Cunningham sat down with Collins, Canning, Hayes, Iarla Tannian and others to test their mindset and see if they'd fit into his template. You can call it a chat, or an interview, but the overriding message was clear – change was in the air. Those players who survived the cull would have to move with him.

There was an element of the iron fist at the start, but Cunningham showed subtlety too. While five of the winning 2011 under-21 side were blooded, their introduction was tactfully managed alongside seasoned campaigners such as Hayes, Collins, Fergal Moore and Tony Óg Regan. And for all the talk of clear-outs, twelve of the side hammered by Waterford in the 2011 All-Ireland senior quarter-final survived.

Blending youth and experience wasn't easy, though, and the difficulty of the balancing act showed in the league, Galway suffering three defeats during which they looked leg-weary and rudderless before capitulating to Kilkenny in a twenty-five-point humiliation at Nowlan Park.

Seven of the 2011 under-21 side started against Kilkenny that day and they must have pondered the gulf in class and wondered if they would ever bridge it. That defeat, though, proved the launch-pad for the rest of their season.

By the end of spring Cunningham had looked at thirty-three players and handed game time to most of the fledglings – including two minors from 2011. Things were shaping up nicely.

Having beaten Westmeath and Offaly they sat down to forensically scrutinize Kilkenny's game plan. They noted in particular how the Cats attacked opposing half-backs and how their half-backs never abandoned the line. Cunningham decided

Galway would do something about that: they would bring their half-forward line further out and play the game in front of the Kilkenny half-backs. In other words, they would suck the Kilkenny backs out and run at them; they would turn key players like Tommy Walsh and force them to chase.

'The whole season took massive attention to detail and discipline from our players,' Collins recalled. 'We were updating sheets every night and were fitness-tested every three to four weeks. Everything was looked at, from strength and conditioning to flexibility. We were squatting and bench-pressing on our own time. It was the only way we could get to the level that was needed.'

Collins was sad that some of those he had soldiered with didn't get the chance to buy into Cunningham's regime – he reckoned they would have loved it. Still, he knew that had he been two years older he might have suffered the same fate.

It was a serious challenge to match the manager's expectations. Collins worked at Hewlett Packard and used his lunch break to hit the gym for forty-five minutes, working methodically on different muscle groups. When he joined team-mates for running sessions, Mattie Kenny, their coach for 2012 and 2013, would push them without mercy. That was when science took a back seat – the muckier the field the better Mattie liked it, as Collins recalled:

'It was more to see what your mentality was like. If one of us was struggling it was "Help get that lad over that line." The logic was you'd then automatically help him in Croke Park, or wherever. We embraced everything.'

Collins swam in the sea at Blackrock to flush the lactic acid from his legs as the summer became a 24/7 commitment to Galway hurling. His day started at seven o'clock with a five-hundred-metre swim at Blackrock and began to wind down when he returned home from training that night around ten. He reckoned every one of his team-mates was equally consumed: 'We had great team-bonding exercises – weekend boot camps with stuff like helping blindfolded team-mates to navigate. Things like that bring a team together.

'Our attitudes changed. Training was at a higher intensity and more concentrated. Previously, we might have trained for two hours but now it was down to ninety minutes. We don't have a centre of excellence in Galway and so we had to travel to Athlone to work on a fully floodlit sand-based pitch. Anthony realized how important that was very early on. It's still a massive concern to me that we don't have such facilities in Galway but we worked around it. Everyone was tuned in.'

Deep down Collins loved every minute of the torture. Having made his name in 2005, he effectively had to start from scratch after a horrific ankle fracture, incurred while playing for Connacht in the 2007 interprovincial final, sidelined him for two years.

The ankle was dislocated, ligaments shredded, the foot rotated 180 degrees. A consultant told him he would never hurl again, but Collins couldn't countenance that. He managed his rehab patiently. Even when he regained his feet he delayed his return to hurling, knowing the constant twisting and turning would likely cripple him for once and for all.

When he found he could run in straight lines he tried his hand at ironman triathlons and soon reached international class, competing in three events. At a 'sprint' triathlon in Miami – 750-metre swim, forty-kilometre bike ride and ten-kilometre run – he clocked seventy-one minutes. The individual nature of triathlon was what he struggled with, however, his mind inevitably drifting to hurling, his club – Liam Mellows – and Galway.

Collins missed the 2008 and 2009 seasons and while he was gone Galway marched east and entered the Leinster championship for the first time in 2009. He made his way back into the team for 2010 and two years later they won a first Leinster title – particularly satisfying for a player who had been among those campaigning for the move east: 'I got a huge kick from winning that provincial title because we had a hard struggle getting there. We only got in after winning a vote by fifty-eight to fifty-six.

'I went into the board meeting and spoke on behalf of the players, told them we needed more games – beating Laois and Antrim by twenty points was of no benefit to anyone. From there we would go into an All-Ireland quarter-final against provincial final losers and have our arses handed back to us because we weren't at the tempo required. We needed to be at the best level from a long way out. It took us four years to win the Leinster championship but it gave us a target to reach for.'

There was, however, bad as well as good in winning that first Leinster title. The good? As Damien Hayes remarked, they put in a brilliant seventy minutes: 'From the first minute we believed we would win. Kilkenny had already beaten us twice that year and they probably didn't expect anything from us. We definitely came in under the radar – we had just avoided relegation to Dublin – and it was a fabulous game to be part of.'

Collins's job was made easier by the movement of Hayes and the other forwards: 'Any time we got the ball in the backs we could see at least three Galway forwards in front of their markers and it was easy pickings for us. We were able to push up and I managed a point myself because there was no one within an ass's roar of me.'

The win was celebrated but only for one night. Then the hype was nipped at source, said Hayes: 'When we got off the bus in

Galway on the Monday we didn't see the Bob O'Keeffe Cup again.'

The downside to that win? Even though they outplayed Galway in the second half, Kilkenny remained sufficiently scorned to want to come back hard at them and emerge victorious from a dramatic All-Ireland final and replay.

There was a hint of anticlimax even before the final. Galway's stats dropped sharply; in the semi-final against Cork they made only half the number of hooks, blocks and tackles. Still, they were confident ahead of the final, so confident that Collins almost dozed off getting an ankle strapped by their physio, the Brazilian Roberto Krug.

For most of this young team it was their first senior final but their preparation was down to a T. Management and senior players compiled a checklist to prepare the younger players for what was ahead. One by one they ticked the relevant boxes. Six tickets per player – let the families divvy them out. Say no to anyone else who asks or you will be mentally drained. Fifteen hundred calories of chicken and pasta every day at midday. The warm-up at Na Fianna. How to fill the twenty-two unforgiving minutes from 3.08 p.m. until throw-in. How to walk in the parade and how to stay warm.

'We just tried to make sure lads wouldn't be shellshocked,' Collins said. 'The biggest thing was realizing that you would be goosed after a few minutes and your first run. The crowd roaring like you never heard them before. The energy draining from your legs. And then everything settles. It's grand for Kilkenny – they play in Croke Park all the time. They go flat out from the word go, like Dublin in football.

'The other thing was that we were asked if we had blown our cover in the Leinster final and it's easy to say, yeah, we blew it open big time. Everyone expected huge things of us again, but that's the pressure you have to deal with. In the Leinster final we went out to lay down a marker and we had that done by half-time. But what can you do? There was an All-Ireland final to be played and it was a different ball game – the stats show that you get no more than six possessions in an All-Ireland and that's twelve plays between you and your marker. That's the level of pressure on players – if you get only two balls in a half and make a mess of one you feel like an idiot.'

Kilkenny started slowly and were dragged about the place again but for all Galway's dominance they were only five points ahead when they should have been out of sight. Single-handedly Henry Shefflin dragged Kilkenny back into that game, winning frees and directing the play.

'We could have done a lot to win in the first twenty-five minutes but we didn't put them away,' Collins sighed. 'I overcarried, Johnny Coen gave away a free too and we conceded three points before the break and went in five up instead of eight.'

In the end, after a pulsating second-half, it was left to Canning to save the day with a last-gasp pointed free. In the rematch Galway again started brightly but as the game went on there was only one winner.

'We were going well when Cyril rattled in a goal but it was ruled out for an earlier free and that changed things,' said Damien Hayes. 'They got a score and then a few more. We hung in there for a while but it was a nightmare feeling near the end knowing we had lost.'

As the game drew its last breath, Collins drove forward on a solo run: 'I got to midfield and ran into Jackie [Tyrrell]. Mother of God, did he meet me with some hit! I didn't go down because I didn't want to show I was hurt, but I was hurt bad. The point is that they were seven points up with five minutes to go and they were still tackling like madmen. We didn't hit them like that, though, and if we are to go up a level we have to do that.'

Sadly, the only level they found in 2013 was one below. The year closed with the tragic passing of young Niall Donohue, which made the disappointments of the season seem hardly relevant. Still, as sportsmen will, they plough on in relentless search of realizing a dream.

'Maybe in our heads we were back in the 2013 final again before we actually started the season,' Collins surmised. 'But that's not the way it works. I learned that over the years. Now the younger lads have learned it too. You can't tell a guy stuff like that – he must learn it himself.

'The worrying thing for all of us is that the average inter-county career is down to about six years. I'm convinced we'll win an All-Ireland but we'd want to be taking the next chance that comes.'

The only option is to stay chasing and remain honest. Sport, after all, keeps offering opportunities for redemption. Galway remain haunted and driven as ever in the search for it.

11

Newer Model Built for Speed

How Wexford ripped up the playbook
and started again

When Wexford beat Tipperary in the 1960 All-Ireland final, Billy Rackard climbed the steps of the Hogan Stand, placed his hands on the Liam MacCarthy Cup and raised it aloft. A wild cheer rolled around Croke Park and out over the rooftops of north Dublin as the Wexford captain reached for the microphone and addressed an ecstatic crowd below in ringing words: 'Hurling is safe in Wexford and more young fellas will follow us! There is nothing to worry about now! There will be more All-Irelands!'

Turns out there was plenty to worry about. In the following fifty-three years Wexford would win just two more All-Ireland titles, in 1968 and 1996. They last claimed a senior provincial title in 2004.

When last they celebrated a national breakthrough, in 1996, most of Planet Hurling joined the purple-and-gold carnival. Wexford were colourful, their men were blessed with charisma, and they played with passion and verve. How could they miss?

Their manager, Liam Griffin, was a beacon of positivity, a quote machine, a walking, talking advertisement for the world's greatest field game.

Griffin, though, would eventually look back in some anger. In his view, '96 was a missed opportunity. When the excitement and hype died down, they had failed to build on their new status and found themselves in a hole – one they were still trying to claw their way out of almost two decades later.

'1996 should have been a platform,' he said. 'Look at the Clare team of 1997 – five of their current [2013] senior team are from Clonlara and that club was inspired by what the county team achieved in '97. Clonlara was a barren ground for hurling and now they have five All-Ireland senior winners there. It's incredible considering the big drive only started there in the late 1990s. They didn't get a kickback for years either; they didn't win an under-21 championship match between 2000 and 2007, until they changed their underage system.

'Meanwhile, I just felt that all we were doing in Wexford was whingeing and I was fed up of it. Everyone was yapping and complaining but what were they doing? One thing is for definite – we weren't capitalizing on 1996. We were too laid back about it.'

Ten years on from that glorious coup, Griffin, long the con-science and unofficial godfather of Wexford hurling, felt that for progress to be made the class of '96 was still needed. And so, at his prompting, Liam Dunne, Tom Dempsey and Martin Storey were dispatched to strengthen underage foundations. Dave Guiney and George O'Connor, two other All-Ireland winners, were given a brief to drag coaching and all the finer points of fitness and skills training into the twenty-first century.

But, said Griffin, the efforts of those men continued to be

largely wasted: 'It was not the fault of any of them; it was the fault of our system here in Wexford. Since the back door came into hurling – and I was involved with the GAA's Hurling Development Committee in setting it up – Wexford was always the county most affected by it because we try to play both hurling and Gaelic football. Therefore our allegiances lie in both codes, and as there is no geographical divide between hurling and football areas, everyone suffers. So the system is not conducive to producing hurlers here.'

Since 1997 the Wexford leagues and championships were, uniquely, run on a week-on, week-off basis. Griffin made the point that in the likes of Kilkenny they focus on one sport all summer long; and so in order to catch up, Wexford would need to be playing twice as many games as the Kilkenny lads – instead they're playing half as many.

So they soon lost ground, and no matter who they recruited to the set-up, however iconic the names brought on board, they had to tackle their organization before progress could be made.

In 2012 Griffin's son, Rory, played a key role in identifying fault lines in the county. He conducted a wide-ranging review, looking into the very soul of Wexford hurling, and perhaps the most enlightening aspect of that survey was a comparative analysis with other hurling counties which threw up some stark findings. It forced a change of outlook; for years the good people of Wexford had blathered and blustered about what was wrong with the set-up, every man and woman having his or her own theory. Now they were presented with facts that could not be disputed.

At schools, for instance, they discovered that 4,300 young Kilkenny players experienced A-grade championship hurling over ten years. During that same period only 1,300 Wexford boys tasted top-tier competition.

Top Cats. Two of the greats of the modern game – Henry Shefflin and Brian Cody.

Left D. J. Carey and manager Brian Cody celebrate victory in the 2002 All-Ireland SHC final.

Centre Kilkenny's Eddie Brennan pursued by Shane McGrath of Tipperary in the 2009 All-Ireland SHC final.

Bottom Kilkenny's T. J. Reid and 'Cha' Fitzpatrick tackle Tipp's Brendan Maher in the 2010 All-Ireland SHC final.

Above Galway's Damien Hayes shortens his grip and prepares to strike to avoid a block from Michael Rice, Kilkenny.

Below Donal O'Grady, Limerick, drawing close attention from Henry Shefflin and Aidan Fogarty of Kilkenny.

Above Joy unconfined. Anthony Daly and David 'Dotsy' O'Callaghan show their delight after the semi-final replay on 29 June 2013, when Dublin secured their first win over Kilkenny in the Leinster championship since 1942.

Below Dublin's Ryan O'Dwyer and Liam Rushe show what it means to win the Leinster senior hurling championship after a fifty-two-year wait. O, happy day!

Left An emotional Brendan Cummins departs the field at Nowlan Park following Tipp's championship defeat to Kilkenny on 6 July 2013.

Below Multiple All Star winner John Mullane, Waterford, gets the sliotar away as Cork's John Gardiner closes in.

Galway's talisman Joe Canning takes a sideline cut under the watchful eye of manager Anthony Cunningham.

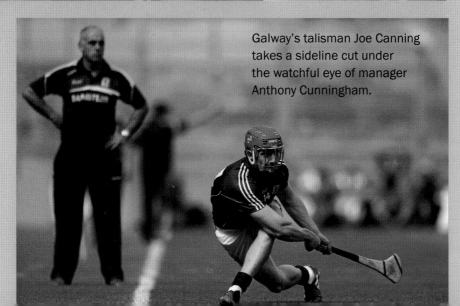

Above The hero returns. Cork manager Jimmy Barry-Murphy walks out at Croke Park on All-Ireland final day, 8 September 2013.

Above Tugging on the badge, Clare manager Davy Fitzgerald signals his passion.

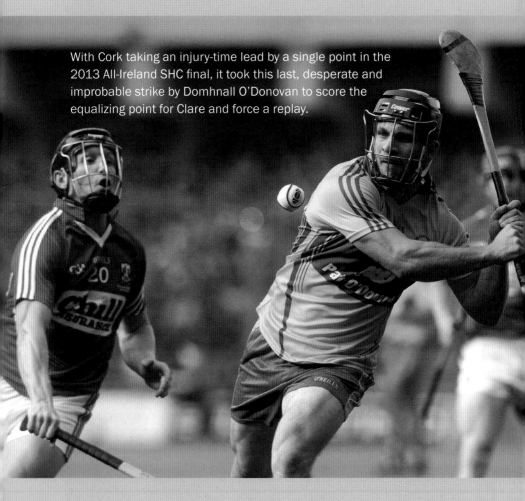

With Cork taking an injury-time lead by a single point in the 2013 All-Ireland SHC final, it took this last, desperate and improbable strike by Domhnall O'Donovan to score the equalizing point for Clare and force a replay.

Pádraic 'Podge' Collins goes on a run with Cork's Stephen O'Donnell in close pursuit.

Above 'Cometh the hour . . .' Heading goalward, Clare's Shane O'Donnell bends his way past Cork's Shane O'Neill.

Below After two classic games at the end of a magnificent championship, the Clare panel celebrate as the 2013 All-Ireland Senior Hurling Champions.

The report highlighted how schools like St Flannan's in Ennis and Ardscoil Rís in Limerick helped their young talent develop. Griffin senior didn't require a signpost to tell him it was a route Wexford also needed to follow.

Meantime, Griffin junior also found that in Tipperary, Kilkenny, Galway, Waterford and Cork youngsters played on average seventy hours of hurling, including games and training, from May to August. In Wexford, because of the two-code structure, they managed thirty-five hours, not all of it competitive. So before they even pulled on a minor shirt the Model County's next generation were way behind. That much was painfully illustrated in 2007 when Carlow beat them in the Leinster minor championship.

'Immediately, you saw from the survey that more Kilkenny youngsters were exposed to a higher standard of competition, which explained a lot,' Griffin reflected.

Clearly, Wexford had enough obstacles in the way of under-age development, and yet in 2013 Griffin pointed to another startling, if purely accidental, one – the fact that in Wexford's best hurling schools many of the youngsters getting the benefit of elite competition were not from the county at all: 'At our main colleges, St Peter's and Good Counsel, there were ten Kilkenny hurlers in those school teams even though Kilkenny have five teams in the A championship themselves. Also, we faced an unreal battle to get combined colleges status – we have it now so hopefully it will get us going again.'

Griffin cited the 2013 All-Ireland minor final as classic proof of how the combined colleges template helped Waterford (a joint Dungarvan colleges side had won the All-Ireland championship and their second Harty Cup in a row earlier that season) and of how it might also help his county. In that 2013 decider Waterford beat Galway well. It was the first time in sixty-five years they had come into a final with more big-game experience than their neighbours – and that came from their players winning college medals.

While the younger Griffin compiled his report, Griffin senior formed 'Hurling 365', an action plan to fund the purchase of camáns and sliotars and nets and suchlike for schools and generally increase hurling participation in clubs as well as schools.

'The plan is that hurling is a three-hundred-and-sixty-five-days-a-year commitment for up-and-coming players,' he explained. 'If that's not there, then down the line we won't compete. Fact. Wexford could be finished as a hurling power at minor, under-21 and senior if this plan is not given a fair shot. We're not bad people but our structures are wrong. Hurling 365 is our new mission statement.'

They launched it on 19 September 2013 and asked twenty clubs to sign up. They also set about looking at a glaring urban black spot: Wexford town with its population of 20,000. Bizarre to report, Rathnure with only seven hundred souls could field senior, junior and intermediate teams, but the county town, for all its bustle, had just a senior team. The county board had a broad acreage to cultivate – even if much of it was under tarmac.

'It's a must to improve this area and bring it into line with Kilkenny and Waterford cities, where hurling is thriving,' Griffin said in 2013. 'A lot of effort has gone into restoring the county over the past ten years but to be honest the real work is only starting.'

Despite these massive challenges expectations have always been high in the county. Wexford people demand success, and when it arrives they turn out in their thousands, illuminating stadiums with their dazzling colours and vibrant good nature, as Griffin acknowledged.

'We're great when we win. But the Blackstairs Mountains stand between us and other counties and at times we're a little republic here; we're very insular. My blood boils when I think of what we could achieve – the time for pussyfooting has stopped.'

Liam Dunne smiled when Griffin's words were relayed to him. Griffin was a huge influence not only on Dunne's hurling but also on his life apart from hurling, and both men share an unabashed love for Wexford. The master was highly influential in the student taking on the job of managing the county seniors in late 2011.

'When I got the job I thought I was after taking over a pot of gold,' Dunne grinned wryly. 'Ah, I knew the task at hand, knew it was a tough one, but I didn't have to be convinced. We needed rebuilding and I wanted to be there for that.'

Dunne had spent three seasons presiding over Oulart-the-Ballagh and was looking forward to a fourth term when his county came calling. The speed of the recruitment process may have set a world record: it involved a brief meeting with the Wexford management committee and a few words with Griffin. 'Only took twenty minutes,' he revealed. 'The cup of tea hadn't gone cold by the time I agreed.'

Observers wondered if the timing was opportune. With the local talent pool at a relatively low ebb, Dunne the manager risked sacrificing an iconic legacy as one of the county's greatest-ever players. Besides, he had been formulating an alternative plan: to go back to coaching at underage – he had spent a couple of seasons with the under-16s and two more with the minors.

'When I managed Oulart-the-Ballagh, I listened to county players saying they were delighted to be back with the club,' he said. 'They probably thought they were saying the right thing to me but I found that very disappointing. I didn't want to hear that at all. It's demoralizing to hear of bad vibes in any county set-up. It should be a privilege to play for Wexford. But we were light years behind everyone else. It didn't surprise me where we were.'

Dunne had retired from playing in 2003, and the following year the county embarked on a bleak and torrid seven-year spell, playing thirty championship games and winning eleven – and several of those wins were against Antrim, Carlow, Laois and Westmeath. When you took the gristle away from the meat, they won six championship games of note in those seven years.

The new manager set to work in November 2011, four and a half months after Limerick had beaten them by six points in the qualifiers. Aware that they were off the pace and that many of the best specialist coaches had already been snapped up elsewhere, Dunne quickly got his backroom for 2012 assembled but also lined up people for twelve months down the line.

They held three sessions before Christmas and the wheel started turning quickly. Dunne recruited the renowned trainer Seán Collier. Soon he had Gerry Fitzpatrick, Paudie Butler and Enda McNulty committed to come on board for 2013.

'I let them know what my ambitions were and planned a year ahead. In my first year I just asked the players would we continue to be whipping boys and live on past reputations or did we want to change that perception.'

Fourteen of the panel for that Limerick game opted out. Dunne insists they were free to come back but he also felt a few were better off moving on. There were no official retirements or sackings but neither did any of them ever feature again. It was in effect a resounding first crack of the whip, but one the new manager felt was necessary.

'I got no shit for it. Well, I didn't hear it anyway – I probably got some behind my back. Some big names went, some good lads too, given the commitment they'd put in, and I respected that. But I had come in to try and push on the best I could. There was a massive turnover. Lads were emigrating, moving on, going back to their clubs. But I didn't retire anybody.'

He wanted guys to up their commitment but refused to issue codes of conduct and rigid targets. He felt if he laid down rules they would only be broken and that would place him in a predicament, especially if one or more of his best players stepped out of line: 'The GAA make rules and then change them all the time and it doesn't look good. I just encouraged the players to draw up their own code and then buy into it.'

Considering there were up to nine Oulart men with Wexford at the time, lads he had played alongside for over a decade, it was probably a wise move. With the team given charge of their own discipline and challenging themselves, Dunne could hardly be accused of favouritism. He had enough on his plate anyhow, such as convincing what was a young group that they were actually better than they thought they were.

'A lot of fellas had taken so many knocks that they were accepting defeat too easily and I knew where they were coming from. If I was from another county and going to play against Wexford over the previous few years I'd have said, look, they're there for the taking – there's a soft underbelly to those fuckers.'

While the seniors went about rebuilding, the underage and minor squads sought gradual improvement, though the project wasn't helped by a serious surfeit of dual players on the panels. The competing magnetic fields of hurling and football were threatening to tear the county apart, and so Griffin enlisted a coach or former player from almost every generation of Wexford hurling to drive youth development, from Adrian Fenlon and Darragh Ryan to Tom Dempsey and Billy Byrne. Interestingly, these men had all played football as well as hurling for Wexford.

They knew that the time for relying on schoolteachers and FÁS coaches was over. For too long the chinks of light that sporadically appeared had been quickly blotted out by the perennial gloom. It was there in 2005 when they had a miserable year, again in 2010, when they lost both their games, and again in 2012, when they fell to Offaly and then Cork in the qualifiers.

Four days after they lost to Cork in July 2012, Dunne called a meeting of the panel, told the players again of his vision for Wexford hurling and explained how they would reach the destination. He also ordered fitness tests.

Earlier in the year Gerry Fitzpatrick had run similar tests – agility, speed off the mark, general fitness – but the results were so poor that Dunne withheld them from the squad until after the Cork match. Effectively, Fitzpatrick's data indicated they would last the pace for only forty-five minutes against top-tier teams.

They were tested again in December and again the following March. Three weeks before playing Dublin in the 2013 Leinster championship, they spent a weekend at Faithlegg House and, said Dunne, the overall improvement was dramatic. Average body fat, formerly at 22.8 per cent, was down to 11.5. A couple of players clocked 8 per cent. Much of the transformation was down to Dr Sharon Madigan, who had worked with the Irish Olympic boxing team.

The stats showed that within a year of Dunne taking charge, Wexford could, on paper, motor with the best teams for seventy minutes. That, however, wasn't enough for Dunne, who said wryly: 'We found out in 2013 that we need to go for eighty.'

And yet the progress was palpable in 2013. First, they came from a long way behind – 0-1 to 0-6 – to draw with the eventual Leinster champions. 'It was only then we remembered what we were all about,' Dunne said. 'Then we put them on the ropes – five of their forwards were taken off. We realized what we had trained for from the previous November until June, put our own system to work and pulled that first game with Dublin back out of the fire – and not with the use of ash like we were accused of. The stats show that we got twenty frees that day and they got ten and yet all the talk was about Dublin, how good they were and how rough we were.'

Even though he had been utterly serene in his new role, Dunne's firebrand reputation as a player had followed him into management. Pundits suggested Wexford were going out to rough up opponents, by fair means or foul, just as their manager had done back in the nineties. On the grounds he could hardly control what others thought of him, Dunne shrugged his shoulders.

'I'm calm on the line despite what people think of me. After the replay against Dublin much was made of how we played in "Dunne's particular style". Michael Duignan had a good lash at me on RTÉ and so did others. I don't mind getting flaked but I thought it was unbalanced and biased.

'I got three red cards in eighteen years' hurling for the county and still people just see me as a dirty bastard. But you can't approach management unless you're totally settled on discipline. Against Clare, for example, Gareth Sinnott was lucky to stay on the field after a couple of tackles and in the end I took him off. He'll learn from that.'

Bobby Kenny was also booked in the first half of that game before being sent off, something Dunne said would no longer be tolerated: 'It's not good enough. I was put off myself in my own career and we talked about that, the two of us. He just needed a quiet word. No one ever came to tell me I was being a fucking eejit by collecting cards. I needed to be told to cop on, that I was acting the clown. I said that to Bobby – spoke of how I went drinking for three months, feeling sorry for myself, after those red cards when all I was doing was being a complete gobshite.'

In the past, losing a man would often spur the remaining fourteen players to match-winning heroics, but in the modern game a red card is more or less curtains; the opposition will revert to short passing and work the ball around you.

'Teams are set up so well that it will kill you,' Dunne acknowledged. 'Besides which, the game has changed: you could hit a fella a belt some years ago and half kill him and play would move on. But in 2013 Pat Horgan, Henry Shefflin and Ryan O'Dwyer were all sent off for nothing. There's so much pressure on referees now and they're cracking. When I saw O'Dwyer being sent off for a shoulder against Cork I was just dismayed.

'It's easy for a manager to lose the rag at that. So you're probably better off up in the stands because if you put one foot over the line and on to the pitch there's a €500 fine straight away. Your players can't hear you shouting instructions so you step on to the field. I wore the Maor Fóirne bib in 2012, just to try and get my messages across to the players, but I was slated for that. I'll have to come up with something new now. Maybe I'll just go out in a suit and stand there on the line. Look, it's the learning curve I'm on. The inches are crucial – that's the level you have to get to.'

The future looks promising. Apart from pushing Dublin in their drawn game they brought Clare – who would drive on to become All-Ireland champions – to extra time in July 2013, a further glimpse of what could be achieved. They must be realistic, though. Wexford drew with Dublin when they were nowhere near the levels they later reached against Kilkenny, Galway and Cork. For most of the game with Clare the Munster men were streets ahead and should never have been caught for extra time.

Every leap forward has seemed to entail a backward stumble and that needs to be stopped. Oulart's failure to beat Mount Leinster Rangers in the 2013 provincial final was a sickening blow to club and county. There have been other knock-backs. Tomás Waters, a fine full-back in the making, severely injured a cruciate ligament in that game against Clare and six months later was still unsure if it would affect him down the line.

Meanwhile, Wexford's promising team had an average age of twenty-four and included Jack Guiney, one of the most exciting young players in the land, as well as others needing maybe a year or two to mature and prosper: Podge Doran, Paul Morris, Andrew Shore, Eoin Moore and Harry Murphy. Patience would be the keyword, something Dunne reiterated.

'We're only tipping the iceberg here; we were way behind other teams. I have to be realistic – it took us nineteen years to win a Leinster title and twenty-eight years to win an All-Ireland, so the law of averages suggests we're not going to be winning lots of titles any time soon. But we need lads to compete and that's my aim.

'The bar has gone up significantly since my playing days. I probably wouldn't be able to hurl intercounty now the way it's gone. You either dedicate your whole life to it or you fuck off. Things have changed so much. In our time you hurled for the club or the county team and went back to the local and had a few pints. That just doesn't happen any more.'

Dealing with the younger player was bound to be a challenge for Dunne and it didn't help that the day after he landed the Wexford job, in November 2012, he was made redundant from another one: his sales executive role with Cemex. He eventually set about looking for another day job but soon concluded that his appointment as county hurling boss was a deterrent to potential employers.

'When I first lost my job, I was able to devote all my time to Wexford hurling and make sure I had good people in and around the scene. I wanted to manage it my way and I wanted to monitor and know everything. If you wanted it to be 24/7 it could be. Initially, it helped distract me from losing my job with Cemex.'

Then the reality of being gainfully unemployed dawned. He saw what Griffin and company were doing behind the scenes to lift Wexford hurling. He also noticed the character of decent young hurlers coming through to his team. He was their figurehead; he would have to stand and address those players – teachers and students and farmers among them – and he would have to lead them, guide them, chastise them and challenge them.

'And there was just no hiding the fact that I was unemployed,' he said. 'Look, it was very hard. It killed me. I was the one being asked to put this set-up in the right direction and on the first few nights I spoke I wondered what they must be thinking of me. A man with no job telling highly qualified people what to do. Would they listen to me? Or respect me? All those thoughts went through my head.

'I put off signing on the dole for seven weeks because I just didn't want to do it but eventually, from January to May 2013, I signed on and I found that very demoralizing. You walked into a dressing room where thirty-two fellas were looking at you – lads training to be schoolteachers or working as medical reps – and I had to lecture them and try to command their respect. And I couldn't get a job myself. It felt awful.'

He had worked in sales for seventeen years, before that as a carpenter for ten, and had never previously been jobless. Application forms were filled in and CVs dispatched and letters of reply came back – but hard offers were few or none.

'People reckoned I would have no bother finding a job being manager of Wexford but it worked the other way: employers felt I wouldn't have time to devote to any job. The irony was that free time was all I had then.'

After six months of searching he landed a position as a regional representative with St John of Gods, the international healthcare organization. It put him at ease again and allowed him to enjoy the Wexford job a little more.

Meanwhile, a county waited impatiently for that pot of gold Dunne was also pursuing. After they beat Antrim in the 2013 qualifiers, in a game where they created ten goal chances, blooded five young subs and won handily after a stuttering start, Dunne was asked on local radio if there was any improvement in the team. He bit his lip before pointing out the age profile of the squad, mentioning that a gifted young keeper had been drafted in behind a highly promising young full-back, and noting the absence of household names on the team to nursemaid the tyros. Rather than get sharp with the interviewer he used the opportunity to solicit more help from the GAA for Wexford's effort to regain the big time.

'I think we've been let down miserably by the Leinster Council,' he said later. 'Their focus has clearly been on Dublin, and while it's great that Dublin are doing so well the truth is that in the past ten years Wexford, Offaly and Laois have been dying on their feet.'

In 2010, the Tipperary hurlers took their expenditure past €1m, most of which went on their senior team. In 2012 Dunne had to work off a budget of €240,000, which was reduced by 15 per cent in 2013. That may sound generous when said quickly, but meals and travel expenses alone cost up to €12,000 a month, and a training weekend away, including hotel, sets them back about €5,000.

'It's not all about money either,' said Dunne. 'But if there is money provided from above we can use it in certain ways to improve our set-up and team.'

They've certainly tried hard to kick-start things themselves. Billy Walsh, the wizard behind Irish amateur boxing, has spoken at their seminars. Before Christmas 2012, every Wexford manager from under-16 up was invited to a 7 a.m. breakfast meeting at the Ferrycarrig Hotel. Communication lines were opened. Liam Griffin reckoned it was the first time in the history of Wexford hurling that all of the managers had met in conclave.

Among other ideas, it was mooted that some sixteen-year-olds be brought into the minor squad, so that by the time they hit eighteen they could form the nucleus of an evolving team. Even if they didn't have schools or colleges medals they would have three years' minor experience behind them, and corresponding belief.

'Everyone left that breakfast with an understanding of the pathway that was needed to make your way from the under-16 side to the senior team,' Griffin recalled. 'They learned about the optimal times to develop strength and conditioning programmes with youngsters, how to properly build up bone density and how to nurture talent and pass it on to the next development squad. They spoke of their strengths, weaknesses and opportunities. And also the threats – such as a recruitment drive from Leinster rugby looking for some of their best talent.'

Another threat discussed was that from football. During 2013 the county hurling and football squads seemed to be embroiled in one big, season-long tug of love, Lee Chin being a particular focus. In early July, the hurlers were to play Clare at 5 p.m. and the footballers were to play Longford two hours later. As it happened, a chronic knee problem ruled Chin out of both games, which was just as well, for the player admitted his head had been 'melted all week' over who to line out for.

Dunne told Chin he had the makings of a top-class hurler and should focus on that code. At the end of the 2013 season, Dunne finally made the call, ruling out dual players from his plans for the remainder of his term in charge and so saving players such as Chin the agony of indecision.

'Lee's a grand young fella,' Dunne said, 'but he was in and out of games and he was tired. Something had to be done.'

Chin was part of the 2013 under-21 team that won the Leinster hurling title and allowed a county to dream again after years of trial and tribulation. While beating Kilkenny needed to be celebrated – and it certainly was – Wexford got totally carried away, perhaps forgetting that they had barely beaten the Cats – and Carlow before them. A local jeweller presented the team with watches, and there was no escaping the feeling that the hype was overblown. They were duly dumped out of the All-Ireland semi-final by Antrim. One step forward, one step back.

'That Leinster title was against the head,' said Griffin. 'But we now have three good under-21 teams coming down the tracks. The 2013 provincial title was a bonus – I was ecstatic.

'But getting pieces of jewellery? Ah no. I was delighted we won, but commercial people will always walk up and ask you to call in for a free meal, maybe get a photo taken, all that stuff. Was it worth it? I only hope we learn.'

Dunne insists the lesson will be learned: 'You always want players to be rewarded, but reward them all in good time. Present them with nice bits of jewellery after the season is over. Maybe we took the foot off the pedal, and bearing in mind where we are coming from over the last ten years, the truth is we can't take anyone for granted.'

Yet four to five players from that side will most likely slot into the senior team. Dunne would like to be part of their development odyssey: 'I don't know where this journey is going to bring us but if the players want it badly enough it will happen quickly enough. The Donegal footballers proved that – if a group of men are committed to the cause anything can happen. Our fellas are not too bad but the sooner we play better teams the better we'll be. We weren't ready for the big boys but we are now.'

12

Back to the Drawing Board

Two counties of contrasting pedigree but
facing similar challenges

Offaly

Almost twenty-five years after he was launched from the bench
by the Offaly management to try and salvage an All-Ireland semi-
final from the clutches of Antrim, Brian Whelahan responded to
another call to arms from his county in late 2013.

Whelahan was Offaly's greatest player; now they needed him
to become their greatest-ever manager. He had been on the verge
of taking over the Offaly minors in late 2013 when the county
board presented him with an alternative: the seniors. It felt right
for him, the fans lapped up the prospect, and it got the county
board out of a jam; the appointment of such an iconic figure gave
them credibility, breathing space, the hope of better days ahead.

Optimism ruled, but, as articulated by David Franks, who
retired from the Offaly team in 2012 after thirteen years' service,
the consensus was that Whelahan should be given some slack:

'They need to leave him be for five years. He's our greatest-ever player so he will command the respect of everyone. But people shouldn't get carried away – there's only so much one man can do and he needs time to build his own style and bring the right personnel in. But it's a big boost.'

And boy did they need a shot in the arm. Offaly had been poor since 2001, but after Whelahan, the only twenty-first-century hurler to be selected on the Team of the Millennium, announced his retirement in 2007, they have been but a pale shadow of former generations. The Birr man's feats are legendary, but the notion that the parched soil of Offaly hurling will suddenly bloom again, simply by virtue of his presence, stretches credibility. And yet if his return does nothing else, it has given the Faithful County a lift. Something to believe in again.

'If you listen to the shite around the country, we are a lost cause, but the truth is Brian has raw materials to work with too,' Franks added. 'We get a rough time in the media but we are not as bad as people think. There are some fine players aged between nineteen and twenty-two. Stephen Quirke stands out, but these guys need to be worked on in terms of strength and conditioning. They need a couple of years' development and then we'll be in a position to compete again. We had a decent display against Kilkenny in the 2013 championship and should have beaten Waterford in the qualifiers. So it's not all bad.'

In fact, they had Kilkenny on the ropes for quite a while; they hit four goals and could have driven on but ultimately seemed resigned to losing, dogged by the lack of belief that, according to Franks, has plagued them for years: 'It's certainly not for want of fitness; it's because we've won nothing at underage. Meanwhile, Kilkenny, Tipp, Clare and Galway are so used to winning at that level. There's the gap.'

After that joust with Kilkenny, the Offaly players were patted on the head, praised for rattling the big Cats' cage and then hardly mentioned again in the dreamy summer of hurling glory. They should have used that game as a launch-pad, but instead they again suffered a late brain-freeze against Waterford. With twenty-five minutes left on the clock, they had clawed back a four-point deficit only to then butcher a terrific goal chance and let the Déise dictate the endgame. Once more they were out of contention by late June, left looking in at the party from outside.

They have grown sick of the hard-luck stories, and sick too of the long-time stereotyping as easy-going beer-lovers. Young, educated professionals like Rory Hanniffy and Brian Carroll had given the bones of a decade's service to the county team but, come 2014, had yet to see game time in August, never mind September.

Whelahan is inexperienced at the top level so he'll have to learn to walk the land quickly. He half managed the Offaly team even in his playing days – and played a part in switching himself from the half-back line to full-forward, with devastating effect, in the 1998 All-Ireland final. He was flu-struck that day, and like himself Offaly were struggling for oxygen until he moved up to the attack, scored 1-6 and effectively won an All-Ireland title for his team.

He had garnered proper managerial experience by cutting his teeth slowly at club level with Camross and Kiltormer. Now stability must be the watchword for Offaly. Whelahan may be a rookie at this level but at least he is one of their own and an icon to boot. That's a big issue – they have had too many first-time managers over the years and the locals would argue that too few have been Offaly men.

Whelahan himself played under ten county senior managers and only four of them were natives. In his first three years, from

1989 to 1992, he had three different bosses, including his father. Eamon Cregan, Michael Bond and Pat Fleury all got a shot. Fr Tom Fogarty, Mike McNamara and John McIntyre all got a shot. And when Whelahan retired, Joe Dooley and Ollie Baker took stints in the hot seat.

One argument for drinking from their own source is that in Offaly they do things differently, as the long-serving Brian Carroll has observed: 'We have our own way of hurling and people need to realize that. I look at Cork and it's admirable how they tried to do their own thing and play their own running game at a time when Kilkenny dominated the game.

'That's been a fault here in Offaly – we have tried to match Kilkenny's way of playing. There has been a lot of dissent over the recent Offaly style. It's been, "Give it long to Big Joe [Bergin] and see how he goes."

'We need to get away from that. And we need to get away from this thing, this lazy journalism, that we're a one-man team. That's not taking away from Shane [Dooley], who is a top-class hurler. But people forget the likes of Rory Hanniffy – the best hurler I have played with. He doesn't get that same attention at all; he goes about his own business and we need him badly. We need to start hurling as a team more.'

An intriguing contrast would seem to beckon. The modern game has been all about possession, whereas Offaly were long noted for moving the ball at speed, a style that made them not only dangerous but also easy on the eye. Regrettably, that way had latterly become a thing of the past; they were trying to copy Kilkenny by getting physical and winning balls in the air. The problem was they lacked the players to execute that approach. A return to the fast ball would be widely welcomed – though Franks is not so sure.

'That might be a bit naive. It's all about retaining possession now and we shouldn't be falling over ourselves trying to get the ball away. Cork and Clare are even content to work the ball backwards if it means going for a long-range score – they won't square a fifty–fifty ball. We shouldn't necessarily go back to the use of the ball on the ground, or the quick ball in.'

Others might argue it is better to fail in originality than to fail in imitation. Copying Kilkenny was never going to work. Carroll looked on in envy as the Clare team jinked and danced their way to All-Ireland glory in the heady summer and shimmering autumn of 2013: 'Their system looked so fluid – it would be great if we were to try something like that. We'd have to evolve, but I had to do that just to survive at intercounty level. I started out as a nifty corner-forward, idolizing the likes of D. J. Carey, Seánie McGrath and Joe Deane. Then suddenly there was no place for that type of player. Now, thanks to Clare and Cork, that player has a chance again.

'Meanwhile, I had to either adapt or go home. I gradually moved out to the wing and tried to pick up breaks, worked hard to get around the field. And then the last management decided they wanted tall ball winners in the half-forward line, which is not my strength. I'm not six foot four and I never will be, so I changed tack again and found a home at midfield.

'The sad thing is, I have seen lads I started off with, guys with great careers ahead of them, and they're not there now. You have to take personal pride if nothing else in trying to reinvent your style and maybe now, with the style Clare have brought, we could see a different approach for the next few seasons. I think it would suit us. There was a period of five to six years when we were in the gym, obsessed with weight training, and our hurling suffered. It would be great to get back to basics again – that's what suits us.'

Considering his lengthy service to the cause, it's sad that the

Coolderry man has only once made it as far as an All-Ireland quarter-final and that was as far back as 2003. They had other chances over the years but failed to click, as he acknowledged: 'Our ship could sink a little too easily at times when we fell behind in games. Human nature being what it is, maybe we lost shape and players started doing their own thing.

'My own club had that. We had a great set of lads but we were just not achieving until Ken Hogan came in as manager and rammed it home to give the ball to the guy in the best position. Look at Richie Hogan and Aidan Fogarty of Kilkenny, who have made careers out of doing that. Soon, with Ken on to us, we felt just as good about popping a pass as we did about scoring ourselves. That helped us reach an All-Ireland final.'

On his appointment, Whelahan immediately set about working on the Offaly players' attitudes. In early January 2014 they played Antrim, his first game in charge, and trailed by six points but rallied to win by the same margin – the result was no great shakes but it at least featured a fightback the likes of which they had seldom if ever produced in recent years. For Franks, the burning question for Offaly would be the support available to the manager: 'The finances are not there so we need to work on that. If we had a million euros to spend on the senior team I'd say we would see huge development within a year. But we don't. The underage set-up is not producing much at all for us either and we lack coaches at that level. Most managers these days have a backroom team of at least twelve people and Brian would need that support as much as anyone else. He can't do it all on his own. I'm not so sure what support staff we can afford, though.'

They have lagged a fair distance behind other counties in terms of development. There have been three different directors of underage hurling – Johnny Flaherty, Pádraig Horan and Pat Cleary – in the ten years up to 2014, another illustration of the lack of continuity. The Offaly academy was unveiled amid much hype and fanfare but the fruits have made for slim pickings. They certainly progressed at underage football in the same decade, but their hurling fortunes were in reverse – the failure to reach a Leinster minor final since the academy's founding a salient statistic.

Indeed, all the way up through the ranks, they seemingly forgot how to win. In 2012, the minor hurlers tumbled to a 2-13 to 2-10 loss against Laois. In 2013 against the same opponents that gap had widened: 4-16 to 0-13 in the Leinster minor quarter-final. To find their last provincial title at any underage level you had to trawl back to 2000, when they won provincial minor and under-21 crowns.

It didn't help Offaly hurling that so many of the 1990s team faded from the scene more or less simultaneously. Most of the fifteen that started in the 2000 All-Ireland final had retired by the end of 2002.

Perhaps the single biggest loss was Johnny Dooley. He played his last game for the county in the 2002 qualifiers at Portlaoise, arriving off the bench at thirty years of age against Tipperary, who won 2-19 to 1-9. It was sad to see a great hurler virtually hobbling around the field after years of persistent knee trouble. Maybe that cameo was his only chance to bid farewell, but Dooley deserved a better backdrop for his valediction.

That was the start of many dark days for the county. They lost to Wexford in 2003 when Carroll missed a close-range free, and a succession of butchered frees cost them the 2004 Leinster final. Had Dooley been there, even blindfolded, he would surely have floated those frees over. That 2004 title seemed well within their grasp, but besides squandering points they also made a hero of the Wexford goalminder Damien Fitzhenry that day.

A win then might have had a knock-on effect and left a positive legacy. Instead the losing habit that had already infected the squad became a reflex. What followed was a veritable downward spiral that left nothing for the kids to aspire to. Young Offaly teams became used to a losing culture, the exact opposite of what had prevailed in the eighties and nineties. Things reached such a nadir that the former county player Daithí Regan was quoted in print to the effect that they were in danger of becoming a Christy Ring Cup side within five years.

'There is a lot of negativity out there,' Franks said. 'And some of it is justified in terms of what is being done to improve things, but we are too proud a county to drop to the Christy Ring Cup – no offence to the competition but I just don't think it will ever happen.'

Carroll, one of those who had observed at close quarters the ten-year slump, said the big danger was that players would be infected by the general pessimism: 'I saw all the stuff about potentially going back to the Christy Ring Cup and it made for good headlines but there are two sides to it. Over the last ten years we have just not done things right as a county, but it hasn't been for the want of trying by the players. There is a realization there that we do need to wake up – all of us – because we have been burying heads in the sand, especially at underage. If we don't properly develop our underage structures we're in trouble.

'There aren't as many male teachers around the county as there were in the past and that's not helping. Perhaps a lot of clubs have focused very hard on the club championship too and maybe some players feel they don't need the hardship of being handed a beating at intercounty so they just choose to stay put instead of relishing the challenge.

'Hopefully players will come in and look at the bigger picture. At the moment a lot of people are only worrying about their own little patch. The way recent Offaly championships have panned out – four different winners in four years – almost every club sees a chance of success. Maybe then lads think they are much better off staying with their clubs. That would be dangerous territory.

'I saw it with Coolderry, how the whole thing can threaten to take over. To win two county titles and a Leinster championship and reach an All-Ireland within eighteen months showed us what could be done.'

After they won their first county title, Carroll brought the cup to his grandmother, the mother of his late father, and Offaly great, Pat. He saw the buzz it gave her and how much she enjoyed having her picture taken with the club. After they won the Leinster title he intended to return with the latest piece of silverware but his grandmother passed away that day.

'At least I saw the joy it had brought her. She was a stalwart. But one point I would make is how united we were. All the Coolderry lads were away on Kevin Brady's stag party in Lahinch and they left Clare at 9 a.m. to come back for the funeral. I thought so highly of them for doing that. I suppose it does show you too how the club can take over.'

Offaly hurling also suffered cruelly in the economic recession. Ten of the 2012 panel didn't return in 2013. Conor Hernon and goalkeeper Eoin Kelly had gone to London in search of work. Six others felt that because of work pressure or college pressure or both they could no longer give the commitment needed. The experienced Brendan Murphy and David Franks retired. The fear was that when the likes of Hanniffy, Carroll and Kevin Brady moved on, their experience and fieldcraft would be impossible to replace.

With all this turmoil, a wedge was driven between players and followers. As the team shed its never-say-die image, fans drifted away. For bad measure, a sense of injustice rankled among the hurling people of south Offaly, aggrieved that all senior inter-county games continued to be played in Tullamore and not Birr, long the spiritual home of Offaly hurling.

The county board would need to come up with a way to solve this problem because, peripheral as it may seem, it has split a county with a small-enough hurling constituency and damaged the sense of identity.

Carroll has had no doubt the issue is huge in its ramifications: 'The hurling area of south Offaly is small and everyone is living on top of each other. We are probably equivalent to one of the divisional areas in Tipp and so clubs know each other's junior teams, never mind senior teams. I could name most of the sur-rounding junior team line-ups.

'So moving to Tullamore has had a huge effect on attend-ances in our league games and it hasn't helped the team either. I totally understand that championship matches have to be played in Tullamore, and I fully accept that the facilities are top class, way ahead of Birr, and therefore when the likes of Waterford and Kilkenny come here on a summer's day the games have to go to Tullamore. But for some league games we'd be lucky to get a thousand people at Tullamore and the opposition team would sometimes have more support. People from south Offaly won't travel and they make the point that there might be five thousand at the game if it was held in Birr.

'The truth is that the locals have seen more ladies' football matches than Offaly hurling matches at Birr in recent times. I asked some of the under-16 development squad how many of them had seen Offaly play in the 2013 league and only three of them had seen us. But they can look at ladies' football every few weekends.

'Are you killing hurling by not having it where the audience is? To a certain extent you are. We need those development squads to see the senior team and have something to aspire to.'

And yet, as 2014 dawned and the evenings stretched, the belief persists that they can become a top-six team again.

'The way hurling is gone, you just never know,' Carroll said. 'I really feel a pressure to try and help turn things around. That pressure was always there and how well I dealt with it I don't know. To a certain extent I've dealt with it and to a certain extent I haven't.

'I suppose being Pat's son I have always felt a weight on my shoulders. I never knew Dad but yet I grew up watching videos of him playing hurling. I think I saw the 1981 All-Ireland a hundred times. My ultimate aim was always to win an All-Ireland with Offaly.

'All my early years were spent finding out stuff about my dad and listening to other hurlers talking about him, so his passing was very personal to me. I went to St Kieran's to hurl and then off to UL [University of Limerick] to hurl just as much as study. I wanted it more and more. I nearly got there with the club. If all of my dreams are not to be realized then that will be hard to come to terms with. I'm coming to the end of my career and I'm running out of time to honour Dad's memory – and win for myself and Offaly. And yet you never know. Did George O'Connor ever give up with Wexford? Did Damien Martin give up with Offaly? You just never know. That's what keeps you going.'

Still, Carroll has twelve seasons under his belt and there is a slow realization that his career may not receive the Hollywood ending he always chased.

As the summer of 2014 loomed, the long, arduous task of rebuilding a proud hurling county had started in earnest, however. Sparks had been few and far between in Offaly hurling but, despite a dire Division 1B league campaign, the fire was not yet quenched.

Antrim

Offaly, though it would pain them to admit it, also have a special place in Antrim's story. The Ulstermen have seldom had a problem producing heroes and role models for their young hurlers and the biggest achievement of their history was defeating the Faithful County in 1989 to make the All-Ireland final for only the second time.

It was a massive achievement but it remains unrepeated. In 1982 the northern side, then campaigning at senior B, proposed that Ulster teams be offered a direct path to the All-Ireland semi-finals, GAA Congress agreed, and when Antrim went on to reach that '89 All-Ireland final, players like Terence 'Sambo' McNaughton, Niall Patterson, Ciarán Barr and Olcan McFetridge became household names.

That is where the link to Offaly stops, however. The Leinster men went on to win two All-Ireland and three Leinster titles after that but in the following three decades, while they continued to produce impressive hurlers, Antrim suffered a perennial succession of internal strife, indiscipline and more than a few hammerings. An immensely proud tribe, they have nevertheless been long in need of help.

Thirty-two years on, Pat Daly, the GAA's Director of Games, pondered what progress had been made since that boardroom motion was passed: 'Are they still where they were in 1982? They are. There have been plenty of structural changes in the hurling championship system since, but with the exception of 1989 there has been no breakthrough. So it's not a structural fault.

'They need to take a more cohesive approach, a more joined-up approach. At the moment it's north Antrim here, Belfast there, south-west Antrim down there. They need less of the isolation thing – this repeated view that no one cares about them. Yes, they are away from the hurling heartland and no doubt there are issues with that, but if they want to be a force they can be. They've already proven that at club level. There's no reason why it cannot be replicated at intercounty level.'

Daly's frank assessment of the situation in the Glens mirrors that of many southerners: isolated, perennial victims, enigmas, cannon fodder – the list goes on.

Perceptions aside, here are some facts. In the sixteen years following the inaugural All-Ireland minor quarter-finals, Antrim represented Ulster in that series every year bar two, when Derry and Down were sent south into the lions' den. From an Ulster perspective, the results have been horrific – sixteen games and sixteen losses. The smallest defeat came when Antrim ran Limerick to a point in 2005. The biggest setback was in 2011, when Galway trampled on them by thirty-eight points. The Ulster champions racked up a grand total of 14-135 over those sixteen shootouts, but conceded an eye-watering 54-285. Whatever way you add it up, it's a cumulative defeat of 270 points, the average margin a morale-sapping seventeen points.

At senior, it's been a wee bit better for Antrim but very little to write home about. Time and again they have taken counties like Carlow, Westmeath, Laois, Down and even Dublin, a team they beat in 2010. But they have endured wild pummellings too, the worst being the 8-26 to 1-15 annihilation by Limerick in June 2012.

And yet, each time they suffered a hammer-blow, they seemed

to strike back when it was least expected. In 2013, with only nine or ten players turning up to training and a series of club football games fixed for the same weekend as their All-Ireland under-21 semi-final, their young team travelled south and pulled off one of the biggest shocks the competition had ever seen, somehow beating Wexford to qualify for the final.

Twenty-three players were listed in the official match programme but just twenty travelled. On the Thursday night before that game they had only fourteen going through the motions in training. Beating Wexford looked as likely as Henry Shefflin declaring for Tipperary.

Come the final, they hadn't a prayer of beating Clare and they were duly thrashed, but imagine how much better they might have fared if a full squad had trained together regularly?

Pat Daly was not far wrong; if they could not get their own house in order, why should we listen to them blaming others? And they often did.

'That whole fixture clash could have been handled better, no doubt about that,' said Neil McManus, a senior player doubling up as under-21 selector, in reference to that campaign. 'It didn't look good for us, it put the young lads in an awful situation, and we've spoken to the county board about the whole affair. There should never be a clash of fixtures like it again if we reach that stage of a national championship.'

Mickey McCullogh, Ulster hurling development officer and a former Antrim minor hurler, also acknowledged the internal weaknesses, not least a certain apathy in the playing ranks: 'Much has been made of Antrim's achievement in reaching the under-21 final. Was it down to sheer hard work? Were there thirty-plus lads training hard at every session? The answer is no. Kevin Ryan, their under-21 and senior manager, said he was often dealing with nine, ten or twelve players at times. Is that how success is achieved?

'The semi-final win over Wexford does show there is talent in the county if it could just be harnessed properly. But take into consideration that some players weren't even at the Wexford game – for one reason or another – and it really throws the coaching manual out the window.'

The final against Clare saw the resumption of normal service. The Munster men had won most of their 2013 under-21 games by nine points or less but they won the final by twenty-two. That hammering took some of the gloss off Antrim's undoubted achievement in reaching the final.

'Look, we were playing against one of the greatest under-21 teams ever and we take heart from the fact that we made the final, though we badly need to build on that,' said McManus. 'Still, we got to that stage of the championship because we were a better team than Wexford in the semi-final.

'The GAA then brought us down to play Clare at Thurles and we thought that showed a lack of tact. But for the team's sake we got on with it and made light of it. We had to. Still, it was a huge opportunity to use the spectacle to develop the game in Ulster and that Clare team would have had no great qualms about coming up north to play that final.

'It was a trick missed. Belfast is the second-largest city in this country and there's so much untapped hurling potential here it's unreal. Antrim actually have the numbers to copy the underage models that Dublin and Clare are thriving with, but we've seen a total lack of investment up here. So all that promise will go by the wayside.'

It's hard to blame the GAA for not investing as much as they could. Down through the years, there has always been some controversy or other surrounding Antrim's biggest games. In

2009, a group of players, including the highly talented Shane McNaughton, went on holidays before they tackled Laois in a crucial qualifier game. They duly lost and would have been relegated from the top tier, only for the GAA to intervene and scrap relegation that year. Speaking to journalists the following year, McNaughton was big and honest enough to admit it had been 'an immature move, that it was no one else's fault and that they had learned from the episode'. Frosty relations between the clubs hasn't helped the dynamic either. Some years ago a group of coaches from Cork went to Cushendall and after a meeting one of the coaches asked a Cushendall official what would constitute a successful season. A county title? An Ulster title? Perhaps an All-Ireland title?

'Don't mind any of them,' the clubman said. 'As long as we beat Loughgiel we'll be happy.'

'Well,' said the southern-based coach. 'That explains so why Antrim never win anything. That's a joke of an attitude to have.'

It must have been the first time in a while that the clubmen had been told a few home truths because a few weeks later that coach was asked back up again.

Still, it's pitiful to see the raw passion that exists for club hurling in the Glens and yet the disregard and apathy that is there for all to see when these clubs combine and pull on a saffron shirt. An intercounty manager was driving through Loughgiel one Sunday afternoon on his way to take a coaching session elsewhere. He saw hundreds of cars parked along the side of the road and stopped to enquire what was going on. He was told Loughgiel Shamrocks were playing Cushendall. He couldn't believe the crowd or the interest levels. It was the same in Parnell Park in 2011 when every man, woman and child attended the Loughgiel versus O'Loughlin Gaels All-Ireland semi-final. The place was simply thronged with Loughgiel supporters. Only a few months earlier, however, Antrim had played Offaly in the same venue for a Leinster championship match and there were scarcely fifty Antrim shirts to be seen in the stands.

Yet, it burns McManus up inside to see his county – and province – 'neglected' by the powers that be. In 2013 the GAA pledged €15m for the redevelopment of Casement Park, the rejuvenation of a venue in dire need of a makeover. McManus would have appreciated it if just a fraction of that colossal sum had been redirected towards Antrim underage teams instead of into a stadium that could – like so many others – sit largely empty for much of the season.

'This is my eighth season with the senior team and to be honest I don't see any major help given to us by Croke Park at all. I stand to be corrected on that but nothing springs to mind. The point I'm making is that we have so much to offer but we are most definitely disadvantaged geographically and in its simplest form that creates expenditure problems because we are always travelling. Any time we go down south to play it costs money, and to make any county structure worthwhile you need to plough resources into the underage system. Our under-21 and minor teams need to be in the Leinster championship if we are to make any progress, and so the harsh reality is that we require financial support – but we're not getting it.

'When Sambo [McNaughton] and Woody [Dominic McKinley] took over the Antrim minors a few years ago the team travelled up and down the country to play challenge matches against the best. They derived funds from their own friends and business people who lived about the Glens. That's why we were able to compete. There's no mad science to any of this. We need support to play against the best counties. And when we play regularly against them we have shown that we improve. It's no big shock if we beat any of them.'

*

Maybe that lack of support is explained by Antrim's long-running internal weaknesses, actual or perceived – non-committal players and shambolic structures the most obvious ones. In 2012 Jerry Wallace, then senior manager, left the job twice. He resigned after they lost to Westmeath by two points, only to reappear a couple of weeks later taking the warm-up before a challenge game against Wexford. It was as if he had never been away. The players, though, didn't even know he was returning. Local newspapers reported that neither did the interim boss, Jim Nelson, expect the Corkman's return. Nor did the county chairman, Jim Murray, and both Nelson and Murray were left red-faced.

Wallace's brief comeback lasted through the Wexford game and just two further training sessions before he left again. It prompted Shane McNaughton to describe the managerial shenanigans as a joke and 'the most amateurish thing you could get'.

When asked what responsibility the county board accepted for the breakdown in communication – not to mention other cock-ups, such as fixing club football games to coincide with the aforementioned All-Ireland under-21 hurling semi-final, McManus was slow to apportion blame.

'The bottom line is that there are some diligent hurling men on the county board working hard for us and doing all they can to look after us but they don't always get the necessary support from other powers that be in the county. But where is the point in going around looking for war? I know there are good men fighting for us, to little avail, but what's the point in having a go at them?

'We simply have to focus instead on the fact that we have a core group of players coming through that want to hurl for Antrim and love training. Their honesty and integrity is testament to those who coached them up through the juvenile ranks. But to go a step further we need to be in Leinster championships from under-16 upwards and build from there. The only way you win is by being competitive on a regular basis and to develop stronger people.'

The Cushendall man accepted that the 2012 and 2013 seasons threw up various issues but said he was totally satisfied they were now historic. It remains to be seen if that is the case. Numerous big-name players didn't participate in 2013, including the county's best forward, Liam Watson from Loughgiel Shamrocks. Watson had been seen as a divisive figure in the county over the previous eight years. But such a sublime talent was bound to be sorely missed. In 2012 he shot 3-7 on All-Ireland club final day to help his side past Coolderry but was hardly seen in an Antrim shirt thereafter. There wasn't exactly a clamour to get him back either. Watson is for ever perched on a thin line that divides calm and storm. The best hurler in Ulster, and in the top bracket across the country, Watson, who is thirty, hasn't ruled out retirement, but he is happier with his club. He knows there are several players in the Antrim dressing room who don't want him back. His case is symptomatic of the county's complexities over the years.

'I was asked to commit to training and it was turning out to be six days a week and I couldn't sign up for that. I am thirty, I train very hard with my club and I have to look out for myself,' Watson said. 'I asked Kevin Ryan for leeway and got none. I was told the panel was closed and I would have to wait for someone to drop off or get injured. I'm still waiting. Players left and were brought in all during 2013. But they obviously don't want me, some of the team don't want me either, and the bottom line is that I have far less headaches just playing for my club.'

Watson remembers a recent awards ceremony where he was approached by another Antrim hurler. The Loughgiel man had won three honours that night but clearly not everyone was thrilled for him.

'Your man had an award, a vase, smashed in two which he thought was mine,' Watson recalled. 'He asked what I thought of that, but I reassured him my awards were safely tucked away in my hotel room. So he must have broken someone else's! That's what some people in my own team think of me!

'Look, I'm not ruling out going back to Antrim, but as it hasn't happened by now I can't see it coming under the current manager anyway. I would love for us to get our act together as a county but I can't see that happening either. We don't invest in the underage system properly. I feel the footballers get preferential treatment from the county board and we are going around throwing millions of pounds at a stadium which will become just another Ulster football venue. Some of that money should be used to get former hurlers into the coaching set-up but there is not enough respect for hurling here. Few enough people at the top care enough about Antrim hurling. So I think that Pat Daly is dead right in what he says – we always blame other people for our troubles but the blame lies squarely within.

'The great talk now is of a great under-21 team coming through and I sincerely hope that is the case but only eight or nine lads were turning up to training in the lead-up to that semi-final with Wexford. I don't know how we beat them that night; Wexford must have thought they had the game won before they even turned up. But down the line that win won't paper over any cracks, wait and see.'

Without Watson in tow, McManus at twenty-five was the oldest player on the team of 2013, so clearly the manager, Kevin Ryan, was putting faith in youth and moving on without their star man. It took Ryan some time, however, to 'get' the Antrim mentality.

Appointed in late 2012, he was seriously underwhelmed by first impressions. Trials were called but the response was lukewarm; in the age of instant communications and blanket social media, phonecalls went unanswered and some players proved uncontactable.

Bewildered, Ryan eventually went public with his frustrations, going so far as to call into question the reputed love of hurling in the Glens. In early November 2012, as he contemplated another gruelling five-hundred-mile round trek from his home in Waterford to coach the county senior and under-21 teams, he told a reporter: 'The perception I would have had was the undying passion Antrim people have for hurling. But some of the excuses I've been getting have been ridiculous. I would be very disappointed in the overall commitment.'

When it became clear the no-shows were not going to have a change of heart, Ryan went with what he had – a committed panel top heavy with youthful brim. They survived in a competitive Division 1B league section and Ryan was happy with that. His enthusiasm for the job increased with every passing week.

A year into Ryan's tenure, McManus was full of praise: 'Enthusiasm is one thing, and Kevin has that in spades, but more importantly he brought organization too, which is what we need most. He radiated professionalism and his ideas on building structures were top class. He threw himself into the under-21 set-up as well. We'd be hopeful that he will stick around for a while and see this project through. It's hugely important that he does.

'Because of him our commitment is just not in question any more. I get as much personal pride from pulling on the shirt as the Kilkenny boys do putting on the black and amber, and the lads feel the same. I grew up in Cushendall immersed in hurling and there's a serious history of the game in my parish alone.

It's very special for me to play for the county and we know that young kids around the place look up to us.

'Over the years we have had players who simply just looked out for themselves and didn't show the necessary attitude but all the right people are involved now. It's not going to happen over-night, but we want to be competitive on a steady basis. A little bit of support from HQ would help us get there quicker.'

It has been argued that, if Antrim cannot change the minds of those who hold the purse strings below in Croke Park, perhaps they should consider changing their own approach. The notion of a combined Ulster team has been talked about in recent times and it's an interesting concept, certainly one that should be tried out at schools or minor level.

From 2008, northern schools held a virtual six-year monopoly on the All-Ireland B competition, St Mary's Belfast, St Patrick's Maghera and Cross and Passion Ballycastle lifting five O'Keefe Cups between them. But it did little to raise Ulster's standards at intercounty, and that's where the combined A colleges model came into play.

Ulster schools made use of that model in 2013 and it allowed them to be truly competitive. A squad of thirty-eight was drafted from several institutions. McManus himself took them for several coaching sessions and McCullogh was joint manager. To prepare for the competition they played big hitters like the Tipperary minors and held their own. They only lost the All-Ireland quarter-final to Mercy College Galway when Shane Caulfield hit the winning point from midfield to put the Westerners through.

But, just as they looked like making a statement for the future, GAA Central decided to restructure their post-primary competitions and it meant the province could no longer pursue the combined-colleges model. And yet, surely a northern team deserved a chance to stay in situ for the 2014 championship. If there really is a will to see Ulster hurling combine and thrive there are two paths forward: the first to revisit the concept of 'Ulster Colleges' and let them strive to improve as a unit; the second to form a combined provincial minor team and let them compete in the All-Ireland championships.

Unfortunately, such proposals have caused a huge stir in Antrim and around the province and have generally been met with a wall of negativity. They stand little chance of ever being put into action.

McManus himself is only half open to the idea of underage combinations and deems the idea totally impractical at senior level: 'The concept is probably against everything we stand for and I don't see how it can work. I just cannot grasp the concept from a logistical point of view. How could players from Cushendall and players from north Donegal meet for regular training? How many hours would be involved in making even just one session? Would playing for the combined province team stop you from representing your county? I don't think the idea has even been fleshed out properly.

'Look, I enjoyed the combined Ulster colleges idea and maybe there might be something in that, but once again the powers that be have decided to get rid of it. So what do you do?'

The frustration remains that within Antrim there is so much talent if only it were nurtured. Loughgiel Shamrocks won the All-Ireland club championship in 2012 and came close to retaining it in 2013. O'Donovan Rossa were national Féile na nGael Division 2 champions in 2013, beating Offaly's St Rynagh's by a point in the final.

But what happens now? Is the county board doing enough to nurture the talent that is obviously there? How can the players improve at county level? One solution would be not to force their best young players to choose between club football fixtures and a national semi-final, as was done – it would hardly have happened anywhere else.

The fact that Antrim hadn't played the 2013 Ulster final, against Down, by the close of the calendar year and beyond is a further indication of official apathy. That game was originally postponed because of Down's run in the Christy Ring Cup, but the shambles prompted McManus to reiterate that it could be time for Antrim to concentrate solely on the Leinster championship: 'We've certainly been competitive within Leinster since we've been involved and it has improved us, there's no doubt about that.'

Wearing his hurling-development cap, McCullogh wouldn't disagree: 'A lot has been made of the fact there was no Ulster senior final in 2013 and blame was laid squarely at the door of the Ulster Council, but is that fair? The Ulster Council are also accused of not pushing the development of hurling in the province. But if the two counties involved don't agree to a date there's little the provincial body can do.

'The reason for the small window in which the Ulster hurling championship can be played is directly linked to Antrim's participation in the Leinster championship. Now the question needs to be asked: would the Ulster championship become a more competitive competition if Antrim moved root-and-branch to Leinster? Instead of having one team clear with very little competition, you would instead have three teams of a similar standard leading the way, followed by two to three other teams that on their day would fancy a shock against the sides above them. In a flash you would go from a one-team-dominant competition to a six-team knockout event.'

McCullogh has suggested another option for Antrim would

be to name and grade twenty lads to play solely in the Leinster senior championship. That would rule them out of the Ulster championship but the provincial series could be used to form a developmental Antrim senior squad, comprising minors and under-21 players, to be given competitive action.

McCullogh has also strongly favoured giving the combined Ulster template a shot: 'If we always do what we have always done then we will always get what we have always got. You could explore options at the various levels. At minor level in the past three years Antrim have been beaten by twenty points, Down were beaten by twenty-two, and Antrim beaten again by thirty-eight points. Keep going further back it doesn't get any better.

'So is there an avenue for playing an Ulster minor championship in April or May and then selecting a combined squad that will go forward to represent the province in the All-Ireland quarter-final? There is some great talent emerging in the weaker counties but with no avenue for them to challenge or test themselves against the very best. I feel an Ulster squad coming together mid-June to prepare together could definitely win an All-Ireland quarter-final within three years. Then buses could head south to support our own as opposed to bringing kids to Croke Park to watch players they have no link to at all.'

He insisted the combined-colleges venture was the best idea he had seen for some time: 'It gave players from every Ulster county an opportunity. It was tried. Did it work? Did it make an Ulster team competitive? Definitely. Why was this not pursued? As for third level, none of our universities compete in the Fitzgibbon Cup, which is widely accepted as the next level below Liam MacCarthy. We have to ask if there is an avenue to bring Queen's, University of Ulster Jordanstown, St Mary's and the rest together with one squad playing Fitzgibbon, a B squad in the Ryan Cup and so on. Antrim reached the

All-Ireland under-21 final in 2013 but how many of them will now continue to improve and play Fitzgibbon Cup? None is the answer.

'Before people come out and reject the idea of a combined Ulster team at senior level they should at least consider the options above. Maybe an Ulster senior team could be formed by the eight counties aside from Antrim. Gareth "Magic" Johnson, Conor Woods, Paul Braniff, Ruairi Convery, Declan Coulter, Alan Grant, Liam Hinphy and Joe Boyle deserve the chance to show their talents off at the very highest level.'

Liam Watson, however, says there is no way a combined Ulster team would work. 'Not a hope of it. Not alone is there too much club rivalry in Antrim but there's no way players from other Ulster counties would link up and play with each other. Not a chance. It will never happen.'

McCullogh is undaunted, though, and has pledged to continue trying to change mindsets.

'All I'll ask is where is the breakthrough coming from if we don't try something new? No team from Ulster challenges in A level at national under-14, 15, 16, 17, minor, colleges or under-21. We're not there at university or senior level either. Do we expect that to just change one day? Or should we be looking to try something new to see that change?'

People like McCullogh, McManus and Ryan are intent on hauling Antrim – and with it Ulster – hurling up by its bootstraps. Ryan has targeted an All-Ireland under-21 title win by 2015. That's a lofty goal and you can accuse him of dreaming but he, better than anyone, realizes that the road to any sort of success in Antrim has been potholed with problems beyond his remit.

The hurling fraternity needs way more organized support.

And the GAA powerbrokers should divert some funds away from stadia development and into fertilizing the grass roots in the Glens.

But they need to get their own act together too. Otherwise, the game will lose its heartbeat up there.

13

Little Fishes Swimming Upstream

Why the small fry of Laois and Carlow can
keep hoping to make waves

Carlow

At the far end of the country in early November 2012, John
Meyler left home in Douglas, in the southern suburbs of Cork.
He pointed his car towards the M8, the contours and cambers
of which are as familiar to him as the face that greets him in the
mirror each morning.

That time was upon him again: a twice-weekly, 270-kilometre,
return trek to Carlow, an odyssey potholed with uncertainty and
no clear end destination in sight. Still, there is little in life, and
certainly nothing in hurling, that Meyler is half-hearted about.
And so he bade farewell to his family and drove away with the
enthusiasm of a man who has volts coursing through his body.

Meyler is an unsung hurling man, a former Wexford player
and All-Ireland club winner with St Finbarr's in his adopted

city. He loves backing an underdog and seems to operate on the principle that you haven't lived until you've done something for someone who can never repay you.

In 1992, he breathed life into a Kerry hurling team gasping for oxygen, most of the available air long ago sucked away by the county's religious devotion to all things football. Undaunted, he found a committed few, preached salvation and led them out of the desert and to their most famous win, over Waterford in the 1993 Munster senior championship.

In 2006, he began a two-year stint with his native Wexford but was prematurely culled before returning to Kerry for a second spell in 2010, this one lasting three and a half years, during which he masterminded their first Christy Ring title and three successive All-Ireland under-21 B titles.

Fuelled by an infectious desire that enables him to see out challenges others would abandon, he's as straight as a spirit level and can spot bluffers the length of a hurling field. There is seldom middle ground. So, when in late 2012 word of Carlow's interest reached him, his response was uncomplicated: they either wanted him on board or they didn't.

'I had two chats with them before I took the job,' he said. 'First, I went to meet the county board and two players, Des Shaw and Shane Kavanagh, both solid men. Next, I spoke to the board and seven players and I think I ended up doing the interviewing.

'Things are different nowadays; you're better off going talking to the players than the county board – they're the ones who have to invest the commitment, bring the right attitude, and try to fit in work in between. There's no point in the board giving you a ringing endorsement if the players are not buying in.'

One glance at the infertile hurling landscape in Carlow would have deterred all but the keenest planters, but Meyler saw scope for cultivation and growth. Rather than being daunted by the task ahead, he studied the barren spots that were everywhere signposted and went about working on them.

There were only seven senior and six intermediate clubs in the county and yet a 2012 domestic championship that started on April 28 did not finish until late October. Something was not right there. Incidentally, some of those intermediate outfits were second-string representatives of the senior clubs. In other words, the pockets of hurling were extremely small and compressed. And while the county jostled the broad, successful shoulders of Kilkenny, with just over half the population of their next-door neighbours – 55,000 against 95,000 – they lacked numerical clout.

To make matters worse, only a small proportion of Carlow's population follow hurling and fewer still actually play the game. The county is V-shaped on the map, and hurling is confined almost entirely to the thin end of that wedge. Draw a line from Bagenalstown to Myshall, and north of it you'll struggle to find a county hurler.

The good news for Meyler was that much hard work had been invested in development squads – at juvenile clubs as well as schools – and this had provided continuity, allowing underage teams to test themselves with some success.

The minors, for example, made a historic first-ever Leinster final appearance in 2006, beating Laois, Wexford and Offaly along the way. Kilkenny whipped them out the gate in the final, but that same year, Eoin Garvey led Pres De La Salle from Muine Bheag to the All-Ireland Colleges B title. Four All-Ireland minor B titles in a row around the turn of the century suggested a county finally coming to terms with its potential.

Garvey took the Carlow seniors to the 2006 Christy Ring final, where they were badly burned by Antrim.

The former Waterford hurler Jim Greene put his shoulder to the wheel in 2007 and 2008. During his first meeting with the Carlow players, Greene told them how he had driven up through Ballyhale, where there were great hurlers, past Kilkenny city, where there were more great hurlers, then out to Gowran, where there were yet more great hurlers, then to Paulstown, with its own share of great hurlers, and then after a few miles, he met a large roadside sign: 'Welcome to County Carlow'. Greene looked hard at the players in front of him and paused before continuing. No, he said, he had no intention, simply because he had crossed a county boundary, of driving over the edge of a cliff, or anything like it – Carlow too could produce great players. But first they had to get their heads in the right place.

He oversaw the first of their Christy Ring titles in 2008. They retained that trophy in 2009 under Kevin Ryan. And in the 2010 National Hurling League they beat Wexford, a result of seismic proportions given they had lost by twenty-five points to the same opposition a year earlier.

At the end of that impressive league campaign, they were managing to coax seventy youngsters out of their Saturday-morning beds and on to the paddock for minor trials. And by the season's close they had Brian Cody across to launch Ceatharlach Óg, an initiative aimed at bringing elite coaching to under-13s, 14s, 15s and 16s.

Following ten years of sustained graft, Ryan's steady watch ensured stability, and in March 2012 Mount Leinster Rangers – a combination of the parishes of Borris, Rathanna and Bally-murphy – claimed the All-Ireland intermediate title and then sensationally landed the senior provincial championship and reached the All-Ireland senior final two seasons later. Also in 2013, the county under-21s would send shock waves rippling along the east coast when they took Dublin out of the Leinster championship.

So by the time Meyler landed in the county, green shoots of promise were pushing up all over the place, and he had a clear plan of campaign.

'The first aim was to get inside the lads' heads. You have to find out what the culture of a group is. What's the social life like up there? Is education a big thing among the panel? Find out who's working and who's not.

'You had to look at the other sports and see where the threat was. In Carlow they play rugby, soccer, Gaelic football – even darts is a big thing. That's what a weaker county always faces, an array of sports that could drag your best hurlers away.

'So I had to study what made these guys tick. I had to find out was a league soccer game more important than an NHL game with Carlow? You vow to pick up a few new players for the following year because they couldn't commit straight away – Paudie Kehoe from St Mullins at centre-forward and Denis Murphy from Mount Leinster Rangers, who was primary school teaching in Scotland.

'In Carlow, you soon discover that pride of place goes to the senior club championship and you must deal with that. Then there are younger lads like Marty Kavanagh, James Doyle and Diarmuid Byrne – they are finishing school and you wonder what's next for them. You look for a scholarship for them and give them resources so that they don't have to go abroad to find work or go working in pubs at weekends for a few spare bob.

'Then you look at the stats and discover that no one from Carlow town played hurling for the county in the past year. And you pledge there and then to rectify that, to get one or two lads out. A townie fella brings a certain something to any squad – maybe a bit more confidence.'

Apart from searching every hamlet for talent, reviving hurling in Carlow town had become a key goal for the county board. Tullow was another hurling wasteland in need of fertilizing. Meyler didn't mind – every port he'd visited had enjoyed a dramatic increase in trade and traffic, and he had always enjoyed a challenge. He had also been around long enough to know that complaining about a lack of resources is like moaning about thin air on a mountaintop – pointless.

And so he set to work, bringing that sense of urgency to a set-up choked by its own history. They were pitted in Division 1B of the 2013 league, and though they went down in every fixture, they did so with their boots and helmets on, fighting to the bitter end and losing to Offaly by only two points, Limerick by three and Wexford by five. Each loss was hellish and every hell was personal for this ultra-competitive manager, but when the post-mortems were complete there was no disguising that progress had been made.

'We were competitive without winning,' Meyler said, the memory of those near misses still enough to bring a grimace of pain. 'Jesus, though, it nearly killed me. Offaly, Limerick, Wexford – those were games we could have won.

'Of course it's a learning curve for the lads. Winning doesn't just happen; you've got to decide to win; you've got to learn how to win. You have to learn how to win while playing badly, especially.

'Still, I couldn't have asked for much more from them. The recession didn't help – I had never seen shift work and money issues impinge so much on training and preparation. And yet we had a full turnout at nearly all the sessions I called – they'd have trained seven days a week if I'd asked them to,' he said, respect for their loyalty palpable in his voice.

It didn't take him long to bond with them.

'I asked the players at our first meeting if they realized what the commitment would involve and we went to work from there, without winning but with a string of moral victories. Fuck it, I have no time for those defeats – they cut me up – but people have to understand that they're sometimes necessary in a rebuilding process.'

Soon after Limerick had won the 2013 Munster final, Carlow's chairman, Michael Meaney, telephoned Meyler and wondered aloud where it had all gone wrong for them, considering they had Limerick dead, if not buried, at the Gaelic Grounds before losing to a flurry of late points, the winners going on to lift the Munster Cup just a few months later.

Meyler, in responding, could hardly suppress a wry smile: 'I remarked that there was a slight difference between ourselves and Limerick.'

Meaney's question did, however, reflect how expectations had risen on this manager's watch.

Those rising expectations became Meyler's food for thought on his regular hike, nearly all of it motorway, between Douglas and Carlow. To and from he had around four hours to mull things over. Sometimes he turned off the phone, the better to juggle with team formations in his head; other times he stayed on speaker for the entire journey, talking to players, fine-tuning arrangements, monitoring the health of the squad and the general set-up.

Among other things, he was looking at maximizing the team's modest budget, and that would require serious thinking outside the box. A lecturer in business at Cork Institute of Technology, Meyler was well-qualified on that front – but also realistic, as he explained.

'The Carlow county board doesn't have the resources Dublin has, for example. Look at the brand of the Dublin jerseys and their market value alone. So we have to be efficient in terms of resources and channel them in the best way to help the team. Dublin get big grants and big deals but we are led by a budget and it's strict. You tailor what you are doing to the few bob you have.'

After Christmas 2012, they trained Friday nights at the Black and Whites complex, where they were able to put thirty lads in for ninety minutes of intensive touch and ball work. Within weeks, several of the team's small and loyal band of followers – parents and siblings, in other words – remarked on the improvement in skills. Meyler then went to work on fitness and strength, but only after they had honed their touch.

'There are things that you take for granted in counties like Kilkenny,' he explained. 'It's a given that any morning of the week Jackie Tyrrell and the boys will be in the gym at seven ready for a weights session. Maybe they're even showered and heading to work at that time. Guys in the so-called weaker counties may not always be able to put the time in off the field, away from training, and that's a problem.'

Meyler understood some of his players were based in Dublin, while others were on shift work or studying, and he knew they would find it hard to fit in the extracurricular work. But after he had been released by Wexford – and more precisely the Wexford players – he conducted a self-assessment exercise.

What more could he have done? Were the players fit enough? Be honest now. No. Were they strong enough? No. Was their touch good enough? No. He determined he would never again answer those questions in the negative. Every box would have to be ticked no matter what job he took after that.

'As a manager you'd have to look at where you went wrong or else you'll learn nothing next time round. Coming to Carlow, I knew what I didn't get right with Wexford – and it wasn't all my fault – but I vowed that our lads here would have more skill than ever before. They would have to be fitter, as well as competing with that improved skill base.

'Setting a team up so that they're hard to beat was another thread to it. I'm still trying to get through to fellas on that – three or four moral victories are not worth a curse to any of us.

'Sometimes on my way back after a match, say when we lost to Limerick or Offaly in the league, I kind of wonder am I ever going to win anything. People down here in Cork must think I'm losing all the time, and maybe people down here think I'm useless. But the reality is that not every manager will take Kerry and Carlow and we're all bursting our asses to make a breakthrough.

'Yes, it gets to me. I wake up some days and ask aloud: "Will I pack this in? Am I wasting my time and the county board's resources? Am I wasting everyone's time?" Like, we're not going to win an All-Ireland.

'Then, take a game like Limerick in the 2013 league. We go down there and have a man sent off but we're only three points down in the last minute. Suddenly, one of our lads has the goal at his mercy and he drops the ball with the net beckoning. We had a famous result within touching distance. And while it's another moral victory, you remind yourself on the way home – with the heart pumping and this brutal feeling in the pit of your stomach – you remind yourself that the team is going somewhere. And the wheel will have to turn sometime.'

It almost turned in the 2013 qualifiers. They were soundly beaten by a resurgent Laois, 2-18 to 0-13, in the Leinster championship but the game had been within their reach for most of the first half – until they had three players sent off.

For the qualifier clash with Wexford, no one gave them a hope but they almost pulled off the shock of the championship, effec-

tively destroying the Wexford midfield until Liam Dunne un-
leashed quality players like Eoin Quigley and David Redmond.
Meyler turned to his bench and grabbed a raw eighteen-year-old
called James Doyle, asked him to do something special and felt
his knees buckle when Doyle grazed the butt of the post with a
scorching effort in the dying embers of the game.

'We were level with a minute to go, then they get two points
and you're there again wondering when the fuck will it turn for
you. I'm from Wexford, I was born there, and I managed them,
but I was baying for a result here. As Carlow manager I had a
job to do. Jesus, though, the dressing room afterwards – fellas
were crying. I'm emotional myself, I always was, but when Eddie
Coady spoke I found it hard to keep it all in.'

Coady, then thirty-four, spoke with the air of a man about
to zip up the kitbag for the last time. If so, he wanted to say
how proud he was to have played with Carlow. That his words
affected Meyler so deeply says much about the Carlow players
themselves.

'Ah, seeing Eddie in bits, trying to talk,' Meyler said. 'Sure
Eddie typifies the weaker counties in a way. And I mean that as
the biggest possible compliment. He's a fella that's as good as any
of the Kilkenny lads but because of circumstances he can't get
to Croke Park and that's hard to take. He puts in as much time,
energy and enthusiasm as any of the Kilkenny boys – probably
more – but there's no reward. Medals are the only tangible reward and there's none of them. I was destroyed for weeks after
losing that.'

He couldn't go down to the Wexford dressing room to con-
gratulate them.

'Arrah, I don't go in for that old shite anyway. I just slid past
Dunne and said thanks. I'll talk to him again. Sure, talking to
fellas on match day is only bullshit. I'll say what I have to say,

but not on the sideline or in the dressing room because I'll be emotional.'

His state of mind wasn't helped when his players huddled together in the middle of the field with their small band of loyal supporters encircling them like a comfort blanket.

'It's kind of unreal in a sense. The team stayed on the field and almost every supporter approached them. I saw old men crying in the middle of Wexford Park. One fella came up and said, "Jesus, you've brought them on a mile. Look at all them young fellas who were able to come down here and compete."

'That only drives me all the more. For all the good work, there are no medals here and there's only one motto in sport – if you win you're right, if you lose you're wrong. People say that's a bit blunt, that I need to chill out, but that's just the way I was brought up.'

As Carlow bowed out in 2013, it was clear the bar needed to be raised yet again. Whether the problem was mental or physical, the players had to ask themselves why they had repeatedly failed to close out tight games.

'The first thing I set out to do was to ensure we would not be hammered,' Meyler said. 'I encouraged the lads to keep their shape no matter what, to keep the opposition from scoring. We then tried to be more clinical with the ball. If we have an extra man in defence we have to be careful we just don't lump it up to our forwards and see it come right back on top of us.

'We know we have to work on our discipline as well because of all counties we had the most players sent off in 2013. I think we picked up nine red cards throughout the season and that baffles me because I wouldn't be like that at all.

'But just look at the yellow cards that were handed out in that championship. In Dublin's All-Ireland semi-final against Cork, Ryan O'Dwyer was sent off for absolutely nothing – the first card was a shocker. We just need to get hurling people to referee hurling matches. Throw the ball in and be as invisible as possible. Stay out of it.

'Three of our lads were sent off against Laois. Then I come back to Cork and everyone says, "Jesus, Meyler, you must be lowering the blade all the time."

'It makes you look like a fucking fool and people ridicule us as sledgers when in fact we're working most of the time on ball touch and control. Okay, we need more discipline, but the GAA needs to show more cop-on too.'

As the winter of 2013 set in, Meyler once more found himself shaking his head at GAA officialdom. The powers that be abandoned controversial proposals to reintroduce Cork and Limerick into Division 1A of the 2014 NHL and instead unveiled a more 'inclusive' plan that cooled tensions across a number of counties who were upset that two big hurling powers had escaped relegation for no good reason.

The new system created two groups of six and guaranteed the top counties quality opposition. It was inclusive all right – as long as you weren't from Carlow or Westmeath, the two obvious losers in this new format.

Though Carlow had lost four Division 1B games by tiny margins and were clearly making progress, this new system effectively booted them back into a Division 3 wasteland. And so, just when Meyler and his team were getting within sight of the mountaintop, they found themselves back at base camp again.

That's sometimes the nature of the GAA. All counties are equal, but some are less equal than others.

'It's a huge setback,' Meyler said. 'We spoke to Croke Park and let them know what progress we were making, how we were pushing the bigger teams. That top-twelve bracket is where we needed to be to continue the progress, but no, they didn't listen.'

Meyler, though, was never one to pick a cause and abandon it easily. And he wouldn't stew in self-pity anyhow. With plenty of motivation they returned to training in October, intent on proving their point and breaking back into hurling's 'Super 12', this time staying there for good.

If Carlow are to stay in the top bracket, Meyler has said, they must build a strategic partnership between county hurling teams and the Carlow Institute of Technology. He expressed dismay that such an alliance had yet to be formed. The Carlow IT campus has facilities any team in Ireland would thrive in: a floodlit pitch complete with stand, an all-weather soccer pitch and an excellent gymnasium.

'The whole relationship should be there between the GAA and education in general, not just in Carlow,' he said. 'And it's not just about facilities either. We must also avail ourselves of the sports science that's on our doorstep. Why not ask a third-level physiotherapy student to take one aspect of our team's preparation as a thesis subject or case study? Why not conduct a mutually beneficial comparison between ourselves and the Kilkenny hurling team?

'Carlow IT should be used as a centre for Carlow hurling, not just for facilities but for research and technology purposes too. How better could fourth-year sports science students, for instance, glean primary information for assignments than by aligning themselves to our team, offering us their expertise as well as drawing down vital data? This way, the students learn and the Carlow hurlers learn.'

Meyler helps coordinate a business Master's programme at Cork Institute of Technology and encourages his students to use live case studies wherever possible.

'You could take the Carlow IT department of media and communications too. Conduct video analysis and feedback; that saves finances for the county board and maybe helps a student with a project.

'I hope this is the road we take. Meanwhile, I have to encourage my young Carlow hurlers to go to college and develop themselves. I have already told three of my lads doing the Leaving Cert that they should go and study further, play Fitzgibbon Cup and improve, both as players and as men. There's not a huge ratio of third-level participation here but it's our only hope of keeping pace with the rest.'

Meyler may be only passing through, but you suspect that, years from now, his name and achievements will still be writ large in Carlow's hurling lore. After all, what legacy is more real and lasting than tireless effort and searing honesty?

Laois

Over the road from Carlow, Pat Critchley and Seamus 'Cheddar' Plunkett had grown weary of it all. Through the previous fifteen years they had seen Laois hurling turn into a soap opera, the plots ranging from wholesale apathy to mudslinging between players, managers and officials. The drama may at times have been colourful but it achieved little except to drag the county into the realm of farce.

After watching so many county teams disintegrate before their eyes, Critchley and Plunkett decided to intervene to try and turn those wounds into wisdom.

Plunkett took charge of the Laois seniors in late 2012 and stated his ambition in modest terms: 'We're making no brash or bold promises, no wild statements of intent, save for an internal pledge that we must try and become more solid after the last few years of disappointment.'

Hardly surprising that he would choose his words. It's a short path that has no puddles, but the road taken by Laois hurling several years earlier had led into a quagmire. Many good people had weighed in with the proverbial rope and towbar, but usually got bogged down themselves.

Paudie Butler, one of the country's most established coaches, was just one who tried to chart a route out of the morass. Taking charge in 2005, he brought structure and enthusiasm, but as with others before him, he could make little or no lasting impact.

Butler went on to become the GAA's first Director of Hurling, a position he held for five years, and on the day he finished his relentless and often lonely crusade, he estimated he had heaped an extra 300,000 miles upon his trusty old Toyota Avensis.

It seemed he had travelled every highway and dirt-track on the map, and a few that weren't, but at the end of his tenure he reflected on how hurling's struggle for critical mass remained just as fraught as it had been in the 1960s, when a report found the game was almost dead in sixteen counties.

If not for himself and a few others, the flickering candle that was Laois hurling would most certainly have been quenched. So many rescue plans had been launched there, it was hard to keep track.

Liam O'Neill, later to become GAA President, unveiled the first such scheme in 1990 but said it was 'effectively ignored'. Soon after, the Leinster Council secretary and Laois native Michael Delaney recommended the county drop out of the league and focus entirely on club hurling. That suggestion, like O'Neill's report, was also ignored.

It's funny, though; when they did apply themselves, Laois could hold their own with almost anyone. They lost to Kilkenny by two points in 1995 and by three in 1998 and beat them in the

1996 league quarter-final. They lost to Offaly by just one point in the 1997 Leinster championship.

Still, consistency and application were foreign currencies – always in demand but usually in short supply. And so the bar was lowered with each passing year.

According to Plunkett, they were unlucky in that while several clubs have had seasons of excellence, those spells seldom coincided: 'We had different clubs doing well at different times – Portlaoise, Camross, Mountrath, Borris-in-Ossory. But they never came at the one time. We maybe got five good club teams over thirty years. Imagine if some of those clubs had emerged at the same time.'

That synchronicity never happened. And as the noughties wore on, further rehab efforts were deemed vital. In 2003, the 'Hurling for Laois' programme was unveiled and Butler, senior manager at the time, expressed in ringing words the renewed vision of 'a successful and proud county that has its young people going to bed dreaming of playing hurling for Laois'.

The youngsters were dreaming all right, but mostly of the county footballers, who won that year's Leinster title. The hope was that the hurlers could surf the waves of the footballers' success, but either the tide was simply not strong enough to carry them or they never got to the surge in time.

In 2005, they rolled out another plan: 'Hurling to the Top' – it cost €250,000. The county board chairman, Dick Miller, remarked at the time that Laois hurling was 'in dire straits'. But if things were bad then, the next eight years were gruesome altogether. The county was essentially on life support and in danger of flat-lining.

Meanwhile, teams like Dublin, for so long close rivals, were in robust health. The Dubs had received hefty funding to complement their strong commitment to development, and very soon the green shoots of promise were showing across the capital. But while such traditional equals prospered, Laois wilted. Indeed, even Carlow and Westmeath, teams Laois would always have expected to beat, were now disappearing over the horizon.

In 2011, the rut in which Laois were stuck became a yawning crater. Antrim beat them in the championship, and Cork put ten goals past them in the qualifiers, inflicting a merciless thirty-four-point mauling.

Brendan Fennelly was in charge and didn't spare the players. They didn't spare him either – and so as the dressing room seethed with tension and unrest, Fennelly moved on. A week after that savaging by Cork, Wexford hit Laois for seven goals in the under-21 championship.

Teddy McCarthy was next to take over. And though Laois were relegated to Division 2, they regained some pride with a handsome defeat of Carlow in the Leinster championship. That, however, was a small puff of oxygen in a season that would almost suffocate them – they were ruthlessly whipped by Dublin in the quarter-final, the margin twenty-two points, and hammered 6-21 to 1-11 by Limerick in the qualifiers. Of that 1-11, Willie Hyland, their captain and talisman, scored 1-10.

Only twenty-three, Hyland went on record for the *Sunday Independent* about his unhappiness at the mess. Asserting he could not face another year like it, he cited the merry-go-round of managers, apathy in the squad, the cumulative humiliation of heavy defeats and shortcomings within the county board. He recalled among other fiascos one painful aftermath of exiting the championship when, on the homebound bus, a team official laughed loudly and repeatedly into his mobile phone. Hyland slumped silently in his seat, devastated that his summer had ended.

James Young, a two-time All Star nominee and, like Hyland,

one of the finest players to ever wear the blue and white, ended his career on a sour note. He left the squad after being suspended for two years over his part in a fracas following a club match, but he didn't go without having spoken his mind. In July 2011, following that disastrous concession of seventeen goals in two games, he had called for the heads of board officials, saying they should resign on the back of several seasons marred by disastrous results and lack of commitment.

Meantime, key players like Cahir Healy, Zane Keenan, Eoin Browne, Joe Phelan, Shane Dollard and Shane Phelan were all missing, for a plethora of reasons, from the first team.

Things reached the nadir in September 2012, when shortly after being relegated from Division 1B, Laois were offered the chance to drop down a level to the 2013 Christy Ring Cup, and so find respite from the perennial batterings.

With sulphur in the air, McCarthy stepped aside and a crisis meeting was held for a team with no manager. Well, it may have been a crisis meeting for some, but only eight players out of the entire thirty-six-man panel bothered to show up. Clearly, not only could the outside world hardly care less about the team, most of the players didn't give a hoot either.

The meeting was chaired by Plunkett, who at the time had charge of the Laois minors. He and Paul Cuddy, a highly re-spected former player, were asked to mediate between board and playing squad. But where could they go?

Plunkett recognized the gravity of the crisis: 'We just wanted to get things back on track. The bottom line was that things needed to improve quickly or we were facing into the abyss.'

Certainly, the players had to shoulder much of the blame, but over the years managers had come and gone, some with disastrous effect, so the players could not be faulted for everything. The county had long needed someone possessing both the clout and the personality to unite all factions, modernize preparations and regenerate confidence.

Damian Fox, a progressive coach from Offaly, shouldered the burden in 2006 and looked like the man for the long haul, but a chaotic training session in June 2008 left him with no option but to walk.

Fox had asked the former player Niall Rigney to take the session, but by the time it was due to start just four players were togged and ready to go. Over the next twenty minutes a dozen or so more rolled up, but Fox, his patience already stretched, had had enough. He chatted with the backroom team and it was mutually agreed there was little point in his continuing.

Fox had come to Laois brimming with hope and optimism, so much so that he could handle – and frequently did – as few as twelve lads showing up for training. Four, though, on the night he asked Rigney in to coach, was the last straw. He'd had a decent response from the squad initially and led them out of Division 2 in his first year, but when momentum started to wane he wasn't going to stick around and be disrespected.

Rigney himself took over then; he was a solid, up-and-coming coach who had already devoted much of his life to the county. Like Fox, he often left training sessions thinking there was more in these fellows. He got a huge response at first, but yet again it did not last. Players might text to say they couldn't make a session knowing training was already well underway. Others wouldn't phone or text at all. One fellow, in particular, had Rigney flummoxed. This guy played in seven out of seven league games, but two weeks before the championship started he texted Rigney to say he had lost interest.

Such seepage of talent and energy was happening at underage too. Laois were beaten by Carlow in the 2002 and 2006 minor championships. In 2010 and 2011 they lost to Westmeath. It was becoming easier to expect nothing – that way the failures would be easier to take.

Yet a small few remained positive, enduring the summers of discontent in the hope of a bright new springtime. They remembered days when Laois were competitive in Leinster – days, it's true, that were fast receding into the archives.

But the 1980s had been decent; Laois reached the 1985 provincial final and earned a place in the Centenary Cup final. Camross and Portlaoise were leading the way in club championships and Pat Critchley had won the county's only hurling All Star in 1985.

Critchley – the kind of man who admires the stars while others are cursing the darkness. It was probably always his destiny to be the rainmaker. His achievements and personality have long since been woven into the fabric of Laois hurling, although he has little time for nostalgia.

A soft-spoken, quietly heroic hurling man, he had spent ten years sowing seeds of rejuvenation around the county for whom he played both hurling and football. Apart from that hurling All Star, he also landed an All-Ireland club football medal in 1983 and was selected on the GAA's official team of the 1980s.

In 2003, while the seniors were taking to the lifeboats, Critchley was below decks with the youngsters, frantically stemming the leaks and working the pumps. That was the year he set up development squads for ten- to thirteen-year-olds, academies now known collectively as the 'Setanta Programme'.

'Setanta stood for three things,' he explained to the first batch of kids that joined the programme. 'Anyone know what they are?'

'He was good at hurling,' replied one eager lad.

'He was,' Critchley smiled. 'But Setanta was also big and strong and able to look out for himself, and he was able to catch a ball and hit it long and hard. Anything else?'

'He killed a dog,' another bright spark shouted.

'He did, but only in self-defence, and it was more a beast than a dog. After that, he stood guard for Culainn and kept an eye out for others. So he was brave, skilful and reliable.'

Those three qualities – bravery, skill and dependability – were, said Critchley, what they aimed to inculcate in every child who joined up: 'And that's enough for them at that age. We don't want to overburden them with psychology.'

They decided against selecting individuals and holding trials. Laois hurling was in no position to be elitist, and there is no indication it would be even if it could – the set-up has been welcoming and inclusive as youngsters of diverse backgrounds and aptitudes come together to learn the basics of the ancient game.

'A few years ago, we had an under-13 tournament and lads couldn't rise the ball,' Critchley said in 2013. 'Now, the under-nines at our "Go Games" get so bored with the ground hurling that we let them rise the ball in the second half and they love it. It's been a huge shift.'

A decade on from its inauguration, the first graduates of the programme made their way on to the Laois senior team – Stephen 'Picky' Maher, a fantastic hurler, probably the best-known. Joe Campion and Dwayne Palmer made their names as minors. These guys did as Critchley asked: they learned to get stronger, play the game well and, more importantly, look out for each other. In time they became the ones narrating the legend of Setanta as parents drove up and presented their kids for the first time.

The follow-up to Setanta, the 'Cúchulainn Programme', came into being a few years later to cater for fourteen- to sixteen-year-olds, and when that module ends, those talented enough graduate to the Laois minors. Some make that grade with three years to spare, meaning they've been in the system for ten years by the time they hit minor.

Critchley has been well-placed to observe the benefits: 'They are family at that stage and it's a huge thing. We have a long road to go but we're keeping them with us. These lads are not used to beatings – in fact it's the opposite; they're used to the best of coaching, the tightest of friendships, great wins and a common purpose. They are the future of Laois hurling.'

With solid structures finally in place, they could at last build toward the clouds and it wasn't long before tangible rewards came. For two decades, Laois had been perennial also-rans in the Tony Forristal Cup – hurling's premier under-14 series – but since 2007 they have claimed three B titles in four attempts (losing the final the other year) and have graduated to the A grade. Meanwhile, their under-16s have beaten the likes of Waterford, Dublin, Limerick, North Tipp and Mid Tipp and drawn with Kilkenny. In 2013, they lost just one game.

The 2013 under-15s also took big scalps – including Kilkenny, Tipperary, Limerick and Cork: revolutionary progress.

Most heartening has been that 85 per cent of these under-age players started out as under-10s in the Setanta Programme, where they learned not just to hone skills but also to get along with each other. In a county where club rivalries had so often boiled over and local feuds stunted progress, the tide turned, which an anecdote from Critchley illustrates:

'At an under-14 club semi-final recently a lad from the Setanta Programme got an awful slap to his leg. Another boy from Setanta, but on the opposing team, ran over, tapped his friend and enquired if he was okay. That brought a smile to my face.'

While the development squads have been running smoothly, Critchley would admit that recruiting competent coaches has remained a challenge. To that end funding is vital, and he has pledged that if Croke Park took up the slack, he would ensure the money trail could be traced from top to bottom.

Plunkett underlined the need for resources: 'What's required to grow the game is enough quality underage players and enough good coaches, and while there are plenty of really good coaches in Laois, we need more. Coaches in clubs are not able to go into schools any more, so there's a weakness there for a start.'

They've taken the first steps to recovery themselves and the GAA has offered some hope in the shape of a five-year plan for four weaker counties worth €45,000 per annum. But they will need a bigger push on than that.

In seven years, almost €7 million was awarded from Irish Sports Council funding to develop hurling and other projects in Dublin. The Laois boys would bite off John Treacy's hand for a fraction of that sum.

In 2011, an internal report estimated Laois were ten years behind the Dubs, who have won four Leinster minor and three under-21 titles in eight years, not to mention the success enjoyed by their seniors.

Laois have clearly lacked the financial resources of their big-city rivals and need help, but they are honest enough to admit that the time for shuffling a deck of excuses and throwing one of them on the table every so often is over.

'Every county has to do what's right for itself,' Critchley has said. 'Fair play to Dublin. But it would be great to get some help like that in Laois too because we have everything ready to drive things on.'

Critchley may have been the driving force at underage and development level but it's Cheddar Plunkett, one of his closest friends, who has been the figurehead.

Plunkett, along with Paul Cuddy, was asked to scout for a new manager to replace McCarthy but they couldn't find anyone suitable and so, after much soul-searching, Plunkett took the job himself, passing his role with the minors to Critchley. In any other county, such a reshuffle might be deemed cronyism, but in Laois the close cooperation of the pair has clearly been a blessing.

Plunkett's name, unlike his nickname, was not of the household variety but he was a native, a respected former club and county player who debuted for Laois with a goal against Kilkenny in Nowlan Park in November 1980 and won several club medals afterwards when Portlaoise were in their pomp.

Upon taking the senior gig, he set about meeting players on the verge of walking away, his aim being to reignite their fervour and hammer into shape a team that had played third-tier hurling and just endured two seasons of purgatory.

After he had done the rounds and doorstepped numerous players in December 2012, the joke was that he would have turned blue in the face had he seen even one more slice of Christmas cake.

'Those lads would have given their right hand to play for Laois,' he said. 'All they wanted was to see that things would be done to their very best – that we'd have a chance to compete.

'Take Willie Hyland. He said what he wanted to say, but Willie is Laois to the bone. He'd cut off his hand to play for you. He just wanted a bit of hope.'

They are still miles off where they aspire to be, as Plunkett admitted a year into his tenure: 'Look, there are going to be a lot of bumps along the road – we have a lot of ground to make up – but I would say there are no lads in Ireland hungrier to play for their county.'

Hope springs, especially in the light of how 2013 unfolded. Plunkett kicked off the season by taking them to the Rock of

Dunamase, a defensive stronghold dating back to the Norman invasions of Ireland. The players were told to look around and be aware of who they were, to remember that Laois people had fought and rebelled in times of adversity. It was time to be proud of the Laois jersey again.

A few weeks later they were promoted from Division 2A and gave Galway an almighty fright in the Leinster championship. Afterwards they were given a rousing ovation by the supporters – an early sign that the old bonds were being renewed.

They returned to hurling's 'Super 12' and contested a minor and under-21 provincial final in the space of a year. The clouds were slowly dispersing after almost two decades of cold and sun-less summers.

Setbacks, such as the loss of Cahir Healy, who went travelling and missed the 2014 season, are inevitable as they follow the road to redemption, but those involved know it's always going to be a struggle.

Laois were on a seemingly relentless race to the bottom, but Critchley and Plunkett have managed to interrupt that headlong descent and initiate a U-turn. They may be years behind most of the opposition but they are on track. Not least of their achievements, these men have helped restore pride.

'The biggest sign of progress came at the VHI Cúl Camps in the summer of 2013,' Critchley remarked. 'Usually we'd be asked for Joe Canning, or kids would be wondering which Kilkenny hurler was coming to visit. This time there wasn't one request for a Kilkenny or Galway hurler. All I heard was, "Is Matthew Whelan coming?" or "What about Willie Hyland?"

'It was the first time I heard them asking for their local heroes. That made everything worthwhile.'

Three

NEW CHALLENGES FOR
THE OLD ORDER

14

The Era That Never Was

Why Tipperary's glorious one-in-a-row
flattered to deceive

When, on a balmy September evening in 2010, Paudie Maher raised aloft the Cross of Cashel Cup, much of his life in hurling flashed before his eyes. And for the Tipperary under-21 captain, the slideshow was a succession of brilliant highlights. Back-to-back All-Ireland minor titles in 2006 and 2007 and now an under-21 title for good measure – Tipp's first since 1995 – and clinched in Thurles itself, just six days after Maher had been part of the team that defeated Kilkenny in the All-Ireland senior final.

Maher must have felt like he'd bought a ticket for a roller-coaster ride that never dipped. Why wouldn't he? Led by himself, Séamus Hennessy and Brian O'Meara, Tipp had just flayed Galway 5-22 to 0-12, the biggest-ever winning margin in an under-21 final. Quite simply, they were unplayable that night.

Eight of those under-21s were on the panel which had just

stopped Kilkenny's seniors from achieving the coveted five-in-a-row. All things considered, Tipp were looking in fair fettle to take off on their own glorious, extended run of success. There was even loose talk of going boldly where Kilkenny had failed to reach – all the way to a five-in-a-row themselves.

As contented fans shuffled out of Semple Stadium that night, even the severest barstool critic, the most jaundiced hurler on the ditch, would have conceded that the path ahead was strewn with nothing but promise. Tipp were well-equipped to win more; it seemed they had just signed up to a long-term lease on Winners' Row.

Very soon, however, that contract was shown to be full of loopholes. Glorious September had barely given way to October when Liam Sheedy stepped down as senior manager and with his shock resignation the players, senior as well as upcoming under-21s, lost an edge. In the three years that followed, they never replicated the feats of 2010.

Commitment wasn't the main problem but discipline was. A small group of players – not all of them first-teamers – lost focus on what it took to stay at the top, and ultimately the malaise affected the group and dragged the rest down.

'It was the era that never was,' sighed Brendan Cummins, the county's most decorated goalkeeper. 'We can dress it up anyway we like but that's the truth of it.'

Paul Curran, the most experienced defender on the Tipp team, also looked back wistfully: 'Like most others I walked out of that under-21 final in Thurles feeling we would win more over the following two to three years. I wasn't getting overly excited about it – I'm too long in the tooth for that – but I did think the next year or two would be ours. And then Liam and the lads left . . .'

With Sheedy's exit, and the subsequent departures of selector

Mick Ryan and coach Eamon O'Shea, everything changed. It may seem melodramatic to suggest the health of the county suffered so badly just because three men left. But besides ruling with an iron will, that troika had built structures on which the hopes of the county rested. They had nurtured a culture of excellence. The players' every possible need was addressed; from personal development to training weekends, from game plans to holidays, they were looked after, spoon-fed even. In 2010, they had the best backroom team in the land: the best coach in O'Shea, one of the best physios in John Casey. The system was as professional as an amateur sportsman could hope for.

Little wonder then that as the players took in the news of Sheedy's departure some treated it like a death in the family. It needed weeks and months before they could get their heads around it. Maybe some never managed to. Meanwhile, as they waited for a new manager, idleness became a danger.

'We had the best set-up in the country,' Curran stated flatly. 'We went into games with Kilkenny and Cork knowing we would beat them. But the boys left and it took the county board six weeks to replace them. The next appointment was crucial and not many were putting their hands up for it, hence the delay.

'That was just enough time for some lads to lose the run of themselves and slip back into a rut. They were used to being kept on a short leash. Some needed a tighter rein than others – every squad is like that – and for the first time in ages they didn't have an intense manager breathing down their necks. For six to seven weeks lads cut loose and maybe found it hard to get back.'

Sheedy's exit on 10 October 2010 was Tipp hurling's JFK moment. All concerned remember where they were when the news broke. Sheedy had wanted to phone the players individually, but before he could do so, word of his imminent departure started to leak, and so the Portroe man was left with no choice but to go to the county board and get a statement out while texting the squad.

Having heard the news, Cummins arrived home from work with his head in a spin and went to bed groggy with anguish. He woke up despondent, stayed rooted to the pillow and couldn't countenance going to work. He was unfit for civilized company.

Curran was getting ready for class at St Mary's NS in Clonmel when the proverbial sky fell in. Flummoxed, he texted Lar Corbett but Corbett was so upset he could hardly communicate. On Sheedy's watch, Corbett, especially, had blossomed from mercurial enigma to the best forward in the land. He admitted he burst into tears when the news came through. It took him some time – and a frank discussion with Sheedy, whom he more or less accused of a type of betrayal – before he saw the former manager's point of view.

'I felt sick myself,' Curran admitted. 'I wanted to go home, but there was a full day's class ahead. We rang around, tried to get Darren [Gleeson, a clubmate of Sheedy's and Tipp's sub-goalkeeper] to have a word with Liam, but Darren said we were wasting our time.

'I'll be completely honest,' Curran added. 'When Liam took over I had my doubts about him. He had been part of Michael Doyle's backroom team in 2003 when things had not gone well for Tipp at all. I was worried about him being in again, but Darren assured me he was the right man. And he was.'

If Curran and Corbett struggled to get their heads around the exits, Cummins went a step further and instantly questioned his own future.

'Sure it was no wonder Kilkenny were winning all the time,' Cummins observed. 'They were well good enough to win all that they did anyway, but the other counties definitely helped clear the road for them. Teams like ourselves were building up over several years to get that family atmosphere you need to win, to strive for the discipline and continuity of management Kilkenny had. And just as they got near those levels a manager would walk, or get the road. All of a sudden they would have to start the building process all over again.'

That had been exactly the case with Tipp in 2002 when Nicky English left.

'Nicky built the whole thing up and we were All-Ireland champions within three years of him taking over,' Cummins recalled. 'Then we arrived against Kilkenny in 2002 and, Tipperary being Tipperary, we were not as well-prepared as we should have been because the high of the previous year was still there. When you win an All-Ireland, the whole thing shuts down here.'

Curran felt that 2002 semi-final, ultimately decided by a trademark D. J. Carey pass to Jimmy Coogan, who goaled splendidly, was a watershed that separated two teams with little between them. If both were at a crossroads that day, it was Kilkenny who took the correct path. Tipp rambled down a side road and it set them back years.

'I just felt we weren't disappointed enough after losing that semi-final, which was strange,' Curran said. 'Lads were not as devastated as they should have been. Maybe we thought we'd get back to the top, but after that Kilkenny just went one way and we went another. If we had won that day, who knows? Would they have gone off on that amazing run of theirs? We might have won more too. I went on to play for another six senior managers and I'm only on the scene since 2001. That made it tough to find continuity.'

It took Tipp another eight years to build back up to where they wanted to be.

'Sheedy finally brought the Kilkenny mentality into our

set-up,' Cummins stated. 'In Kilkenny, everyone is plugged into Cody's principles. His demands are just a given; the manager rules and that's it. Those lads might go for a few drinks here and there but they know the "guardian" is watching. Also, when you play hurling for Kilkenny you're no longer a "normal" person – you don't do "normal" things any more. They understand that if they do "normal" things – like socializing and standard training – they won't be playing for Kilkenny for long. Sure, what are three All-Ireland medals worth over there? Hardly even acknowledged. They're All-Ireland champions for three months and then the circus closes down and they restart training again. In Tipp, we never had that.'

Cummins chooses a specific word for Tipp's trajectory between 2002 and 2010 – drifting: 'Our managers came in, took the job and to be fair they did exactly what every other manager in Ireland was doing. But Sheedy went above all that. He was a maverick with a completely different approach; he was like a Premier League soccer manager. I was thirteen years involved when he came in and he completely changed everyone's role. He put the structures in, gave talks on motivation and then stepped back and let Eamon coach and work on tactics. Liam oversaw everything but his lack of ego set the tone.'

Like most of his team-mates, Cummins reacted enthusiastically to the bar being raised. When he appeared at Sheedy's first pre-season camp, tests at the University of Limerick showed him to be the fittest on the panel, and he left that night with a new clarity of purpose. Sheedy had communicated to all his very clear vision of what he wanted to do with the team. Everyone knew his own job: the physio, psychologist, dietician, trainers, coaches and, most importantly, the players.

*

But if the manager had opened Cummins's mind, the coach – and subsequent manager – O'Shea simply blew him away. Sometimes O'Shea would take Cummins aside in training, bring him behind the goalposts and ask him to look out on to the pitch, not necessarily to hit a puck-out, but instead to picture a team-mate making a run.

Initially, Cummins wondered if this was part of some harebrained, airy-fairy, new-fangled coaching theory, but he gradually discovered that a visualized move in training became easier to execute and replicate on match days. Throughout his stellar career, and despite some astounding feats between the posts, Cummins sporadically took flak, especially from managers, over his puck-out repertoire, which Babs Keating, for example, deemed one-dimensional and static.

Under O'Shea, though, he began peppering short pucks to his half-backs or arrowing them into the grateful paws of his half-forwards, who, in response to the coach's vision, had either crossed wings or used space made by a team-mate to find the puck-out.

It was fascinating to watch O'Shea conduct a training session. His calling card was movement and he empowered all the players to achieve that. After working with Cummins on practice nights in Semple Stadium, he would amble along to the half-backs and give them their roaming brief, encouraging them to drop off markers and collect possession.

After that he might saunter along to the midfielders, remind them to hit the gas whenever Cummins got the sliotar. Half-forwards were pulled aside – or, as with Patrick 'Bonner' Maher, taken to Cloughjordan, O'Shea's home pitch – and shown how to create space by switching wings, or how to split to enable a lethal full-forward line to receive primary possession.

As for Corbett, he was given two simple instructions: 'Start from deep but keep making runs behind enemy lines and stay unpredictable.' If Noel McGrath got possession, Corbett was to run even faster to make something happen. The two soon developed telepathic lines of communication.

Thus, without a ball in sight, Tipp players in every line of the field learned to think and act as a unit. The coach preached how the collective would always beat the individual. His belief in them culminated in the pièce de résistance of the 2010 All-Ireland final, when they hit five goals against the greatest team of all time.

'Maybe Eamon didn't even know he was doing it, but he totally transformed the way we saw the game,' Cummins reflected. 'That's why losing him, Liam and Mick was so tough.'

Declan Ryan and Tommy Dunne took over and led Tipperary to the 2011 Munster title in spectacular style but the team never turned up for battle in that year's All-Ireland final and that's what they were ultimately judged on.

Losing that final was hard to bear, but it wasn't as awful as the 2012 All-Ireland semi-final loss, also against Kilkenny, when Tipp went down by eighteen points and Corbett spent much of the afternoon trailing Tommy Walsh – instead of it being the other way around – and was temporarily installed as public enemy number one in the county.

Cummins put that down as the worst day of his entire Tipp career, recalling that each time he went to take a puck-out he couldn't fail to see Tipp fans throwing match programmes away in disgust as they made for the exits, furious with the tactics du jour.

'Hopefully that was a watershed moment; I sincerely hope it was anyway,' he said. 'It wasn't frustration from the terraces; it was pure anger.'

The 2012 campaign had been unsteady all year. Corbett quit temporarily before being enticed back but it was obvious to many that internal unity was sorely lacking. The harmony Tipp crave requires perseverance and commitment, of the kind the Cork football team of the early 1990s had – so strong was their bond that they met religiously every Christmas Eve for drinks, even if it meant flying in from abroad for the occasion.

'You need really strong relationships with almost everyone to win,' said Curran. 'Maybe Declan and Tommy felt the players would come training with their boots and gear, work hard, go home and then play a match at the weekend, but you nearly have to be a sports psychologist now as a manager. Some of our lads need a lot more attention than that – arm around the shoulder stuff. Maybe they had it too good with Liam and the lads. One thing is for sure: 2012 was tough.'

Curran reckoned Dunne and Ryan were brave to put their hands up for the job: 'Those two lads were on a hiding to nothing in many ways. We were on autopilot during that 2011 season – seven goals against Waterford in the Munster final. It was super, but it wasn't good enough in the end.

'In the All-Ireland Kilkenny beat us and it was all of our fault because we didn't show up on the day. After being tested so hard by Dublin in the semi-final, we should have been hopping. I don't know why it was flat, but the players have to take responsibility too.'

Cummins believed the origins of that below-par finale to 2012 were easily traceable: 'Life had changed for a lot of the boys. Most of 2011 was spent going around to schools, opening this and that. A text would arrive from a team-mate looking for you to visit his club and at some stage you would ask the same of them. The concentration might have gone out the window.'

He kept a diary throughout every season of his career and

looking back on 2011 he wondered how they managed to reach the final. He found himself out and about way more often than was desirable, and it was difficult to balance his own training with requests to coach fifty school kids. His 2010 and 2011 diaries were like night and day.

'In 2010, everyone was training but in 2011 injuries stacked up and fellas seemed to be tired and weary from bringing the cup here, there and everywhere. In that sense, Kilkenny probably have an advantage in that their clubs and schools are sick of seeing the Liam MacCarthy Cup.'

On the Thursday before the 2011 final, Cummins received a Facebook message asking him to get the team to sign a hurley for a cancer research fundraiser. Cummins didn't want to disappoint, so he rounded up the signatures and drove to Cahir, the designated meeting point, but found no sign of the other party. Back home to Ardfinnan, where the hurley was eventually collected at 10.30 p.m. – just three nights before the All-Ireland final.

'I wouldn't have dreamed of doing it the year before and I should have been selfish, ignorant maybe. But that was the change; your life wasn't your own any more.'

For Cummins, that period was a low point in his Tipp career. But for protracted difficulty, his lowest spell in the blue and gold coincided with an unpredictable and turbulent period for the team in general. Through the early to mid-noughties, Tipp could be either a joy or a mess, but they were seldom average. Before they played Limerick in the 2007 replayed Munster championship clash, Cummins was dropped from the starting team by Babs Keating. It was an astonishing and inexplicable move, one that reflected the general chaos in the county at the time.

It seemed Keating found Cummins difficult to mentor and felt the keeper was ignoring his advice on puck-out strategies, so about two hours before the championship opener with Limerick he dropped the bombshell – and his All Star keeper with it. Cummins was replaced with the rookie Gerry Kennedy, a fine young goalie whose intercounty career would suffer thereafter, perhaps because of that premature promotion.

A few weeks down the line, against Wexford, Eoin Kelly got the boot too, and camp insiders surmised that Keating was keen to take his best two players down a notch, for whatever reason. Both were model hurlers and born leaders. Cummins had started his first league game in 1993 and would last all the way to the end of the 2013 season before retiring. Kelly was virtually a one-man band up front at the time, performing hit after hit often with a bare minimum of backing support, repeatedly winning games almost single-handedly.

The stature and profile of those two stars meant massive scrutiny was heaped upon the county. In Tipp the hurling team has always had a singular grip on the popular psyche, and they were now enduring a new controversy with almost every passing week.

Before Babs took charge, the players had forced the curtailment of Michael Doyle's reign, letting it be known they wanted him gone after just one season. Ken Hogan, too, saw his term come to an abrupt end after two years. So it wasn't just Keating who reckoned a number of players needed to be shown their place in the natural order – many in the stands and on the terraces would have supported that view, and some would feel the problem persists. Not many, though, would have considered Kelly or Cummins the ones in need of a lesson.

As a county minor, Cummins registered 11 per cent on the body-fat index. When he retired twenty years later he was still at an exceptional 16 per cent. His days were a treadmill of routine – porridge in the morning, two litres of water through the day, lunch and a snack before training, most likely a couple of energy bars or a bag of popcorn. Semple Stadium forty-five minutes before training and back home at 10.30 p.m. for a cup of tea and a sandwich. Over the fridge was a bowl of fresh fruit and the kitchen was a chocolate-free zone. On rare evenings off, he would put his feet under the sofa and do a hundred sit-ups while watching TV. Each winter, before the team gathered for pre-season training, he clocked six weeks of four-mile runs three nights a week – just to make sure he set the tone early for others.

Despite the manager's eccentric style and left-field tactics, everyone continued to put shoulders to the wheel, but as Curran later acknowledged, they knew deep down that things weren't right: 'We were nowhere near challenging for titles at that stage. It was only when time had passed that you looked back and actually saw how far away we were.'

The following year, under Sheedy, the team won league and Munster titles and reached an All-Ireland semi-final. Cummins bounced back from his term in the wilderness and went on to win two further All Stars before calling time on his career. The slate had been wiped clean and rewritten.

On the night the 2007 All Stars were picked, Cummins had been in the throes of a training regime an Army Ranger might have winced at. He had won All Star awards in 2000 and 2001 and 2003 but had lately been surplus to requirements and, worse still, he was aware many of his erstwhile team-mates were well off the pace and drifting aimlessly. That night in Ardfinnan, as he reeled off laps of the field in murky darkness, he set clear goals for himself: 'I said that this time next year, on the same night, the team would be back in contention and I would be part of it – and an All Star again.'

Sure enough, Cummins arrived home from Dublin in 2008 with his fourth All Star, drove down to the Ardfinnan pitch and placed the trophy in the middle of the field. Another promise kept. That night he looked back on his 2007 diary one last time and waved goodbye to the madness of it all.

'I have a fifty-five-page Word document on everything that went on in '07: how training was going, what people said to me when I got the bullet. I gave a half-hour every day at end of work updating it before I went home. That might seem strange but it kept me going.'

After regaining his place he went on to win an All-Ireland, four more Munster titles and those All Stars, and yet he retired with a keen sense of the lost years. Though Tipp bowed out of the 2013 championship with some bit of dignity, losing an epic battle to Kilkenny at Nowlan Park, the charge remained that the team had badly underachieved. The widespread perception was that too many of the squad lacked discipline off the field and drank too much, though as Séamus Hennessy insisted, to tar the whole group with the same brush would be unfair.

'Some of those lads led lives of a consummate professional,' Hennessy stated. 'There were a few incidents, mostly after matches – no point in saying otherwise – and it led to the whole squad getting a reputation. That's not right. People say X and Y were out and did this and that and they assume Z was with them too, but you can't just assume stuff. That's what happened though.'

As Cummins has expressed it, the problem is a sign of the times: 'There was an issue with discipline there. It was a lifestyle thing. The average age of an intercounty hurler has dropped to about twenty-four and for continued success you need a strict code of conduct. Twenty years' experience of this game tells me you give a lad a chance but if he lets you down then its curtains no matter how good he is. It never works out if there is no discipline.

'Managers are caught in that regard. They need results and just one bad apple can affect the whole barrel. We're in danger now of losing a generation of under-21s from 2010 and we've already lost a few, that's the reality. It's up to them to change it. It's up to players to take responsibility.

'In our last three championship matches we lost twice to Kilkenny, once by eighteen points, and we lost to Limerick despite being four points up in the second half. We need to reset slightly. There might be some attrition when it comes to picking a team for 2014 but to make an omelette you must break eggs.'

Hennessy makes the point, though, that, apart from Limerick in 2013, Tipp were beaten by only one other team, Kilkenny, in championship hurling since 2010, something often forgotten when criticism rains down on former team-mates.

Tipperary added a new crop of youngsters to the set-up at the end of 2013 and, as Curran saw it, further changes in personnel would be inevitable over the following few years. Reflecting on the previous ten years, the Mullinahone man could foresee just as many ups and downs to come, but he also sensed renewed optimism, an air of better days ahead.

'There was a togetherness in the dressing room at Nowlan Park after we lost in 2013 and that's a real good sign. I always feel Tipperary can challenge in any given year. I know things have to be right but we have the hurlers and the tradition. We have a way of playing, a way that the Tipp supporters want, and we don't fear playing anyone. The main thing is that the whole squad is united.'

*

Perhaps the cruellest loss to the Tipp collective was that of Hennessy, whose career had been repeatedly stalled for three years with a knee cartilage that needed two operations and several visits to specialists. He had been fit for only three months of intercounty hurling out of thirty-six and also went all that time without starting a championship game for his club. And when injury struck again in the Waterford Crystal League final of 2013 it came, barring medical miracles, as the definitive blow.

Hennessy won a county junior B medal with Kilruane MacDonaghs at fourteen and had to be held back from playing senior by his father when he was fifteen. A Masters graduate from NUI Galway, he holds two All-Ireland minor medals, a Fitzgibbon Cup, one under-21 and one senior medal.

While others debated where to socialize after matches, Hennessy was trying to salvage his career. A born leader and proven match winner, he was one player who always called others into line when it was needed. His absence was bound to be sorely felt.

'A huge loss,' Cummins reflected. 'The influence he had on his peers; he just did everything right. Fellas were going out and not eating the right stuff, or not training enough, but Fez, as we call him, would come in and be in peak condition at all times of year and would put you to shame. He had no problem telling fellas to cop on.

'I was close to him on the night he got the news that his knee was in trouble again. He realized he was in huge bother that night and you could nearly cry for him. He had put huge rehab work in but he couldn't turn or twist. That loss of character and ability hurt us. He played well every day but he did things right – that's why.'

Hennessy himself accepted his likely fate with characteristic good grace: 'Look, if this is it for me I'm grateful to have won what I did. From fifteen to twenty-one it was "Win a title and now what's next?" The last three years have taken my career from me but thankfully I threw myself into college work, I have a good job, and I have worked with Pieta House and coached with college teams and the club here too so I've seen how to transfer certain qualities into different areas.

'The lads are still young, we have some fine hurlers in the county and I can see signs that players are starting to step up. Even though we've been heavily criticized I can see signs of a maturity there. Brendan Maher and Noel McGrath [the 2014 captain and vice-captain] drove a fundraising run for Eddie Connolly [the Tipperary and Loughmore-Castleiney hurler, who had an operation to remove a brain tumour] in December 2013 and for me that was a clear sign of unity. It was excellent. I take that as a huge positive.'

Several of the 2013 under-21 side particularly impressed O'Shea, who brought them into his senior squad, but the most urgent task as the year ended would be replacing Cummins – the obvious successors being Darren Gleeson, Darragh Egan, and the young contender James Logue – and building the team from there.

After twenty years of valiant service with one of the least predictable teams around, it was ironic that Cummins bowed out at the beginning of July 2013 in the most choreographed of scenarios.

The drama of the evening ran high: Nowlan Park, a vital qualifier game between sworn enemies, and a capacity 23,000 in attendance on one of the hottest nights of the summer. When it was announced Henry Shefflin would be among the substitutes, a wild cheer almost pierced the ozone layer. The stage was set for what was always going to be a Kilkenny win.

'It brought me back to when we played Clare in 1999 and 2000 and, oh my God, how I wish I could play those games for ever,' Cummins smiled. 'If I had one last breath, I'd ask to be taken back to those days or else Nowlan Park in 2013.

'When we played Clare it was genuine hatred. I met Davy Fitzgerald in Ballina around that time and cars were nearly swerving off the road to hit him. Loughnane, of course, was winding the whole thing up in the background.

'Clare were battling against everything that we stood for. The tradition, Nicky smiling in 1993 – they used everything. One of our players, Philly O'Dwyer, was cleaned out during the National Anthem, before the game even began. The game in Kilkenny was just like that.'

Tipp may not have won, but it was some way for one of the great hurling keepers – perhaps the greatest – to bid farewell. After the game he walked off disconsolate at losing, and equally upset at the thought of never again pulling on the blue and gold. Behind the faceguard he was weeping.

A Kilkenny woman and her daughter approached him looking for a hurl to be signed. When Cummins unclipped his helmet to oblige, revealing a tear-stained visage, the two autograph hunters were visibly upset.

'The poor daughter looked like she wanted the ground to open up and swallow her,' he recalled. 'I just said, "Well done and good luck the next day." I just walked into the dressing room, put a towel over my head and cried my eyes out. It was a milestone.'

For Cummins, with the exception of the 2009 final, that was the worst dressing room he had ever been in. Back in 2009 though, there had been the sense of a dynamic team emerging. Before that night ended, Sheedy had reassured everyone at the final banquet that Liam MacCarthy would be on the table twelve months later. The final act of 2013 was less gung-ho.

*

The future was in no way joyless, however; shoots of positivity are perennial within the Premier County. Since 2006, Tipp had won three minor All-Irelands – though in 2013 Eamon O'Shea was still remaining loyal to a large core of relative veterans.

There was also the Paudie Maher factor. The rock on which a winning team could be built, he has increasingly been the one opponents seek, with ever more sophisticated strategies, to nullify, and Tipp would need to respond to those threats.

And so as Cummins walked out of Nowlan Park that July Saturday evening in 2013, it was difficult to predict what lay ahead for the county to which he had given long and heroic service. Of course, even in defeat the Tipp faithful, born and bred to the game and steeped in a tradition of achievement, would live in hope of the next victory, the next glorious campaign.

15

Third-Level Playing Fields

How Cork looked to the colleges for
suitably qualified talent

When Tom Kenny stepped off the Cork hurling carousel in late 2013, he left Brian Murphy behind him as the sole survivor of the 2005 All-Ireland-winning team. Kenny was only thirty-two when he walked, still as nimble as a gymnast. He had seen plenty of game time during a lengthy 2013 season but had surrendered his starting place by the end of that tumultuous campaign and was unlikely to ever reclaim it.

Just a few weeks after his retirement, however, the Cork hurling trainer David Matthews reckoned Kenny could have continued for another season at least. Matthews recounted how he kept using the word 'perfect' to describe everything Kenny did in training. Team-mates would laugh conspiratorially at mention of the 'p' word, leaving Matthews frequently bemused. It was only after some months that he learned Kenny's nickname was indeed 'Perfect Tom' – it had stuck to him ten years previously.

Kenny was such a role model that Matthews would often

pick him from a line-up of the usual suspects and have him demonstrate a skill or a new drill. Quite simply, he was a guy who did everything right: a sprinter and middle-distance runner rolled into one, with perfect stride, foot plant, balance and cadence. He was a bloody good hurler too.

While Matthews could see no reason for Kenny to retire, the player himself clearly discerned the writing on the pitch. As deft and dynamic as he was, the game itself had moved on. Clare's all-action forwards had frequently rampaged past Cork defenders in both finals – draw and replay. The average age of the Clare team was twenty-three, of the Cork team twenty-four. Kenny was a decade beyond that and felt his time was up. He moved on without rancour between himself and management – an amicable separation, perhaps unlike others, during the first two years of Jimmy Barry-Murphy's second coming with Cork.

As the former coach Ger Cunningham put it, change is always hard, but in Cork it is essential to ensure a future: 'In general if you put two lads up against each other for a place, Jimmy [Barry-Murphy] will always go for the younger fella. He won an All-Ireland in 1999 operating on that basis and that's the way it has been during his second stint in charge too.'

Not all Kenny's former team-mates departed the battleground so quietly. When he was left off the squad, Dónal Óg Cusack felt he could have battled his way back into contention for the number one shirt, or at least should have been given the chance to try. Cusack suffered a horrific Achilles tendon injury but recovered by dint of high-intensity rehab. When Barry-Murphy sat into his car and told the Cloyne man his time was up their conversation was brief.

Cusack felt he deserved better. He had been the main architect of the county's 2004 and 2005 All-Ireland wins. He was not only their last line of defence but also their first source of attack, revolutionizing and extending the goalkeeper's role. By the time he left he had turned the duties of the number one into those of a quarterback.

Yet hindsight would vindicate Barry-Murphy. Cusack's replacement, Anthony Nash, won back-to-back All Stars and captured the imagination of the public, selling more replica jerseys in a season than the rest of the team combined. He also brought the goalkeeper's remit even further, becoming a primary source of scores with his deadly accurate long-range and lethal short-range frees.

Like Cusack, the equally iconic Seán Óg Ó hAilpín was offered minimal sympathy when made surplus to requirements and decided to retire. He was initially scathing of the manager's decision but by the time his autobiography was published the Na Piarsaigh man had seen Barry-Murphy's vision for the future and had softened.

Seánie McGrath retired from the top flight at twenty-eight years of age and ten years later was back as a selector helping to mentor the players of the future. Team-mates that backboned the 1999 side had all departed and few left without some upset. McGrath has said, however, that deep down they recognized the need for rebuilding: 'When Jimmy took over a lot of the older lads were still involved and it was hard to change and hard for them to change too. Before they walked away – or were let go – they probably would have read between the lines and realized what was happening. We had to go with youth.'

McGrath won underage and senior crowns with some of those who were jettisoned and then was part of the management team that cut them free. He admitted the ruptures were awkward but would claim there was no lingering animosity: 'I would have no problem with any of those lads. I wouldn't socialize with them frequently but we'd always chat away when we'd meet. I was gone myself from the intercounty stage at twenty-eight, which was young, and I had been away from the scene for ten years, so when I came back into it I didn't really have any baggage. It's never easy to be let go when you've given such service and commitment and you pledge yourself to the cause.'

Of all the players left out, John Gardiner was possibly the one with most cause for grievance, having been cut adrift before he even hit thirty. Gardiner could feasibly have played some type of defensive role in 2013 and would have brought some much-needed steel to the ranks, but his cards were folded for him.

The experienced Niall McCarthy also drifted from the scene. The O'Connor twins walked off into the sunset with a catalogue of golden memories. One by one the all-conquering team of the nineties had disappeared.

'And they were some team,' said D. J. Carey. 'When you beat them and won an All-Ireland you knew you deserved it. They found a way to combat the Kilkenny game plan and they were brave enough to stick to their guns. They had their own problems over the years with the three strikes and the high-profile departures but at the end of the day there is massive respect for them out there. They were slated for short puck-outs and short passes, but they held firm and it won two All-Irelands for them.'

Cusack, Ó hAilpín and Brian Corcoran all devoted chunks of autobiographies to their irresistible running game, as well as the equally groundbreaking strikes against the county board that ensued. Years on, some of the wounds inflicted by those walkouts were still taking time to heal. But there remained numerous differences of opinion between former friends and colleagues that may never be reconciled.

The legacy of those strikes proved a shocking one. A team

that had won all before them at underage graduated to senior and within six years landed three All-Ireland titles. Tragically, they came to feel disrespected and undervalued by a county board they saw, rightly or wrongly, as tight, insensitive and anti-player. The players went on the offensive and appeared to spend more time dealing with solicitors and mediators than wielding hurleys. By the time they took on the board for a third round of wrangling, the entire GAA world, never mind the good people of Cork, had grown weary of the saga.

Meanwhile, the county board, already found wanting in several areas, took their eye off the ball in terms of underage development. From the early noughties and on into the current decade, Cork, apart from winning a few provincial titles at minor and under-21, made little mark on the national stage. But the slide went largely unnoticed because, when they lost, it was often by only a point or two. It wasn't until July 2013 that the cracks became a sinkhole, revealing foundations of rubble.

It was left to the under-21 manager, Ger Fitzgerald, to take the heat. Under a searing Thurles sun his team wilted to a humiliating defeat by Tipperary in the Munster semi-final, the margin 5-19 to 2-13. As supporters packed up and departed the stadium, that damning final tally still flashed on the electronic scoreboard, mocking any Corkman or Corkwoman careless enough to glance up.

Fitzgerald took the rap but he had been badly served by a parched academy system. Tipp may have underachieved at senior but they were still churning out the cream of young talent. Cork's supply, in contrast, was running dry.

Fitzgerald apologized in the wake of that shocking setback. There was little to hide behind but, unlike other county board officials and some former managers, he had the testicular fortitude to stand up and be counted. One of the proudest hurling counties was in the throes of an underage crisis and he didn't fudge the issue: 'It certainly wasn't a good sign. And I don't know if this was just a one-off, because we thought we had a really strong team and a strong panel, and I never saw it coming. I can't put my finger on the reason why we didn't perform. We were so inept. I still believe there are good hurlers coming through in Cork – maybe not enough of them – but we are in a downward spiral at the moment, and we're finding it very difficult to get out of it.'

That result told you all you needed to know about the Cork underage scene. Moral victories in the years leading up to the collapse had allowed all involved to convince themselves they weren't too far off the pace. The Tipp game finally blew away those illusions.

Most of the under-21 players that suffered that five-goal humiliation had grown up with no peers to emulate and formed part of a faltering academy that had failed to win an All-Ireland minor title since 2001 and had not seen an under-21 crown since 1998. As for Munster titles, the minors hadn't won one since 2008, the under-21s since 2007. A traditional powerhouse had serious developmental flaws.

Critical investigation would have shown that the underage programme lacked structure, cohesion and inspiration. There was no shortage of hardworking people, but they weren't always the right people. Too few past players were putting it back in, and so coaching standards were off too. Against this backdrop even the sheer size of the county proved a hindrance.

The decline of Cork teams in schools competition had long since set in. Famed nurseries that once provided rich pickings for the county's underage selectors – the likes of North Mon, Farranferris, St Colman's and Críost Rí – had regressed. Some even reverted to B competition. The 2014 season, through the emergence of Rochestown College and Hamilton High School, was the first of any promise since 2006, when Midleton CBS, captained by Paudie O'Sullivan and featuring Luke O'Farrell, had last claimed the Harty Cup for a Cork school.

Keeping the flame alight at senior level was hard enough for Barry–Murphy, but the backdrop to the 2013 championship was less certain than it had ever been. Eoin Cadogan announced on Twitter that he would concentrate on football for the foreseeable future. Damien Cahalane also joined the footballers. Darren Sweetnam, who had shown tremendous promise in his debut season, pursued a Munster rugby contract. Niall McCarthy headed to Australia. Then you had Gardiner, only twenty-nine at the time, Cusack and Ó hAilpín, left in no doubt they were out of the loop.

And yet, eighteen months into his second term as boss, Barry–Murphy had Cork back in an All-Ireland final – after three semi-final appearances in five years. As the massed Cork fans gazed out from the lofty vantage points of the Cusack and Hogan stands in September, many must surely have pondered how Barry–Murphy had managed to build so impressively on a proverbial sandbank.

According to Seánie McGrath, much of it has been less about rocket science than about Barry–Murphy's pragmatism and common sense: 'Jimmy just has an ability to click with a player, read him, identify areas to improve on and do it all quickly.'

It's staggering that Cork were but a hair's breadth away from beating Clare in the 2013 drawn All-Ireland final. This, after all, was a Clare team running on the impetus provided by a relentless underage machine; they had reached the All-Ireland minor final in 2010 and landed three under-21 titles since 2009.

Perhaps only Cork could pull off such senior heroics with their own minor and under-21s stuck in the dark ages. And yet, as McGrath would argue, it wasn't entirely an aberration: 'Yes, the progress at senior level came a little earlier than anticipated but we didn't get to the final playing this "we're Cork we can do what we want" card. Any Cork team I was ever involved with had prepared well and worked tirelessly on touch and tactics. After that maybe we could take a bit of encouragement from our tradition, but that won't win you games any more.

'Every major hurling county in Munster is at the same level as ourselves – though ahead of us at underage – so there's little to separate us. I know Clare were better than us in both All-Ireland finals, but I still don't know if they're a better team than us. Time will tell.'

And so a proud county, huge in geographical extent and built on a massive hurling tradition, had to look hard for raw materials. Again, possibly only Cork could have papered over the cracks as they managed to do.

They turned to third-level hurling, and specifically tapped into the Fitzgibbon Cup successes of University College Cork and Cork Institute of Technology, in a bid to thrive again at intercounty. The strategy largely worked. The Fitzgibbon Cup has always been highly regarded in Cork, and in the teens it has effectively kept the county ticking over.

When UCC and CIT met in the 2012 Fitzgibbon Cup final it was only the second time in history two colleges from the same city clashed in a decider, and twenty-six of the forty-two players involved were from the Rebel County. Darren McCarthy, Killian Murphy, William Egan, Conor Lehane and Séamus Harnedy all went on to benefit with the county team from that experience.

Sixteen of the squad beaten in the 2013 All-Ireland final replay studied at UCC and four attended CIT. In all, twenty-seven players from the Cork and Clare teams had recent Fitzgibbon Cup experience.

'And we've a few more lads to come in over the next year or so,' McGrath said. 'The Fitzgibbon Cup was always huge in Cork; it sparked All-Ireland wins for the county in the mid-eighties and the late nineties and beyond. But it's after taking on a life of its own down here now because we've been starved of underage success. We don't specifically go to games, see a guy and just thrust him into the Cork senior squad – most of the fellas who make it would already have been on our radar – but what the competition does is give them the opportunity to mix it on the big stage and it lets us see how they cope from there. They usually cope just grand.'

Harnedy proved a classic example. Hailing from a small junior club, St Ita's in East Cork, he became a Cork senior after excelling for UCC at fresher grade and then Fitzgibbon Cup. From there he went on to become a first-team regular and an All Star. It was a fairytale story.

'That's the job of UCC,' said the college's freshers manager, Ger Cunningham, who stepped down as Cork senior coach at the end of 2013. 'We get them into the ethos of the college straight away; they look after their education and we look after them hurling-wise. Most of the lads are from Cork so they know there's a window to make it. Their clubs will have developed them, but we give them big-game exposure and in the case of Séamus he was able to play against Clare in front of eighty-two thousand people on both All-Ireland final days knowing he had marked Pat O'Connor before at colleges level and had always done very well on him. That's huge belief. Playing for UCC definitely gave him a platform. But he did the rest himself.'

John Grainger, the GAA Development Officer at UCC, has

made the point that the college – and the way it treat its players – offers an overall balance to a student's life that can only help him develop: 'Hurling's age profile is radically changing and that is putting a lot of pressure on younger students.

'When I studied here, I did an arts degree and there wasn't an ounce of pressure on me. These days a lot of the fellas have to combine study, college and intercounty life. If you are thirty playing intercounty you are almost part of a dying breed now so it puts the onus back on these young fellas.

'We treat them great here – there is huge craic – but I go back to the pressure they experience in their overall life. More and more of them would come looking for the chat the odd time. Maybe the studies are getting on top of them, things might not be great at home, and then they have to worry about what to do when they leave here. Jobs are not plentiful and even having a Masters will not guarantee them work, so there's a threat of emigration hanging over them.

'That's the first thing to say – we recognize all those things. Then we have to ensure there are good lines of communication between UCC and the various intercounty managers. But we can help them too. Ger [Cunningham] has had the freshers on top of the charts for the last five years and we can feed Cork and other counties because there's a huge number of young players in the Liam MacCarthy senior championship. Clare, with the exception of two or three, were basically a Fitzgibbon Cup team. Over half of all the panels in the top ten counties are under the age of twenty-one – that's a frightening statistic. Only six years ago it was about twenty per cent.

'For the likes of Cork, who haven't been winning huge amounts at underage, this is a crucial development. We have to step up to the mark at underage.'

With that in mind Barry-Murphy is looking further down the

line than third-level for talent. Hamilton HS caught the eye with a fine 2014 Harty Cup campaign but by the time they figured on the public radar, the Cork manager already had their best player, Michael Cahalane, co-opted to his squad.

Seánie McGrath was a selector with the Cork minors in 2010 and Barry-Murphy has tapped into his connection with the emerging youngsters. Each night at training, walking into a dressing room full of kids, McGrath has seen the continuing evolution at close quarters.

McGrath has also been witness to a sea change in attitudes and lifestyle, a generational thing, but has not at all been fazed by it – indeed he finds it highly entertaining: 'They're gas young lads. Jesus, in my day if you were seen combing your hair you were destroyed. But these lads, they love it. You could say they're metrosexuals. They love the oul muscle tops, gelling up the hair, the clothes they wear. And they don't give a shit if you have a crack at them for it – they just don't care. And though they're not roaring down the walls of the dressing room with big speeches they go out on the field and do the job for us. Hopefully there's a lot more to come from them yet.

'The Fitzgibbon Cup was the first competition Jimmy delved into when he took the job for the second time in 2012. There were no signs of the underage structure making an immediate improvement at that stage so he went with what he saw. And I think he will always go in the direction of youth.'

Unlike the warriors of the past, who downed tools and fought the board for what they believed were basic rights, the emerging youngsters seem blissfully free of political baggage – or indeed any baggage.

'When Limerick beat us in the 2013 Munster final we were very down, but those lads are so young and resilient they bounced straight back,' McGrath recalled. 'On the following Thursday night you'd have sworn we won the game – they were in a terrific frame of mind and they lifted us. We knew when we met Kilkenny a few weeks later we had a great chance of beating them and we did. Things took off from there. That's what youth gives you – fearlessness. And we won't stop.'

By the start of the 2014 championship the county board had finally made some inroads into nurturing its own underage academy by totally restructuring the template. There had been eight divisions in the county, but with population trends shifting families from rural to urban areas, refinement was needed. They changed to six grades at every level of underage hurling, from Premier One and Two (for urban teams) to A and B (for rural teams) to twelve-a-side C and D (for small clubs unable to field full teams). It helped streamline fixtures and help clubs struggling for numbers.

Anomalies were bound to persist, such as clubs sixty miles apart ending up in the same competition, but the eight divisional boards were cut to four, while every club was put in a league where they could compete. The programme would need to be given ten years to work to its optimum, but should ultimately repay the effort.

'It might take some time,' admitted Cunningham in early 2014, 'but I think the first seeds are already coming through. Rochestown College and Hamilton HS did so well in the 2014 Harty Cup, which was a massive achievement, and we seem to have a nice flow of youngsters coming through at all levels.'

Apart from looking after the UCC freshers, Cunningham also oversees the Cork under-15 development squad: 'We're getting organized. Our job with the under-fifteens is to let them know that minor hurling is not too far off the radar. We want to mobilize these lads, and I'm looking forward to passing back some knowledge to them. They're the future and I want to work with them and see what they're thinking, try to talk their language. And more importantly, see what's coming along the production lines in the county. If we don't get these lads through there will be no one to push the lads on the current senior team. That will only lead to a comfort zone. And we don't need that.'

The wheel has been turning. In 2001, for instance, the county board allowed Duhallow to enter the minor championship as a divisional side and they went on to contest three county minor finals and two under-21 finals. In the process players like Anthony Nash, Lorcán McLoughlin, William Egan and Mark Ellis came through.

'You don't necessarily have to be winning finals – but reaching finals – and getting to that stage is paramount at underage level,' said Cunningham.

While Cork waited for the teams of tomorrow to take shape, they were boosted early in 2014 by the return of Eoin Cadogan to their ranks. Aidan Walsh, another dual player, followed him. Mark Collins and Damien Cahalane were being pursued.

'They would be welcomed because I still don't think we played particularly well in either the All-Ireland final or the replay,' McGrath reflected. 'Patrick Horgan was our key forward and I think he got only four touches in the replay.

'But those finals were all about drama, expectation and pressure. That's where Anthony Nash has become a real leader. Think about it – in no sport does a guy have such a long run to the ball [a reference to the keeper's forays upfield for penalties and twenty-metre frees]. He's thinking, where will I put this? Is my hurley okay? Will someone clatter into me on the way up? Will I get back to my goal in time? And then they flood the goal-line with thirteen players and nine times out of ten he will still nail it for you. It's a disgrace that the GAA tried to stop him from what he was doing by looking for rule changes. A lot of that stems from jealousy. All I can say is he is a leader. He is going to drive us on in the years to come. Nash will make sure the youngsters hit their potential.'

Potential is the keyword. Imagine what Cork could achieve with all their best players available and an academy firing on all cylinders.

16

When the Banner
Roared Again

How Clare had to think differently before
they could play differently

Ten years after the crazy highs of the nineties, Clare senior hurling was overhung by dark clouds, and shafts of sunlight were few and faint. The start of the noughties had been a period of stability and grit, an ageing group hanging on in there to reach the 2002 All-Ireland final before the inevitable decline set in.

The latter half of the decade was marked by regression and personality clashes, and the slide got steeper when, in January 2007, the county's iconic goalkeeper, Davy Fitzgerald, had a difference of opinion with the senior team manager, Tony Considine. Fitzgerald pulled out of the squad, and a subsequent clear-the-air meeting between the two brought no resolution.

There was proof of further disharmony when the highly rated trainer Dave Mahedy also severed links with the set-up. At the end of February, Ger Ward, a selector, was next to pull the plug, citing 'business commitments' – whereupon another selector,

Tim Crowe, was moved to lambast those he alleged were 'carrying out a witch-hunt' with the aim of forcing Considine to resign.

March arrived and though the Burren was starting to clothe itself in small riots of springtime colour, the Clare hurling landscape remained bleak with uncertainty. The county board enlisted the services of Martin Lynch to mediate between Considine and Fitzgerald but by April there was still no end to the row.

Considine, meanwhile, still had the board on his back. Everywhere he looked there seemed to be an issue. The executive insisted county players be made available for club games, whereas Considine had told his men not to play club fixtures ahead of their championship date with Cork. Incredibly, at the start of May, just twenty-three days before that Cork shootout, a vote of no confidence was proposed against Considine. It was the last thing he, the team and the county needed.

And yet the plot thickened. Considine survived before the team captain, Frank Lohan, got publicly involved, reiterating his support for the manager, insisting the players would not be distracted by backroom dissension and pleading that they be let get on with the job in hand.

On 27 May, after months of turmoil, Clare got to play Cork and lost by seven points. They did win three games in the qualifiers, but lost to Limerick in an All-Ireland quarter-final – again by seven points – and were out of the championship by July. And Considine, despite those three wins, was out too.

Mike McNamara took over in 2008 and brought the team to a Munster final and an All-Ireland quarter-final, where they lost by two points to Cork. The following season, though, was a disaster, McNamara in turn experiencing serious problems with panellists. He resigned with a heavy heart in December 2009, releasing an emotive statement referring to 'indiscipline', 'lack of quality' and 'agendas' in the set-up.

The Scariff man had been managing, training and coaching intercounty teams for twenty years and had roles in the preparation of eleven teams that reached provincial finals, five of which were victorious. Five of those teams also made All-Ireland finals, three of them winning. The modern-day Clare were going nowhere, however. The entire triumvirate that oversaw their 1995 and 1997 successes – Considine, McNamara and Ger Loughnane, all had stints in charge but the aura of those glory days had well and truly faded.

Against that backdrop, a committee consisting of four former hurlers – Jamesie O'Connor, Seánie McMahon, Brian Quinn and Jim McInerney – convened to redesign the template for development squads. Maybe ruling out hope of senior success any time soon, even though they had won the 2009 All-Ireland under-21 title, they figured they might as well get things right nearer the foundations. At the time Seán O'Halloran, the Clare Bord na nÓg chairman, was virtually ploughing a lone furrow, his job description as wide as the Ardnacrusha dam – he took on every job from seeking out training venues to marking pitches to rounding up volunteers to raising funds.

One summer's evening O'Halloran took a phonecall from an irate parent who had dropped his son to Clare under-14 training only to find the designated mentor or coach conspicuous by his absence. The father on the other end of the line was Gerry O'Connor, a former intermediate full-back for Killanena, normally easygoing, not prone to histrionics, but now demanding answers and quick. The conversation went roughly as follows.

'Seán, what's the story? I dropped the young lad down for training but there was no one to coach them. That's a joke.'

'I couldn't agree more, Gerry. But what about yourself? What are you doing on Thursday night?'

The Bord na nÓg chairman didn't know it at the time but O'Connor was exactly the type of coach he was looking for – open-minded and forward-thinking and representative of a flock of young men that had moved from rural to urban areas like Ennis and suburbs. Just outside Limerick city, for instance, hurling fraternities had started to spring up, and new teams in Cratloe and Clonlara were guided by people such as Joe McGrath, originally from Toomevara in Tipperary, and Colm Collins. Both were coaches who looked for inspiration outside traditional parameters.

O'Connor, though, had had his fill of hurling for a while. Or so he thought. He had recently retired from junior B hurling with Killanena and a new set of golf clubs stood in the garage waiting eagerly to be broken in. He was looking forward to mastering a different game – assuming of course he could cut out the time from a hectic day job, which entailed travelling not only at home but also abroad with the Shannon-based Mincon.

Which was why on the night he phoned O'Halloran to register his protest, coaching was the last thing on his mind and his initial response to the cheeky invitation was blunt: 'No way, Seán. I'm just too busy with work.'

That Thursday evening, however, he became an accidental coach. He went to help a bunch of under-14s and found he couldn't step away. And so fast-forward to 2014, and O'Connor's golfing CV was still disfigured by a handicap of twenty-two. Hurling had not only kept him firmly in its grip; it had brought him places he hardly dreamed of.

'I threw myself into it of course with men like P. J. Kelleher and Eamon Fennessy and we looked after the under-14s and under-15s. Two years later I asked my friend Donal Moloney to come and join us with the under-16s. Back then someone would coach an East Clare under-16 selection and someone else would look after Mid-Clare – they were two independent republics.

'This time we worked together – we played each other in the Nenagh Co-Op under-16 semi-final but worked in unison, which allowed us to look at every possible player. So instead of having twenty-five lads, we looked at sixty. That's where we saw smaller, speedy, skilful guys like Séadna Morey and Cathal O'Connell and how much trouble they gave a bigger, stronger guy. We thought there was something in that.'

Moloney and O'Connor had grown up only eight miles apart but, having moved away and spent time working abroad, hadn't seen each other in twenty years. When they did meet again it was just a nod here and there – usually at their local bar, the Halfway House – until one night they renewed acquaintance, talked about hurling, recognized a shared passion for the game and became friends again.

The friendship strengthened during two years in charge of the Clare under-16s, and they were persuaded to bid for the vacant Clare minor job. They got that and ended up working with the iconic former full-back Brian Lohan. They had no grandiose targets or goals. Mostly they just wanted to change the way Clare did business.

According to Moloney, no one else really wanted that minor job: 'There were lots of big names that had hurled for Clare on the coaching circuit but there weren't too many hands in the air for that particular role – which is probably why we got it.'

Both men came from rural backgrounds, farming stock, and would admit they grew up in a traditional, highly conservative environment. It's remarkable that they helped inject so much freshness and variety into the set-up.

'I'm from the heart of East Clare, from the top of the mountain,' said O'Connor. 'Donal's farm is just up the road. For twenty years we would go down to Thurles to watch Clare and we'd be beat out the gate. Year in, year out, for as long as I can remember. We just wanted to try and change that.

'What we had was a savage interest in the game and an ability to look outside the box for coaching purposes. I was only a club full-back. Donal, in fairness, played underage and senior for Clare – although sporadically as he says himself. But we really had a drive to learn more.'

For good measure the pair brought exceptional business acumen: O'Connor, as noted, a world-travelled manager; Moloney supply-chain director at DePuy Johnson & Johnson in Cork. Time was of the essence for both so they adapted a simple business template to their own sessions.

Management duties would be shared; egos would take a back seat. They would look upon each game in terms of a business target and once the 'quota' was reached – in other words, the game won – they would set about reaching the next quota. Games were reviewed on a business model, data indicating what worked and what didn't.

The results weren't long in showing – you could say they were soon in business – and they have brought a trophy to Clare hurling in almost every year of their involvement. They took the county to successive Munster minor titles and then back-to-back Munster and All-Ireland under-21 titles. And they landed an All-Ireland intermediate title along the way. Previously, Clare had claimed just two Munster minor titles and one Munster under-21 title in their entire history.

And yet O'Connor and Moloney were quick to apportion credit where due. As Moloney has said, for them it's always been about the management 'team': 'Men like Paul Kinnerk, Mikey

Kiely and Jimmy Browne have all come in after we worked with Eamon, P.J. and others. All four of us over those under-21 teams, for instance, had different strengths and weaknesses. But we challenged each other for the benefit of Clare hurling.'

O'Connor agreed: 'I fully believe that if you employ or hire someone for a company, that person has to be able to threaten you in a positive way. We applied the same principles to hurling. We went looking for a coach and asked Alan Cunningham to train our minor team. He couldn't do it, but he put us in touch with Paul Kinnerk, a young Limerick footballer. That guy was way ahead of his time. For the first few weeks before the 2010 minor championship all we did was fight with Paul, but after a while we could see he was right. And boy was he right!'

When Clare were beaten by Waterford in the 2009 Munster minor semi-final, Lohan left the set-up but the two friends hung on, still hoping to get the chance to change the Clare hurling mindset, but fearing their views would be dismissed. They had looked on and seen players on the run hooked repeatedly because they were unable to shorten their grip. There was an ingrained habit of striking off the back foot. Ball to the forwards was often high, wide and aimless, and with Clare not being much of an aerial power, the end product was disastrous – much like the sequence of match results. In short, there was much to work on.

But the Clare board saw enough potential to give the pair the 2010 season, and it was in early May that year that Tony Kelly sealed a famous win – and with it the immediate futures of the co-managers.

Tipperary had travelled to Ennis as unbackable favourites to win a Munster minor play-off and against a Clare team already heavily defeated by Waterford and with their season – and the managerial careers of Moloney and O'Connor – dangling by a thread. With seconds to spare, Kelly posted the winning point. Clare went on to win the provincial final, and though they suffered a heartbreaking loss in the All-Ireland final, the journey had started.

'And that's exactly what this is,' O'Connor said. 'A journey. Look at what those lads have won since and under Davy Fitz at senior level and sure I think those lads are gone past counting medals even now – they just want to see where this journey takes them. We're only a small part of the story; we're just passing through. And had Tony not hit that point in 2010 we would have been an even smaller part of the story.'

Tears flowed in the dressing room after the 2010 All-Ireland minor final but they had developed and nurtured enough talent for the under-21s to deem the year a success. Players were coming through with a specific style. By happy coincidence, Davy Fitzgerald was operating to a similar philosophy below in Waterford. But east being east and west being west, little did people expect the impact those cultures would have three years down the road when eventually the twain did meet.

So what changed along the way? Well, for a start Clare teams stopped pumping snow-covered sliotar down on top of their forwards. The high-powered committee overseeing the rejuvenation of the development squads had long since deduced that aerial skill was a dying art in the county, and so O'Connor and Moloney took stock of the players they had – mostly under six feet, blessed with touch and speed, nifty as terriers in a rabbit warren – and decided they would play to a different beat.

Why try to win ball in the air when you didn't have to? They would work the ball purposefully out of defence, keeping it below head height as much as possible. When the sliotar did go high they would try breaking it to a team-mate rather than contesting the catch.

Back with the minor and under-21s, the joint managers had looked at Ulster football drills to identify a clear tackling strategy they would then bring to the training field for months of refining.

For O'Connor the incongruity of the lofted ball was glaring: 'It's gas – in all the training drills the ball was never above head height. Then you went to play a match and it was in the clouds most of the time. It made no sense. We put a huge emphasis on an aerial game of a different type. In a sense, Podge Collins should not have played at centre-forward on our 2013 under-21 team because he was too small for that position, but it's not about winning possession – it's about directing the ball.'

In the 2013 Munster final, Clare put Collins on Tipp's defensive lynchpin, Tomás Hamill. At the other end they resolved to quieten Niall O'Meara, Tipp's most promising attacker: 'We knew we couldn't beat Tipp if we went out and tried to catch ball over their heads, but that's where Podge came in; he doesn't catch – he holds the hurl at an angle, runs on to it and breaks it for the others.

'The first ball in that final was always going down on top of Hamill. You attack the opposition at the point where they think they are strongest. A high ball came down, it was made for Hamill and up he went for it. Podge shifted his feet, went late off the ground and broke it. Suddenly there were doubts in Tipp heads. You could see the same tactic in the 2013 All-Ireland senior final replay. Everyone expected Clare to look for John Conlon again that day but they fooled Cork by going for Colin Ryan, and he continually brought the ball down on the hurley in front of his man.'

In under-21 training they would split into corners of four:

O'Connor would focus on tackling, Browne on goalkeeping and off-the-ball running, Moloney on the forwards and Kiely on sidestepping and peripheral vision. Every session ended with a five-minute goal-scoring drill. As O'Connor explained, they had seen how Tipperary spurned gilt-edged chances in the 2009 All-Ireland final and were determined not to go there: 'Tipp players were one on one with P. J. Ryan, the Kilkenny goalkeeper, three times but there was no goal. Imagine what that did to the confidence of the Tipp team.'

Their tack would be simple – players homing in on the net have to hammer the sliotar off the sod while forcing the keeper to switch hands to get to it – in other words to plant it to his weak side. Maybe the coolness with which Shane O'Donnell nabbed his hat-trick in the replayed 2013 senior decider came from this drill.

The managers and backroom continued to look for inspiration, and their prayers were answered when Kinnerk came on board. He was a relatively unknown footballer who had studied PE under Dr Cian O'Neill at the University of Limerick and very few about the place had heard of him.

'We soon saw Paul was on a different planet from the rest of us,' said O'Connor. 'Since he arrived in 2010, he has helped us win a Munster championship every year at some level. That's why he soon went to the senior set-up. Davy knows how good Paul is – and he lets him at it. Everything with Paul is done through conditioned games played with manic intensity. It's all match-related. Paul is special and we're lucky to have him.'

It took the punters a while to appreciate what the new-look Clare were about. Former players watched Kinnerk in action, with those choreographed training games where everything related to match situations. He would frequently blow a halt and get players to re-enact a drill until he was happy with it. And everything had to be done at warp speed.

The natives were restless for quite a while. They wondered if he was in the real world at all. Early in Fitzgerald's reign as senior manager in 2012 frustrated fans would berate players for failing to hit it long. Fitzgerald and Co heard the words of abuse, but turned a deaf ear.

What they were doing was quite alien to the traditional Clare way. But save for 1995 and 1997, the traditional Clare way had yielded little in terms of glory or success. So in a sense it suited Fitzgerald at senior – and O'Connor and Moloney at underage – that people disagreed with them: it suggested they might be on to something.

O'Connor and Moloney also took on the Clare intermediates in 2011 and guided them to an All-Ireland title. While that team hasn't won since, it gave David McInerney a first audition at full-back for Clare and Conor Ryan his chance at centre-back. Both players later won All-Ireland senior medals in those positions, despite having started out as forwards. That's some legacy for an intermediate team. But there was more: thirteen of the nineteen intermediates of 2013 were so young they didn't even make the starting fifteen for that year's All Ireland-winning under-21s.

With success flying left, right and centre, Fitzgerald, O'Connor and Moloney worked hard to maintain perspective in the camp. On the Tuesday before the 2013 All-Ireland final Fitzgerald met a close friend and asserted he would have no problem keeping the players' feet on the ground when they won. His friend re-minded him that since there was the small matter of winning still to be negotiated it was surely a case of 'if' rather than 'when', but Fitzgerald was adamant they would indeed win – and how to handle victory was already high on the agenda.

A similar emphasis on balance and self-control was also well established at underage, where, according to O'Connor, the approach was entirely holistic: 'The All Blacks have a saying when someone comes into their camp – no dickheads. That's basically our mantra as well.'

When they played Galway in the 2013 under-21 All-Ireland semi-final the managers noticed that Davy O'Halloran was suffering from corner-forward syndrome – fear of being the first player taken off. O'Halloran didn't figure in the win against Waterford but came on and excelled against Tipp and was rewarded with a start against Galway, but struggled in that game to find the target. And so the backroom team changed tactics on the hoof; they told the youngster to forget about scoring but demanded he execute ten tackles and force five turnovers.

O'Halloran went back on to the field after the half-time break and tackled like a maniac on speed. Indeed, he was so preoccupied with making tackles and reclaiming the ball that he hardly noticed his two points from play.

To help the young players cope with increasing expectations, Moloney and O'Connor had sought counsel from several other coaches over the years – from Kilkenny's underage development maestro Richie Mulrooney to the Tipp manager Eamon O'Shea to the national boxing coach Billy Walsh. One message prevailed: look after players away from sport and other elements will fall into place.

'We see these young lads as more than just a product,' said O'Connor. 'You have to help them in seeking employment, and before you worry about their discipline and how they handle success you have to worry about their personal development –

their academic life, for example. All bar one or two of them are in college.

'Davy Fitzgerald preaches the same message, but this is where Jimmy Browne stands out more than anyone else in Clare hurling. All those lads who have won All-Ireland under-21 and senior medals – Jimmy has career-guided most of those lads in one way or another.'

Browne, vice-president and financial controller at Limerick Institute of Technology, was for ever asking players about their academic choices and long-term plans. He would take guys aside, fellas with over five hundred Leaving Cert points, and get them to think twice about courses they were doing, suggesting alternatives.

'When players see you care about their personal lives they respond,' said Moloney. 'And the parents have seen that with us. We will not just dispose of the lads; our approach is to develop them not alone hurling-wise but personality-wise too. Then they will buy into your discipline code without even thinking about it. If they fail academically and in terms of discipline they will feel as if they've let down a lot of people. Davy has followed on from that by instilling ferocious discipline in his squad and so it's a natural progression.'

O'Connor knows players will move away and fall out of the Clare hurling system, but he hopes their efforts will have set the standard for all those who follow. He is also humble in reflecting on what they've achieved with the academy: 'We have had some of the best players to ever put on a Clare jersey. Sheer natural talent and ability is what they bring. You don't win anything without that. We've been fortunate that our reign coincided with the emergence of these guys. Clare produces the likes of Tony Kelly only once every twenty years – a guy who needs no coaching whatsoever.'

*

When Davy Fitzgerald's term with Waterford ended in late 2011 he was always going to walk straight into the Clare job and with it a set-up that was the pride of the county and envy of the country.

Fitzgerald had started coaching at seventeen but this was the role he had always dreamed of. 'For the first eight or ten years I thought I was a savage coach,' he laughed. 'But I wasn't.'

Over the next fifteen years, he coached teams to twenty-four titles at not only club, college and intercounty hurling but also camogie and Gaelic football. He took on an ageing Waterford side, changed their style and led them to an All-Ireland final just months after they had shafted Justin McCarthy. In 2010, they won a Munster title. It was a good innings and the truth is he was the best qualified to get the Clare senior gig when it arose.

In 2012, he used six of the under-21s nurtured by O'Connor and Moloney. In 2013, there were twenty kids on the extended panel. Very soon Fitzgerald's senior team started looking like a Fitzgibbon Cup side, its average age twenty-two. Only Brendan Bugler and Pat Donnellan were older than that average but those two were ravenous for success and a challenge.

It looked like a dream ticket from the start. The retention of Kinnerk ensured continuity and was perhaps Fitzgerald's smartest move. A top coach in his own right, he deferred to the Limerick man, whose effectiveness with the youngsters he had witnessed.

The 2012 season was full of ups and downs, and fate, inevitably, pitted him against Waterford. Clare lost by two points and at the end of the game John Mullane and Eoin Kelly expressed their glee by sliding on their knees in front of the Clare bench. Tensions bubbled in the dressing room afterwards – the Waterford boys reckoned Fitzgerald spoke about them being finished, while he swore he said nothing of the sort. In any event, Clare dropped to the qualifiers and beat Dublin at home before losing to Limerick in phase three.

'There was unrest at that stage,' admitted Louis Mulqueen, one of Fitzgerald's selectors. 'Most of it was on our own doorstep too. People questioned us and the way we played. A few even wanted us gone out the road after just a year. Can you believe that?'

Fitzgerald thinks of one league game that year. His young team were losing and seemed caught between two game plans. There was short passing – and shorter passing. The crowd were roaring at the manager to press the reset button: 'Fuck off, Fitzgerald! You have Clare ruined!'

But apart from letting up slightly on the short-passing game Fitzgerald wasn't for changing. Mulqueen and the rest of the backroom reassured him he was doing the right thing. The two were always competitive but close. They hop off each other. One Christmas Eve Mulqueen beat his old rival in a game of squash. On Christmas Day Fitzgerald knocked at Mulqueen's door looking to level the score over a game of racquetball. And he wouldn't take no for an answer.

'Davy just needed time to get the new style going at senior level,' said Mulqueen. 'We had guys like Brendan Bugler, who had been used to different tactics – and seventeen-point hammerings against the likes of Tipp – so we had to try and combine the older lads with a group of youngsters who knew nothing but close control and success and had no fear of anyone – Kilkenny, Tipp, no one. That process took time.'

It wasn't until the middle of the 2013 championship that they took off. An average league saw them just about avoid relegation and weeks later they were beaten by Cork in the Munster semifinal. Once more the pressure came on Fitzgerald, who called a meeting in his home on the day after that game. Much was made of the chat they had over MiWadi and goldgrain biscuits. Again, like the videos of players training at 5 a.m. on Christmas Eve, that house session is one of the propaganda snapshots that has become part of the popular narrative.

But Fitzgerald is adamant it was the turning point in their season: 'I just knew from them coming to my house and the attitude they left with that we would drive on. Like, we were creating huge chances in games and we weren't as bad as we were made out to be. I told them we were being flaked to the hilt by people, but we would drive on.'

They met Wexford in the qualifiers and led by five points with five minutes remaining but somehow were left feeling for a faint championship heartbeat as Wexford got a surge of oxygen and almost stole the game. The whistle sounded to signal a draw and extra time.

The notoriously excitable Fitzgerald had worked hard during the season on controlling his emotions and paying close attention to the heart monitor he wears, but he was stunned not to have won: 'I was rattled but I never felt out of control. I had a lot of work done on myself over the year and worked on staying calm. The way it is, over a seventy-five-minute game I'm seen on RTÉ for maybe two minutes and I'm judged on being a lunatic. But look, I have to accept that for what it is. The heart monitor tells where I am and that night against Wexford I just needed to show the lads we were still in control even though Wexford had the wind in their sails.'

He took a few moments to compose himself before entering the dressing room. Clare had been showboating, going for goals instead of taking their points, and in a few skelps of the hurley Wexford had almost made them pay. But Fitzgerald reckoned this was no time for smashing the furniture: 'I just went in and challenged them. I had an idea what was in them but now I wanted to find out. Wexford had finished with 1-1 and had all the momentum; we were in shock. I needed something to get our focus back. I told them that if we overcame Wexford, with all the momentum they had, and turned around a situation like that, we would win the All-Ireland.'

The players dusted themselves down, went back out, got two early goals and buried the game for once and for all. First part of the plan achieved.

Louis Mulqueen reckoned their season took off from there: 'We were not as free-flowing as we would have liked until the midsummer. Suddenly we got a run of games: Laois, Wexford, Galway. Beating Galway was a massive shot in the arm – they had taken Kilkenny to an All-Ireland final replay just ten months earlier. It was huge.'

Ahead of their All-Ireland semi-final clash with Limerick, Ger Canning of RTÉ remarked to Mulqueen on the 'huge crowd' Limerick had brought – as the Croke Park attendance swelled, the green and white outnumbered the saffron and blue three to one. But Mulqueen was undaunted. 'A huge crowd to go home disappointed, Ger,' he replied.

It wasn't out of arrogance he said it, merely a rock-solid conviction the team would not be beaten. Standing on the centre of the pitch, Mulqueen looked at his watch: six minutes till the teams would join the pre-match parade. He juggled two sliotars as he gazed around at the crowd of 62,000 that had turned up for this 'local derby'. Tony Kelly jogged past.

'They're all here to see you, Tony,' said Mulqueen.

Unruffled, Kelly paused, glanced up at the stands and replied, 'I know. Give us a ball there, will you?'

The nineteen-year-old then took three steps, curved the sliotar over the bar and went on to hit four points from play as the game unfolded. Mulqueen wasn't surprised: 'Tony and the boys accepted they were there to perform and entertain. They were doing keepy-uppies in the middle of the field before the game. Sure he was full of jinks and sidesteps the same day. Pressure was just the norm.'

Reaching the All-Ireland final, especially with Kilkenny out of the way, gave them a golden opportunity, one they might not see for a while again. Getting ready for Cork was all about one thing: surprising the opposition. They had played with a sweeper system all year, and Cork worked hard on counteracting that. But at the start of the year Fitzgerald had unveiled six game plans and the squad had worked diligently on each one, trying various tactics in challenge and league games.

By the end of the 2013 season, Fitzgerald had deployed four of those systems – the seventh defender; the out-and-out sweeper; the man marker; and all-out attack with the aim of three quick-fire passes culminating in a shot at the posts – and in the All-Ireland final he was widely expected to pack his defence and batten down the hatches. But instead he sprang a surprise, a 'shackles off' style whereby the players were given licence to attack space. There would be no sweeper for the biggest game of the year.

He had trusted his men in extra time against Wexford and they hadn't let him down. So now he would give them their heads from the start. They would go all out. Cork arrived in Croke Park expecting an intense, compact, tactical arm-wrestle. Instead, they got caught up in a shootout.

To those outside the loop it was a massive risk to change tack so late in the day, but Fitzgerald didn't see it that way: 'The lads are that comfortable they can play to any of the six plans at short notice because we have the work done. I knew we'd be grand.

The backroom staff were brilliant in coming on board with that change too, but I surround myself with ambitious people who want to win. We challenged each other on it but we went with it.'

Fitzgerald has a huge entourage and listens to them all, but he makes the ultimate call. Mulqueen has seen both the public Davy Fitz and the private one and would confirm there are vast differences. What is leaked into the public domain is often deliberate: 'People saw videos and pictures of the cosmetic stuff we had done – running up Carrauntoohil and the like – and probably thought there was a lunatic doing caveman running. But it's so sophisticated and people don't see the half of it.

'We had lots more done than that, all with the ball and all involving mental toughness. We had been in the gym at five some mornings and we would be looking through the players' logs seeing if they had recorded what they ate for breakfast at 4.30, as they were supposed to. That was about mental toughness. We had Cork on the rack but didn't put them away. When they came back and led by a point, that was where we had to demonstrate what we had learned during the year.'

At the end Patrick Horgan had given Cork a one-point edge. Time was officially up. Fitzgerald was pleading for one more minute: 'I just wanted one more chance, one more attack. I knew if we got that we would muster up another shot. I was so proud of how we didn't panic when we got the ball again. Three passes and a shot. Then I saw Dunny [Domhnall O'Donovan] shooting, all the way up from corner-back, and I got weak at the knees. It flew over and I just thanked God. But Dunny is a cool customer – there's not much to rattle him.'

In a deflated dressing room, Fitzgerald asked the team three questions about how they coped with the opposition and certain tactical demands. He hasn't revealed what they were but said the players' answers transformed their outlook. They had been almost inconsolable after losing the lead. Within thirty minutes they were buoyant again.

It prompted the manager to make yet another big call: 'I let them have a few drinks that night. They had only one night of drinking all year long and it may have been a gamble to let them off the hook at that stage but I wanted to show I trusted them. We went back to the Clyde Court Hotel, did the banquet, and then they went off to prepare for the under-21 final.'

Aside from cruising past Antrim in that under-21 final the players did nothing for the next three weeks except to stay limber and sharp. But Fitzgerald and his management had another huge move in the pipeline.

From the first night he came in for trials, against Waterford at UL in the winter of 2012, and hit two goals, Shane O'Donnell had been earmarked for a likely role in any September show-down. They remarked when they first saw him how goals won finals.

For most of the 2013 league he played a lone ranger role up front and struggled to hold form. He slipped out of the first fifteen after they beat Wexford, but two weeks before the All-Ireland final replay, in an A-versus-B game, he grabbed two quickfire goals. So did Pat Donnellan, from centre-back. In fact, the A team had posted 8-9 after twenty-one minutes in what was supposed to be a forty-minute game. Fitzgerald, aware they might peak too early, called time.

That was the night they knew O'Donnell was ready. They decided Darach Honan would miss out for the replay. Cork had done well against Honan in the drawn game and Fitzgerald suspected they would be better prepared for him next time: 'It was a hard thing to do, telling Darach he was out – and I'll be honest, he didn't take it great – but sure what would you expect?

Still, we always say that one fella can pull the whole thing down, and to be fair to Darach he got on with it.'

By the nineteenth minute of the replay O'Donnell had three goals scored. And the manager knew what would follow: 'Cork were going to come back at us. We had that drilled into the boys. And they did. They scored two goals in one half of an All-Ireland final. That's another reason why I'm so proud of those lads – there's not many teams could ship three goals in an All-Ireland final and still be standing at the end.'

Not until Honan came off the bench and nailed their fifth goal could Fitzgerald relax in the certainty they would win: 'It was only when that goal went in – relief coursed through me. People had wondered why I dropped Darach but Shane scored 3-3 and Darach got the goal that won the All-Ireland. I knew in my heart I had made the right decision.

'Some days it works and you're a genius. Other days it doesn't. Back in 2010, Brian O'Halloran was hurling out of his skin for Waterford and I started him against Tipp and it didn't work out at all. But it was still the right move to make. Some days you get lucky.'

There was very little luck in this win, however. Over 140 minutes of two pulsating epics, Cork led for only ninety seconds. O'Donnell had been the goal-scoring hero, but when the chips were down it was Conor McGrath who grabbed the replay in a headlock. He won countless ball, set up attack after attack, nabbed a timely point and scored one of the best goals ever seen in Croke Park for good measure.

From the stands, however, Gerry O'Connor saw the game decided on two plays. After six minutes Pat Donnellan tore upfield with Séamus Harnedy in hot pursuit: 'Podge Collins peeled off to his left for a pass and Shane O'Donnell went to his right but Harnedy gave up the chase – he pulled up because he didn't expect Clare to go for goal. But Donnellan popped the pass and bang.

'Forty minutes later Cork had all the momentum. Christopher Joyce tore up the pitch and Podge tore after him. He ran thirty yards and got a hook in on the forty-five-yard line. Cian Dillon gobbled up possession and gave it to Tony Kelly, who found Shane. He banged over our first point in twenty minutes. It broke their momentum. It broke Cork.'

'Were we in control?' Fitzgerald asked. 'Yeah. Were we the better team? I would say so. But they kept coming back. We just couldn't put them away.

'They took a lot of kicks along the way. I took a lot of kicks but it was fucking worth it to say that we stuck the long road. Fuck everyone else! Before the game we looked each other in the eye. We knew we'd be okay.'

They were okay. And as an epoch-making season ended, they looked in better shape than anyone.

Epilogue

Hurling rebooted for a new generation . . .

The curtains opened on the 2014 championship and a beautiful dawn greeted us. Hurling was in a wonderful place. Fans had enjoyed the thrilling revolution of the previous season and now every major power and would-be power was in search of bounty, confident of a rich harvest after years of assiduous cultivation.

The All-Ireland hurling championship had, for the first time in history, yielded more gate receipts than its football sibling, the camán and sliotar pulling in €12m at the turnstiles in 2013, just ahead of football's €11.9m. Even allowing for the replaying of the final between Clare and Cork, those figures reflected some astonishing performances that had gripped spectators and greatly heightened interest in the sport.

In the aftermath of that unforgettable season, the playing fields have been levelled and the balance of power between several counties looks tantalizingly even. It seems unlikely any county will dominate in the foreseeable future, and while it will be hard to replicate the earthshaking heroics of 2013, there is an undoubted stirring in the land – a rising in the hurling heart-lands.

How will Kilkenny, with heavy mileage on the clock and a set way of playing, adapt to the fluidity, mobility and deftness of the emerging teams? Will they stay true to type and try to dictate their own terms? They love physical confrontation, high fetching and full-on attack, but the 2013 title was won with sliotar pinged from paw to paw and overlaps from deep.

'Kilkenny like to win playing in their way and I think they have to keep that style,' says Brendan Cummins, who swapped the Tipp goal line for RTÉ's *The Sunday Game* studio in 2014. 'Everyone will need to up their levels of fitness because if you can't run with Clare you can't impose your own game. But if people think the big three won't come roaring back again they're mistaken. Go into Croke Park, look at the past winners and you have to go down four steps to see Clare's name. The traditional teams will be gunning to get back on top.'

Historically, Kilkenny have always reacted decisively to reading their own obituary. But the next few years will represent a huge challenge. From 2006 to September 2010 they didn't lose a championship game. In 2012 they lost one and drew one. In 2013 they lost two and drew one. The flame their iconic players carried for years is guttering and the taper is running short. How could it be otherwise?

Whether their cycle of domination is irreparably broken remains to be seen, but when the theatre of 2013 ended, a number of counties were well armed to carry the fight deep into the heart of Kilkenny's fiefdom. One thing is for sure: Brian Cody will endeavour to find a route back to the top for his men, whether by old ways or new.

Galway's David Collins would go so far as to say Kilkenny

are still the team to catch, and adds that only those motivated by what he calls 'pure hatred' have a chance: 'Believe it or not I mean that in a good way. You'd have absolutely huge respect for them first and foremost. My ambition is to win an All-Ireland medal and some of those lads have eight, which you could only admire. So to knock them off the perch you will have to be absolutely manic because they are that desperate to stay winning.

'Our beating them in the 2012 Leinster final took eight months of sustained dedication. You bought into Anthony Cunningham's plan or you didn't buy in at all – that was the ultimatum put to us. Nothing less than wholesale commitment was going to beat Kilkenny, because that's what they have in abundance.'

To illustrate the point, Collins cites a 2004 third-round qualifier in Thurles: 'They beat us by nineteen points that day – murdered us. When they went twelve points up I turned to Richie Power and said, "Richie, will ye ever go and fuck off!" They went on to rattle in two more goals. It's no wonder you want to nail them back – I don't think we feel that aggression towards any other team.'

Limerick's Donal O'Grady says that though Kilkenny under Cody have been the greatest team in history, they must adapt like everyone else: 'Hurling has gone to new heights; the average age of teams has dropped to about twenty-three and the new model of hurling is built upon speed. If you're twenty-six or twenty-seven you're actually near the finishing line career-wise, and that's sad. But we all have hope. The 2013 All-Ireland could have gone to any of four teams. The road ahead is open.'

Cummins sees a seismic shift happening: 'Anyone hitting less than fourteen on bleep tests won't even get a game any more. And the lad who can win ball in the air is no longer a nailed-down starter. Look at Podge Collins, the size of him, and yet the ability of him. Those Clare forwards are not ball winners but their work rate ensures serious turnover around the middle and they love to bring the ball to ground and take you on.'

Dublin's Ryan O'Dwyer hesitates to talk of a revolution, asserting that such developments are cyclical: 'Every couple of years hurling changes – it was the same in Gaelic football when Armagh and Tyrone came through with their defensive ways. As soon as teams found a way of winning an All-Ireland final there was a new game plan in town.

'Hurling's latest one is centred on speed and intensity, keeping possession with high-quality touch. I don't actually see how fitness levels can go much higher. Even in league games players are clocking up to nine kilometres. A tracking device showed that Johnny McCaffrey hit eleven kilometres in one match.'

To put that in perspective, when David Beckham ran sixteen kilometres, over ninety minutes, for England in a game against Greece in 2001, he was held up as some sort of freak. But amateur GAA players are now in the same ballpark – metaphorically of course – in secondary competitions, never mind championship games.

'Everything just seems to be getting quicker and lighter,' O'Grady adds. 'You'll probably see Joe Canning back behind the halfway line, cutting a ball over the bar. Even the sliotars are getting softer, so maybe Joe will put a free over from his own twenty-metre line soon. With the level of skill out there every aspect of the traditional game is under pressure.

'After seeing what Clare did, the self-belief in other teams has sky-rocketed. Conor McGrath scored a top-corner goal in the 2013 All-Ireland final replay and it looked like a play from the Roy of the Rovers. If I scored a goal like that I would still be jumping around, looking to high-five anyone within reach, but McGrath just gave a tiny clench of the fist and ran back into position. Clare will take some beating now. In fact getting out of Munster will be a nightmare for all the teams there.'

Very little now separates the southern counties. From 1983 to 2008 every Munster minor title was won by either Cork or Tipperary. But the old order has been infiltrated – the last three minor titles have gone to Clare, twice, and Waterford. Limerick's schools and underage set-up is flourishing. The only certainty is that nothing is certain any more.

'There's a good chance we'll never again see a hurling year like 2013,' says Davy Fitzgerald. 'I'm not sure how 2014 will go. All I can say for sure is that everyone is coming for us. But my lads will respond over the next few years. There's too much in them not to.'

Across all levels Clare have stolen a march. From 2010 to 2013 inclusive, they lost not one underage game in Thurles, previously a graveyard for Clare hurling. As Gerry O'Connor puts it, 'We love Thurles now – that's where our underage players can express themselves, where they learn to win.' That is some shift in attitude considering the dark days they endured at Semple Stadium.

Meanwhile, anyone who doubts that the Clare players will be able to keep their feet on the ground need only look for reassurance to the likes of Shane O'Donnell, whose three goals in the replayed 2013 All-Ireland final handed him the keys to Ennis, and possibly places beyond – every young man wanted to be him and many a young woman wanted to be with him.

But, as O'Connor affirms, there's no danger of him falling in love with himself: 'He got five hundred and sixty points in the Leaving Cert. He's an intellect; a mathematical guy. He's studying genetics at UCC, but many of his classmates don't care about hurling; their academic studies are their careers. They'll wonder what he's doing "playing that old lark" in his spare time. And so he was grounded very quickly after that All-Ireland final.

'But he's thoughtful way beyond his nineteen years and has a very good family base. His dad is an engineer and his mam an accountant. They're solid, unassuming people. A lot of the guys we're producing are real high achievers. We'll have challenges like any other county but I don't see these guys getting sidetracked any time soon.'

At no stage in the aftermath of their All-Ireland win did the Claremen look like losing the run of themselves. On their homecoming they made it their business to bring the cup to little Liam Foley from Cratloe. It meant the world to the lad and his family. Liam, only six, would pass away in early December.

'We don't want any credit for that,' Fitzgerald said. 'That's part of our job – we make people feel better but we don't want it out in the open. I'm just so proud of the guys that if anyone asks them to help a sick person it's just not a problem. We talk a lot about things as a group. We know how lucky we are.'

They also brought the cup to more than a hundred schools, but didn't just walk in to smile and pose. They distributed leaflets advising the kids how to eat sensibly, how to conduct themselves, how to stand up to bullying and respect their peers. The handout was signed by every member of the Clare set-up.

They took Liam MacCarthy to hospitals and fifty-seven GAA clubs.

'There were nights when Tony Kelly didn't get home from those clubs until one o'clock in the morning,' says Louis Mulqueen. 'Brendan Bugler came in and played the accordion for various people with illnesses. One night we brought the cup to a Brothers of Charity function and I saw some of our players waltz with people sixty years older than them. That's the warm element within. The lads created lots of goodwill around the county – a feel-good factor in a recession.'

They had a few nights to themselves, and a few drinks, but even at their medal presentations there was no excess; they realized they were up there to be shot down. And they know that while the quality of hurling in the All-Ireland final – parts one and two – was exceptional, the defensive efforts of both teams left much to be desired.

'What I saw between ourselves and Cork was pure innocent hurling,' says Mulqueen. 'How many counties would let the likes of Conor Lehane run across you or score the way he did? How many teams would allow Conor McGrath to score the goal he got? The more traditional teams would have cut that off at source. Someone would have met McGrath but Cork tried to hook him. It was just the pureness of those games; we went at it point for point and goal for goal. Would it be as pure against another county? No. Having said that, have we played our best hurling yet? No!'

If Clare's management wanted tangible indicators of their victorious players knuckling back down they hadn't long to wait. They were fitness tested in November 2013, just six weeks after the final replay, and then played four challenge matches before Christmas.

When they returned from a team holiday in Cancun and the US in early January 2014 they resumed training at UL and it was heavy-duty stuff – the fallout included at least one broken finger. Earlier that day, Brendan Bugler had texted Mulqueen asking about the format of the session. These players demand information and standards.

Curious as to which of his players would make a statement by arriving early, Fitzgerald was at the UL dressing rooms by six. Colin Ryan was first in, landing at ten past six for a session scheduled to start at 7.30.

By now the squad were well into pre-season mode, chatting – often via their internal social media mechanism, MetroFit – about injuries, states of mind or nutrition. Some had texted management pictures of their breakfast menu, keen to know if a certain brand of porridge or fruit juice was permitted.

The cover photo on the team's WhatsApp Messenger suggested a team intent on greatness. Over Christmas the app had shown a sandy beach under a blazing sun, hinting the team was in holiday mood. But when Mulqueen checked again on the morning of their first session back, the golden sands were nowhere to be seen, replaced by a picture of the Liam MacCarthy Cup on the dashboard of their team bus. The message was simple – the team would have to go and win it all over again.

The chase is on. The next five years could see five different All-Ireland winners. Breathe these days in. For they are rich in promise.

Acknowledgements

The summer of 2013 took my breath away. Not only was my beautiful daughter Chloe born, but hurling – my main passion in life outside of my family – reached spectacular new heights.

Every Saturday and Sunday I would fill up my car with diesel and hit the highway to take in a game, either as a reporter or spectator. And every night I would return home, my head still spinning – wondering how the game I had just seen could possibly be bettered. And yet it was. With every passing week. Without fail.

That was the glory of the summer of 2013; the most exciting championship we ever had.

The season may have ended in a welter of exhilaration but it was like that all the way through. Mid-summer I looked on as little Laois shook Galway to the bone, while plucky Carlow took Wexford right to the wire just weeks after Wexford had almost beaten Dublin in the Leinster championship. The Tipp-Kilkenny qualifier in Nowlan Park was the most exciting of the lot, and yet the least enjoyable if you come from where I come from!

Still, my deep admiration for Kilkenny only grew that night and again shortly afterwards when they hung on in there one last time against Waterford at Semple Stadium. They were on the ropes that night, but when the bell sounded they regrouped, sucked in the air, and came back out fighting. Just hours before that epic, Clare and Wexford had also gone to extra time in another pulsating qualifier.

I suppose that was the night I decided I had to do something.

To write an account of the 2013 season, absolute justice wouldn't have been possible in the timeframe available, but luckily for me, my publishers at Transworld – Eoin McHugh and Brian Langan – also felt that some statement on the game of hurling needed to be made. And so the first thanks goes to these two men, gents of the highest order, for entrusting me to write *Fields of Fire.*

So here it is. Now, I'm not for one second foolish enough to write off Kilkenny – and just look at how they came out of the blocks in 2014 by winning the Walsh Cup and burning up serious ground in the league. But I wanted this book to demonstrate and document the work that has gone into hurling development around the country as teams endeavoured to catch up with the Cats. And I think that at least two teams have finally caught up with them. Father Time is playing a part too. Even still, I don't expect Kilkenny to stray too far from the winners' podium. The game is just too strong there, at all levels.

I do, however, expect other teams to climb the steps of the Hogan Stand every September with greater frequency over the next few years. This book will indicate exactly who is best equipped to do so.

Fields of Fire would not have been possible without the cooperation of so many players, managers and officials who trusted me, gave me their time and energy. I contacted forty people for help on this project and completed thirty-six meaningful and intimate interviews. Colleagues in my business often complain about access to players and the like, but I have to say I was overwhelmed by the goodwill, respect and sheer kindness extended to me. Overwhelmed, but not surprised for GAA people are extremely decent. I was welcomed into players' homes, introduced to their families and fed at their tables when all I wanted was a few words. It was a most humbling experience. Thanks to these guys below for allowing me to pen this book: I sincerely hope I have not left anyone out.

Dublin – *Niall Corcoran, Ryan O'Dwyer and*
   Johnny McCaffrey.
Galway – *David Collins and Damien Hayes.*
Clare – *Davy Fitzgerald, Louis Mulqueen, Gerry O'Connor,*
   Donal Moloney and Ger Loughnane.
Waterford – *John Mullane, Páraic Fanning, Darragh Duggan*
   and the GAA's Head of Games, Pat Daly.
Cork – *Ger Cunningham, Seánie McGrath and John Grainger.*
Tipperary – *Brendan Cummins, Paul Curran, Séamus Hennessy*
   and Dr Cian O'Neill (adopted Tipp man).
Limerick – *Donal O'Grady (captain), John Allen and*
   Éibhear O'Dea.
Wexford – *Liam Dunne, Liam Griffin and Rory Griffin.*
Offaly – *Brian Carroll and David Franks.*
Kilkenny – *Cha Fitzpatrick, Eddie Brennan, D. J. Carey,*
   John Power, Richie Mulrooney, Pat Treacy, Enda McEvoy
   and Barrie Henriques.
Antrim – *Neil McManus, Liam Watson and Mickey McCullogh.*
Laois – *Cheddar Plunkett and Pat Critchley.*
Carlow – *John Meyler.*

I have to be honest, too, and admit that at times the sheer intensity of this project – the driving, transcribing, interviewing, research and writing – was almost too much. That's why I am so grateful to my friend and colleague, Richard Gallagher, who has supported and encouraged me with every book I have written. Pat Nolan and Denis Hurley both have books of their own in the pipeline and also gave me their stout backing, constructive criticism and an unwavering commitment to this book. They steered me right in so many areas. Thanks also to Damien O'Meara, Declan Bogue, Brian McDonnell, Eddie O'Donnell, John Casey and Jackie Cahill for their words of encouragement and kind deeds. To Kieran Shannon and Christy O'Connor for their loyalty and friendship over the years.

Ruth, my wife, has always supported me and I owe her a massive debt of gratitude. Heading off for six- and seven-hour round trips for interviews and then coming back to transcribe thousands of words (before I even started writing) may have been a labour of love for me, but leaving Ruth with two small children was not easy on her. Not once did she make an issue of it. Without her backing there would have been no book.

I'd also like to thank Mam for passing on her ferocious drive and energy to me, and Dad, a lifelong hurling man, for introducing me to Gaelic Games when I was only a kid.

Finally, an acknowledgement that I've been lucky in life. Hurling and the GAA has opened so many doors for me and I just hope that this book can provide some enjoyment and entertainment for the thousands of supporters who, like me, love this game so much.

Picture Acknowledgements

Page 1
6 July 2013; Brian Cody speaks to Henry Shefflin moments before
he is introduced as a Kilkenny substitute. GAA Hurling All-Ireland
Senior Championship, Phase 2, Kilkenny v. Tipperary, Nowlan Park,
Kilkenny. Ray McManus/SPORTSFILE 768037.

Page 2
Above: All-Ireland Hurling final 8.9.2002.
Kilkenny's D. J. Carey and manager Brian Cody celebrate after the
game. © INPHO/Andrew Paton. INPHO 82902.

Centre: GAA All-Ireland SHC final, Croke Park 6.9.2009. Tipperary
v. Kilkenny. Kilkenny's Eddie Brennan and Seánie McGrath of
Tipperary. © INPHO/Lorraine O'Sullivan. INPHO 391913.

Below: GAA All-Ireland SHC final 5.9.2010. Kilkenny v. Tipperary.
Kilkenny's T. J. Reid and James 'Cha' Fitzpatrick tackle Brendan
Maher of Tipperary. © INPHO/Cathal Noonan. INPHO 455691.

Page 3
Above: 8 July 2012; Damien Hayes, Galway, in action against Michael
Rice, Kilkenny. Leinster GAA SHC final, Croke Park, Dublin. Brian
Lawless/SPORTSFILE 662780.

Below: 29 July 2012; Donal O'Grady, Limerick, in action against Henry Shefflin (left) and Aidan Fogarty, Kilkenny. GAA Hurling All-Ireland SHC quarter-final, Kilkenny v. Limerick, Semple Stadium, Thurles, Co. Tipperary. Brian Lawless/SPORTSFILE 669377.

Page 4

Above: 29 June 2013; Anthony Daly and David O'Callaghan make no attempt to hide their satisfaction after the replay win over Kilkenny in the semi-final of the Leinster SHC 2013. Ray McManus/SPORTSFILE 811818.

Below: 7 July 2013; Dublin's Ryan O'Dwyer and Liam Rushe celebrate after the game. Leinster GAA SHC final, Galway v. Dublin, Croke Park, Dublin. Ray McManus/SPORTSFILE 768350.

Page 5

Above: GAA Hurling All-Ireland SHC Phase 2, Nowlan Park, Co. Kilkenny. 6.7.2013. Kilkenny v. Tipperary. A distraught Brendan Cummins of Tipperary leaves the pitch at the end of the game. © INPHO/Donall Farmer. INPHO 715508.

Centre: 17 July 2010; John Mullane, Waterford, in action against John Gardiner, Cork. Munster GAA SHC final replay, Cork v. Waterford, Semple Stadium, Thurles, Co. Tipperary. Brendan Moran/SPORTSFILE 444160.

Below: 7 July 2013; Joe Canning, Galway, watched by manager Anthony Cunningham during the game. Leinster GAA SHC final, Galway v. Dublin, Croke Park, Dublin. David Maher/SPORTSFILE 768400.

Page 6

Above left: 8 September 2013; Cork manager Jimmy Barry-Murphy. GAA Hurling All-Ireland SHC final, Cork v. Clare, Croke Park, Dublin. Paul Mohan/SPORTSFILE 791108.

PICTURE ACKNOWLEDGEMENTS

Above right: 28 September 2013; Clare manager Davy Fitzgerald celebrates his side's victory. GAA Hurling All-Ireland SHC final replay, Cork v. Clare, Croke Park, Dublin. Barry Cregg/SPORTSFILE 797693.

Below: 8 September 2013; Domhnall O'Donovan, Clare, shoots to score the equalizing point despite the attentions of Stephen White, Cork. GAA Hurling All-Ireland SHC final, Cork v. Clare, Croke Park, Dublin. Brian Lawless/SPORTSFILE 791073.

Page 7
GAA All-Ireland SHC final 8.9.2013. Cork v. Clare. Cork's Stephen McDonnell and Pádraic Collins of Clare. © INPHO/Ryan Byrne. INPHO 734962.

Page 8
Above: 28 September 2013; Shane O'Donnell, Clare, in action against Shane O'Neill, Cork. GAA Hurling All-Ireland SHC final replay, Cork v. Clare, Croke Park, Dublin. Paul Mohan/SPORTSFILE 797548b.

Below: 28 September 2013; Clare players celebrate with the Liam McCarthy cup at the end of the game. GAA All-Ireland SHC final replay, Cork v. Clare, Croke Park, Dublin. David Maher/ SPORTSFILE 797796.

Index

ABOUT THE AUTHOR

Damian Lawlor, from Kilruane in County Tipperary, is an award-winning journalist and Gaelic Games Correspondent for the *Sunday Independent* newspaper. He is a presenter with Setanta Sports and also presented *Take Your Point* on RTÉ Radio One for two years. *Fields of Fire: The Inside Story of Hurling's Great Renaissance* is his fourth book, following the bestselling *I Crossed the Line – the Liam Dunne Story; Working on a Dream – a Year on the Road with the Waterford Footballers,* which was runner-up in the 2009 William Hill Sports Book awards; and *All In My Head,* Lar Corbett's autobiography, which was shortlisted at the Irish Book Awards in 2012.